THE CASE OF MINERVA

Secundus Sulpicius

Book 1

COPYRIGHT – FRANCIS M MULHERN

In writing this book I have attempted to be as true to the time period as possible. However, the telling of a story set in history requires some frames of reference for the reader to ensure consistency with modern terms and names. As such I have used some terms such as hours, minutes, miles etc. to enable the action to be positioned and understood by a modern reader.

In researching the book it was also clear that there is no

definitive nomenclature for the road systems in the City of Rome from this time period and so I have used more conventional names where necessary even though they may not have been named as such within this time period and were introduced much later. I've also used literary sources to indicate possible road names and then utilised that information to create a picture which I have presented below. In this way I hope to be able to give life to what was a growing city and allow the reader to understand the world in which Secundus may have lived. I have included temples and other historically significant sites which give a flavour of the diversity of sacred and religious sites that are known to date. I may have missed some and I may have added them in the wrong location if the details of their exact position could not be found in my research. I hope that these items help you to enjoy reading my books and I welcome feedback.

The hills and roads of Rome in the time of Secundus Sulpicius Merenda. Picture copyright © Francis Mulhern

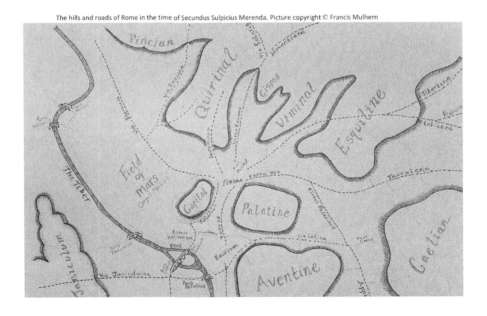

FRANCIS MULHERN

Map2: Locations of action, The case of Minerva

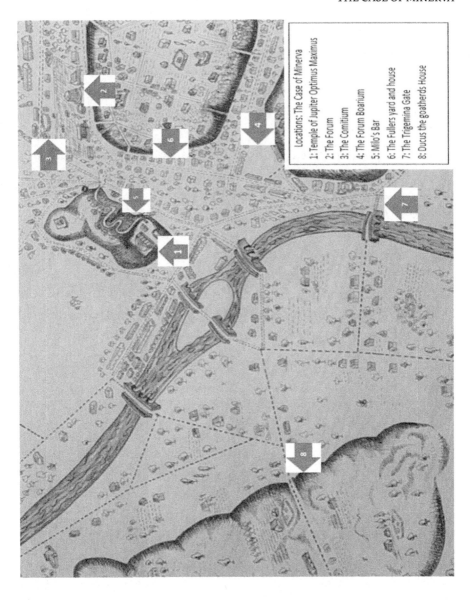

Locations: The Case of Minerva

1: Temple of Jupiter Optimus Maximus
2: The Forum
3: The Comitium
4: The Forum Boarium
5: Milo's Bar
6: The Fullers yard and house
7: The Trigemina Gate
8: Ducus the goatherds House

Minerva was the goddess of wisdom, justice, the law as well as the patron of many tradesmen and crafts in Ancient Rome. From the early Republic she was known for her ability to change her mind and punish those who she had formerly supported. Such cases as

Arachne (who was changed to a spider) and Medusa (turned into a serpent headed monster) stand out. She was worshiped as part of the Capitoline Triad along with Jupiter Optimus Maximus. At her festival in March the first day was said to be the anniversary of her birth and no blood was to be spilt, which gives a great backdrop in which to set a murder mystery.

Janus was the two-faced god of doors, gates and transitions. He is one of the oldest gods of Rome and is linked to all aspects of change and new beginnings, including having a very close link to omens and auguries. There was a small temple, more of a shrine, in the Roman Forum in early Rome. The two-faces of the god are looking forwards and backwards, and there is record of many milestones with the two faces carved into them at each gateway and arch in the old Republic. Such duplicity in the nature of the god and his support of change is fantastic for creating options in a hero who is facing a new beginning. I do hope you enjoy reading the following story.

I

The Fuller, the father of the dead girl, bared his teeth in resentment to my intrusion into his home. His Etruscan features, dark hair and even darker eyes, distorted in anger as he came to stand in front of me, crossed his arms over his considerable chest and stared down his long nose to make it clear that I was not welcome. I know he holds minor plebeian status and as such has some rights within the city and especially within his own house so l need to watch my step. I might be both a patrician and on official business but this bastard is outraged at my arrival and has been in my face from the moment I showed him the official document which closed the case of the murder of his daughter.

I flinch under his glare but stand my ground; he's tall, dark-skinned from his work and the muscled arms that are now waving at me give the impression that he is as strong as an ox.

"You Romans think you can wash over this don't you. Someone killed my girl and I'll find the bastard if you can't." I hesitate at the fury in his voice but I remain firm, grim-faced and stubborn, whilst inside I am rueing my decision to be here and swallow nervously.

Why had I brought the death notice? What sort of fool had I been to bring it here?

My mind flashed back to sitting in the office. I was bored when I heard Graccus asking where the messenger boy was. He had a judgement that needed delivering to the Fullers yard within the next hour. It was because I'd found her, the daughter of the man who now loomed over me, that I'd taken the note and decided to deliver it myself; to close my mind to the death I'd seen; to remove the image that watched me from behind my closed eyelids every night; to try to find the restful sleep that evaded me.

Standing in front of the bull-necked Fuller, I consider my next actions. Is he likely to attack me? He certainly seems angry enough and I've heard stories of the most recent messengers sent back with their tails between their legs and the occasional drenching in piss from one of his fuller's pots. I'm a good wrestler, but against this massive sun-baked Etruscan Pleb and his slaves, I'm out-manned and out-muscled. Two of his workers turned towards me, the thought of giving me a good beating or up-turning one of the brim-full bowls of urine evident in the balling of their fists and tensing muscles. I saw their brown eyes lighting up with glee, the unshaven chins jutting out as they tense their jaws, the taught muscles flexing as they prepare for action.

I held out the death notice once more, feeling the weight of the words written into the thin vellum and understanding the mistake I'd made in taking it from Graccus. I breathed slowly and deeply and stiffened my resolve in the face of an imminent outburst from the father of the dead girl.

"I am only the messenger. I bring the order from the judge and must have your agreement in front of your followers that you have received it," I said in my best *'you don't intimidate me'* voice. I watched the two workers circling and felt my heart start to hammer. One of the men wore odd shoes, the left a darker brown than the other. I wondered why, thinking that maybe it was to do with the fulling process before I cast my thoughts back to my immediate situation. Behind the encroaching men, the slaves continued to slap their feet in the Fuller's dance, the acrid smell of urine flooding my senses as my breathing deepened at the thought that I might have to fight my way out of the Fuller's yard. One of the slaves had pallid yellow skin, his thin frame showing hours of work and little nutrition; his blue lips suggesting he might just stop and sink into the pot of piss he worked in every day at any moment. I stared around at the yard, taking in all the details in my agitated state, feeling the sweat trickling down the back of my neck as I swallow hard again.

In an instant, the Fuller snatched the note from my hand. I saw his fingernails were clogged with dirt as his hand flashed close to my face. "You think this sorts it do you?" he snarled, his considerable height now more evident as he stepped closer and pushed the document like a knife towards my face. "You know it was murder, you bastard" he said as he took another step forward, the noise of feet stamping in unison suddenly dropping to stony silence as several of the slaves leered at the scene with the expectation that their master was about to deal out a punishment to the bringer of bad news.

What a show I will make under his heavy fists. What a fool I am.

In those seconds, as each heartbeat bounced against my ribs like a drum at the festival of Jupiter, I remembered why I was here and cursed my foolhardiness.

I'd found the girl, his daughter, on my drink-sodden slump home a week earlier. She was in a ditch, one hand above her head, legs astride and face turned towards the road as if she was looking for help. I was here because I still saw his daughter's face every night when I closed my eyes and the vision of her visited my dreams. Her still-warm body and lifeless stare still admonished me for seeing her nakedness, for not saving her from whatever fate ended her short life. Her plight had touched a raw nerve, reminding me of the death of my beloved wife and child, reminding me of the chasm I had fallen into and the lack of hope I had for any part of my wretched, unlucky, life. I'd sought solace in any amphora I could get my hands on and had been out of my mind almost every night on good wine, or bad. Since I'd stumbled across his daughter my inability to sleep and my depression at how badly the gods were treating me had become worse. I cursed the gods, and they cursed me in return. Life was shit and Bacchus laughed in my face from the bottom of an empty cup every night, followed swiftly by the image of the dead girl's eyes reminding me of my loss. Every night I dreamt of his daughter and was haunted by the memory of my wife Plaudita as she died in my arms and took my son, and my love, with her. Those dreams had compelled me to be here, to stare uselessly at his shaking fist as it came closer to my face.

The gods had deserted me on the day my wife and child had died and now they mocked me by giving me the arrogance to think that by taking the note from Graccus and delivering it myself to the dead girls family I could rid myself of the dreams and memories that haunted me. Surely the gods hated me as much as my family, why else would they put me here with the Fuller who was about to smash my head to a pulp.

That thought brought my mind back to the shouting man in front of me who was yelling that he would find his daughter's killer, even if he had to beat it out of every man in Rome. His workers and slaves grinned like idiots, nodding at his words and mouthing obscenities towards the justice system that I represent. Me, the fool with a conscience and a death wish. I stepped back as he made a grab for my tunic and mouthed a protest, which went unheeded.

As I adjusted my feet to use his momentum to counter the lunge towards me, a voice rose above the ethereal silence that now hung across the yard.

"What is going on?"

A female voice, formal and sharp. A woman dressed in green had appeared in the doorway behind my attacker, a baby attached to her hip. Her voice commanded enough attention for the slap of feet from the cubicles surrounding the yard to instantly start again and her husband's ire towards me to turn into a hoarse-breathed explanation of how he was going to send me back to the judge with my message rammed up my arse. Her dress flowed to her feet but didn't hide the curves that would happily keep any man warm at night. Leather sandals of the same colour complemented a thin fawn belt at her waist which was the colour of honey. Her fingers were long and thin, her eyes sharp and alive.

My gaze jumped back and forth from the husband to the wife who now faced me with a frown which begged an answer t her questioning gaze. I must have exclaimed in shock at what I saw as her face turned to me. It was her! The image in front of me was so remarkably similar to the dead girl's face which haunted my dreams that I reacted with a gasp. The gaze that captured me was older, but not aged, more defined, with lines that spoke of laughter, gaiety and fun. Yet it was *her* eyes that watched me as the fuller waved the notice in my face once more. The sadness in the eyes of death and the life in the eyes of the mother snatched at my heart. In that moment my dreams came back to haunt me and I realised why I had come, why I had taken the note.

Death is beautiful.

The lifeless stare of my wife and the dead girl I had found in the ditch flashed through my thoughts like a bolt from Jupiter himself. The life I saw in the visage of the mother standing before me filled me with the sorrow of my own loss, the hatred of the gods for taking from me the only good thing I had in my miserable life. Remorse had led to senseless drinking and endless fights with my family. I'd been a fool since Plaudita died. I'd fallen to hedonism. I'd cursed the gods and in reply Somnus, the god of sleep and dreams, had punished me with all-consuming memories that I could almost touch as I screamed at my loss in the dark prison behind my restless eyes. Those night-time terrors had brought me to this place and forced me to make ridiculous decisions like the one that had brought me to the Fullers yard. In the flicker of my thoughts, I could see my head forced into one of the terracotta bowls of foul smelling urine and stamped on by the idiotic, grinning, slaves. I told myself I deserved it for my stupidity and arrogance. It wasn't a lie, it was what the gods had given me as a punishment for ignoring them for the whole of my life and cursing them aloud.

I had missed half the insults hurled at me by the Fuller as I turned my stricken face from the image of the mother to the man in front of me once more. "Go on then" he snarled, his dog-like face bitter at the loss of giving a thrashing to a Patrician. I stood like a statue, dumbstruck, my head twisting back to the mother, who gave me a look of curiosity whilst she bounced her babe on a soft hip. Her face was beautifully symmetrical; her dark hair combed over her ears and braided to show her bright cheeks and large eyes.

"Go" shouted the Fuller, his frustration now at boiling point.

I bowed to him and his wife quickly before turning on my heel and walking with as much integrity as I could muster whilst feeling a desperate need to fill one of his piss bowls with my own full bladder.

II

"It's not your job to deliver messages to the fucking Plebs. That's what we pay these pricks for" shouted a red-faced Scavolo with a wave to a grinning messenger boy hiding in the shadows. Scavolo was my boss, a former Centurion with more phalera on the sash that he wore across his chest than a legion could win in a decade. The man had been a one-man army, and his anger was legend amongst every soldier from the Tiber to the Anio. "You've wasted all afternoon on a fucking wild goose chase. You've got all that" at which his iron ringed finger thrust at the pile of letters I had left on my desk when my stupidity had made me take the note to the Fullers yard, "to finish before you move from that seat. I don't care if you need a shit, you are *not* moving until you finish that work. Do you understand?"

I realised why he'd been such a good soldier. The enemy would wet their tunics under a barrage of his words and his men would rather die in a naked charge at a hundred blood-soaked spears than turn and face the anger of their own Centurion.

I tried to speak as I nodded in response, but only produced a squeak and a cough and felt my cheeks redden in embarrassment. His head was shaking with the sadness of a man who had tried several times to beat sense into a puppy and the beast still didn't learn to sit. He sighed through clenched teeth as his tone dropped and his hands rested on his hips. "If your father wasn't in charge I'd have you out on your arse. Fucking waste of my time." He snapped these final words as he turned and clicked his fingers for the boy to follow him through the doorway.

Bastard, I thought. What right have you to bollock me? I'm the Patrician. You're just a jumped up Pleb with a few sashes for bravery. If you weren't under the protection of my father... I considered walking out and telling him to shove it up his own backside, but in my heart I knew that he was right. What a waste of everyone's time I was. I felt anger turn to hopelessness as I sat on the hard wooden stool and my gaze fell on the pile of wax inscribed notes I had to transcribe to vellum. My head was in my hands and I closed my eyes, depression starting to sink across me like the shadow of Oizys herself bringing darkness and misery to haunt me. I had been here for two months now, at my father's insistence. *Do it or I'll put you in a sack and float you down the Tiber to the Styx* were his exact words one night when I had been dragged home drunk by two door slaves from a local brothel. They'd left a hefty bill for the damage I'd done and I had no memory of the previous three days of drink-sodden recklessness which had brought me back to my family's door. My parents had hidden me away after that, locking me in my room for days to sober up and save their embarrassment as my father had recently been awarded the highest honour our family had ever received on the Cursus Honorum; the role of Quaestores Parriccidii, the second highest judge in the Senate. And then I was placed here so that his dog Scavolo could watch over me and keep me out of the local bars and any trouble which would darken our family name.

The timing of the death of my wife and child and my slide into depravity was a disaster for every member of my family, and I knew it. My grief had caused clan-wide anger and resentment and I'd been forced into hiding to save face and honour. As the Paterfamilias of the family, my father had the absolute right to tell me what to do and expect me to conform at pain of exile or death. I knew my place, and this was it. That bastard Scavolo could shove his prick up my arse and I couldn't argue as long as he had my father's ear. I bent to the work, cursing Scavolo, cursing my family, cursing my luck and cursing the gods who

THE CASE OF MINERVA

had never replied to my bargaining pleas.

Much later, I sloped home rubbing my stiff forearm from the effort of writing; it hurt more than drills with Mancio my sword and wrestling tutor. As I approached the long incline back to the Palatine Hill where we resided, I remembered the vision of the Fuller's wife. As the memory floated into my mind, her beauty was eclipsed by the image of the dead girl and then of Plaudita. I came to a stop and closed my eyes as I felt tears welling up behind my lashes. I cursed under my breath, the desire for wine filling my senses. I sniffed loudly before I let out a slow breath and then tapped my temple to knock sense into my stupid brain. *No,* I screamed in my mind. *No. I will not drink.*

I knew it was a lie, and I knew it would take me back to the brink of destruction.

****

The worst thing about your parent's righteousness is that they are always right. Damn them. Add in the ex-Centurion from my father's time in the legions who was now my task-master as well as an older brother who had been Decurion on three campaigns against the Latins and held a minor role supporting a Senators office, and I was seriously under siege from every vantage point with no defensive position to which to retreat.

The sermon from my father had continued for several long moments. I squeezed my lips so tightly that I could almost feel them closing forever and never coming apart as I held my tongue.

His voice continued to rise and fall like a hammer knocking nails into my skull. Scavolo stood in the corner of the room in silent indignation. He'd run to my father to give him a full account of my latest levels of stupidity and to request, as he had done twice before, that I be removed from my position in his office as a bad influence on the rest of the staff. The *rest of the staff* was a boy called Graccus, whose own misdemeanours were so thoroughly hidden by my total incompetence that he appeared to be a model employee even though the quality and speed of his work was less than half that of my own. In fact I often finished his work because he was too busy chattering on about inane rubbish he'd heard in the forum to finish his own slates.

Needless to say, Graccus wanted me to stay.

My mother tutted loudly every time my father drew breath, her tongue having to be constantly wetted from a large cup of wine to ensure she could create just the right amount of sucking and clicking noises to offend my ears. My brother shook his head continuously with the look that only a brother can give when you aren't living up to his successes and you know that underneath all the frowning and stern gazes he is pissing himself that it isn't him on the end of a lashing from the tongue of our father.

He, doing his duty as a parent in his eyes, continued to explain how I needed to get a grip on my life and find a way to get out of the black hole that I had dropped into since the death of my wife and son. The trio with him backed up his wise words with their mock anger, exasperation and stone-faced stare at my failure to do anything that met their exacting standards.

"Do you understand how bad this looks for me?" my father said to the wall. He couldn't even look at me.

My mother tutted, my brother shook his head, Scavolo, like an heroic sculpture of a Trojan warrior with his chest filled with phalera, did not move or blink.

"I could have you shipped off to the mines for this. How many times..." his hands rose and slapped on his legs as he turned to the painted fresco on the wall in frustration that neither the wall nor I seemed to respond to his words. I couldn't help but notice that his hands were vein-lined and thick with grey hairs. It was strange how I always noted such things. *It's a curse* my mother had always said when I continued to pick out the lines on her friends faces as they lined up to pat my head when I was a small boy. Rude some had called it, observant said others. But all had agreed that it was unwelcomed. As such I had few friends. As the face of the head of the house, the Patres with all-seeing power over my life, turned to the painted plaster once again I wondered if he expected the picture of a bird to answer his question. As the painted creature ignored his pleas he continued with a glance to me, "do we need to have this discussion?" He finished with a shaking head, a sigh and that look in his eye which suggested that strangling me at birth might have been a good option.

From the corner of my eye, I could see my brother shaking his head. My mother tutted and dropped her head to her free hand and Scavolo didn't blink, didn't move and didn't speak but I could tell the bastard was enjoying this.

After a moment of silence, my father placed his hand son his hips, huffed and then sat heavily. At this my brother followed his lead as he sat slowly, crossing his arms over his chest with his head still shaking in mock disappointment. My mother sat with a pained sigh before she sipped her wine and tutted loudly. Scavolo was rigid, elegant in his stone-like state. The rat still didn't blink, his narrow eyes accusing and indignant but hiding his mirth as his lips quivered at the edges.

"The honour bestowed on our family is the greatest in more than six generations. We cannot allow you to ruin this gods-given opportunity, or to create a scene which will embarrass the name of our family in the Senate" continued the head of the house, his righteousness extending to all of the Lares that stared at us from the small busts of my ancestors who were placed on the table under the only window in the room. I glanced across to see my terracotta grandfather glaring at me to show how upset he was. I wondered if he had been a tutter or a head shaker. "We must show unity as a family now more than ever" my father continued as the wall seemed to agree with his words as he turned his face to it once more. "We must have you play your part for the good of us all, for our future. And this" his hands were flapping again and he stood from his chair to emphasise whatever point he was going to make. I saw the hairs in his nostrils flare with the exertion.

My brother stood and shook his head.

My mother stood and sighed loudly as she sipped her wine. At least it was better than tutting.

I didn't look at Scavolo, but I knew he wasn't blinking.

"This stupidity." His voice rose like an orator in the Comitia telling tales of tragedy and loss. "This drinking yourself into the gutter like a base-born criminal every night is…" he grunted before he could finish his sentence as if a punch had taken his breath. His despair was evidenced by his sagging shoulders which suggested I had sucked all the energy from his body.

My mother tutted - I was disappointed that she had changed from the sigh, it seemed more personal.

My brother shook his head - I wanted to rip it off his stupid shoulders.

And Scavolo, well I couldn't be bothered looking at him.

"It's ridiculous" finished my father and sat again, this time crossing his legs and his arms to show that he had reached the end of his rant.

My mother sighed as she sat, sipping the wine before tutting.

My brother sat but was still shaking his head so much I thought he might get dizzy from the effort.

Scavolo was as cold and immoveable as the stone gods in the Temple of Mars.

Then came the final hammer blow. "I've found you a new wife. Marry her, get over Plaudita and move on." It was a command.

That got my attention. The words were delivered with the cold cruelty of someone who is used to death and has little understanding of the despair I feel at my loss. "A what?" I exclaimed.

"A new wife. The gods know you don't deserve her but she will be ten summers in a year and ready for marriage" he waved down my protests by standing and glaring at me as I tried to interrupt.

My brother stood and glared, my mother stood and her eyes almost crossed as she scowled at my words, Scavolo was forgotten, he was a pleb and not important but I could feel the bastard smiling at me from the corner of the room.

"It is a good match for you, and the family have lands and cattle. I've arranged for her to visit on the kalends and you *will* be presentable," he ordered this with a grimace as if he felt me incapable of presenting any face other than that of the drink sodden fool I'd been since the death of Plaudita. "And you will start to act like a member of this family and live up to your breeding." He nodded in declaration of the finality of the order given; the dictator with the final words that we must obey or be damned. I turned my head to the others in the room as my jaw gaped.

My brother nodded curtly.

My mother nodded slowly, with a protruding bottom lip and a pained frown.

Scavolo was fighting the urge to laugh in my face.

****

"Bastards the lot of them" I grumbled to a laughing Graccus the next day. He didn't answer, he never did. What did he know? He was just a pleb with a paid job, not a Patrician with my family history who was under the thumb of his father's ex-Centurion. "How can they do this to me? It's not acceptable" I said, even though I knew there was little I could do to stop it, unless I ran away. The twelve tables were clear on the rule of ownership, and he was the owner of the family, in every sense of the word. I'd considered leaving, running away, but I was too much of a coward to try and live on my own. I'd done nothing but moan about my poor treatment to my work-mate since he'd walked into the room we shared earlier today and eventually I'd taken a breath and given the fool an opportunity to speak.

"You want to try living in my house" Graccus replied with a gap-toothed grin as he wiped his permanently wet nose on a long sleeve.

I ignored him, prick. What did he know? *Patricians and Plebs should not mix*, that's what I'd been taught since I'd been old enough to swear and kick the slaves. Graccus was all right, but he didn't understand how the system worked, he just worked in it. Sending me here and making me mix with him was enough to turn me in a dribbling fool just like the man who sat across from me. I knew he'd learnt to copy text from a Greek tutor as his family owned a pig farm, which is why his family name was Porcius, and had a few ases to spare on educating their children. However, he had nothing to say beyond laughing at my problems and rambling on about gossip in the forum that didn't interest me. His misaligned teeth stared back out of his empty head as he continued talking.

"My father beat me for burning the bread and nearly causing the thatch to catch." His plight at home was clearly as serious as my own. "Look" he exclaimed standing to pull his tunic up and show me a yellowing on his ribs but also give me an unpleasant vision of his genitals. My eyes must have screwed up as he quickly continued with raised eyebrows. "Yeah, it's bad isn't it? But what can we do, eh? Patres have the final word and we just have to do as we're told" he shrugged as if a beating was an everyday occurrence, which it probably was in his household. "I'm keeping my head down from now on." He shook his head at his own sage words, reminding me of my brother.

I shook my head in response and sighed slowly. "Best just get this work done" I said as much to stop listening as to get away from my own dark thoughts. I turned another wooden tablet over and started to read the decision inscribed into the soft wax.

Graccus and I were scribes in the office of the Quaestores Parriccidii, in which there are two judges presiding over the law in the city. Their main role is to investigate all manner of crimes and bring criminals to the public court. Our legal system is built on a form of the Greek style of democracy, but also includes our own twelve tables which describe the boundaries we adhere to as citizens of our new Republic. The twelve tables were written by the Decimvirs and transcribed to bronze tablets which are posted in the forum for all men to see. As criminal cases are judged at court it was our job to transcribe the decision to velum and send these decisions to each party in the case as well as create a record for the future. Most of the time a fine is imposed on the guilty party, but on the odd occasion of murder or treason, the culprit could be exiled or sentenced to death. Only last year there had been such a case and it had been the talk of Rome for weeks, so Graccus said. I had expected this job to be full of gossip and excitement when I'd first been forced into this form of slavery, but now that I'd done it for a few weeks I felt like Sisyphus rolling that damned rock uphill every day. Then I'd found the girl. It was Graccus, my roommate, who had scribed the case of the Fullers daughter and raised the issue of delivering the death notice the day before.

"Are you getting soup for dinner?" asked Graccus after a while, his wet nose dripping. I grunted in answer as he stood and stretched his back. I watched the drip being expertly caught on his sleeve. My roommate was a head shorter than me and stick thin, but similar in age. His dark eyes matched his dark hair and he had several pox scars on his face but was lucky that they didn't show unless you got close enough to see them, by which time the smell of stale sweat would force you to take a step backwards anyway. I'd told him to wash in the Tiber on more than one occasion, but you can't tell these plebs anything, they have their own ways. He'd given me a lecture on the value of rubbing the body with fine sand imported from the desserts across the sea and how it gave the skin a fresh sheen. I'd seen the scratched, red, mess that such new-fangled treatments left on people's skin and the smell of over-ripe sweat remained at a level almost as strong as the Fullers yard. I wasn't going to try it.

"Give me a moment to finish this and I'll come with you" I replied, knowing what the next comment would be and answering before it could be asked. "And yes, I'm buying."

III

"Two" I said to Milo as we arrived and sat with our faces to the street. Graccus liked to people-watch and so this was our usual spot. I listened to Milo's gossip on the Latin League, the fights in the Forum and any other seedy business that was happening in Rome. The man knew everything, or at least he pretended to. Either way, ninety percent of his stories had a grain of truth in them and it wiled away an hour at the hottest time of the day in which the stuffy, airless room, in which we worked became more of a prison cell than usual. To add to that, the fish soup served by Milo, always served on Dies Mercurii, was the best there was without a trip to one of the coastal towns.

Milo greeted us with a flick of his chin and took the lid off the large terracotta pot to ladle out two large helpings. Graccus sniffed and cleaned his nose on his sleeve as the steam rose from the pot and I licked my lips in anticipation, my belly grumbling in expectation.

Milo leant across to slide the bowls to us and then turned to pull a small loaf of barley bread from the cast-iron warmer below his oven, which he placed in-between the two bowls. "Busy today lads?" he asked in his thick Roman accent, a mix of Latin and Sabine dialects. I looked at him. His shaven head, a few cuts from today's razor, shone with sweat from the hot work over the fires of both soup and oven. He had thick black eyebrows, like two beetles scurrying across his face as they rose in greeting. His intelligent face turned to the street and back towards us after he nodded to two men as they ambled past. His arms were thick, his chest tight with strength and his quick moving eyes gave that aura of one who could easily turn to anger as smile with warmth.

"Same crap" I replied. Graccus grunted and slipped his sleeve across his face before he ripped some of the bread from the loaf and dabbed it into the soup. I'd given up trying to explain to him how to eat properly and took my wooden spoon from a pocket in my toga, licking it to make sure it was clean. "There seems to be more crime happening now that the sun is with us for longer" I replied to his smiling face, spring was coming. I dipped my spoon into the soup and blew slowly to cool the hot liquid.

Milo nodded and placed both hands on the counter. "Always been the way in Rome. Always been the way. And" he bent forwards conspiratorially, his eyes scanning the road to see if anyone was listening to the scandal he was clearly going to impart to us. "Heard you were at the Fullers yesterday" he nodded, his chin almost disappearing into his neck as the beetles on his shiny forehead lifted knowingly.

"How the..." I said as I did my best impression of my brother and shook my head in exasperation.

His thin-lipped smile told me that he'd never reveal his source. "Heard you nearly got your arse kicked, had to be rescued by a woman."

"Fuck off" I snorted. "It was nothing like that."

His grin told me he wouldn't believe any story I came up with so I continued shaking my head and slurping my soup, my family would be proud of me. "Any news on his girl?" he continued. "Any idea who did it?" My shaking head gave him the reply he wanted, and he flicked his head in response. "Some right nasty bastards out there, eh. I mean, what did she do to anyone, poor thing? Lovely girl too" he added. "Father's a nasty piece though. He's already going around asking questions and kicking up a stink, saying that Minerva will get the bastards that did it." Minerva was the deity of the Fuller's trade as well as many agricultural occupations and the girl had been found in the early hours of the morning after the night of the festival to the goddess. I'd been out enjoying the festival myself when I'd stumbled into the girl on my way home. There was a goat herder there that morning too, a short grey-beard with no teeth called Ducus, and we'd come across her body together as some of his goats had jumped into the ditch and he'd asked for my help to find them once he'd calmed down at the shock of me appearing out of the fog like a ghost.

Graccus was leering at his already empty bowl as another drip of snot loomed on the end of his nose. His puppy face looked at me and I tutted and rolled my eyes. Bloody hell I was turning into my mother now. "Go on" I said as Milo, ever alert to more profits, slipped the bowl away to refill it. I looked at the street vendor and frowned before asking, "So, what's the story on the street about her death" the vision of the dead girl flashed in my mind again and I saw the green dress and beauty of the mother as I felt my stomach lurch at the memory.

He replaced the over-filled bowl that would cost me another coin and Graccus lifted it to his lips in one movement, his eager lips twitching as they connect to the bowl and he sucked like a new-born having its first feed. "Not much really Secundus" he answered. "One of the slaves said it was a family feud which went wrong. I also heard that she'd been promised to a duck farmer out on the marshes but then the mother changed her mind after the lad had fathered a child. She's the real boss over there." he said with a confidence which suggested he had inside knowledge of the workings of the family. I was watching his beetling eyebrows as they rose and fell to confirm the story.

"I heard that she was seen with a man in the shadows too" Graccus added suddenly as his slurping ceased and he turned his wide eyed face to us. Our questioning looks made him confirm his words. "Said it in one of the reports" he lifted his shoulders in reply and snatched the last piece of bread from under my nose.

"What else did it say?" asked Milo as he bent lower,

conspiratorial in his search for gossip from mem who had worked on the case. Graccus lifted the bowl and Milo huffed, his mock offence taking just a half second to decide if the telling was good enough for a bowl of his soup, before grabbing it from his hands and adding a half ladle of steaming liquid.

I listened to the words without really hearing them. I was consumed with the vision of the naked body and broken skull. I remembered hearing Ducus before I could see him in the half-light and thick mist of early dawn as he shouted for his goats, the old dog he used to keep them in check limping along uselessly at his side as it bit at a thorn or something that hindered its movement. My memory of his shouts for his animals remained as clear as the sky above as they caught my attention as I'd approached the Gate to the city.

"What's up?" I'd asked as he scowled at my appearance, toga covered in dirt from falling over several times. He looked shocked to see me and narrowed his eyes suspiciously at my slurred words as I drew near out of the fog, clearly steaming drunk. I'd stopped several times to throw up remnants of wine on my slow trudge through muddy roads and no doubt I didn't give him the suggestion that I am a patrician and several levels above him in status as I questioned him. Even his dog didn't seemed impressed by my social status as it sniffed at me for a moment before sitting, cocking a leg and licking its balls.

"Lost two goats. You seen them?" he asked in broken Greek, assuming I was a trader out early, and with a nod towards the direction from which I'd come. I said I hadn't and had waved my arms at the thickness of the fog which meant I could only see about ten steps ahead of me, adding that they must be close as they wouldn't just wander off with such an alert creature as the hound that now paused, appeared to frown at my words and then to turned back to sniff its arse as if it the nectar of the gods had just erupted from its orifice. Stupidly I then offered to look and see if they'd fallen in the ditch as I knew that quite often the pig farmers had to climb down and drag their lost hogs back when an unlucky animal had fallen in. I'd slid down on my backside, heedless of my toga, which I'd had to wrap into coils around my shoulders, and then slopped along the bottom in the ankle deep mud and filth calling 'here goat' into the mist until I'd seen a white shape lying half up the side of the far bank.

"It's here" I shouted as I slipped again and my head span with the effort of trying to remain on my feet. I didn't hear his reply, but it was a few choice phrases for sure as I stared helplessly up at the fog and then puked once more just like I'd done at the stone of Janus which marked the road junction from whence I'd come. Then I saw her. My mouth dropped open and my jaw fell slack. I couldn't speak. The half-naked body lay with one arm high above her head and the other behind her back. Her legs were apart, showing areas that a young woman should never show. Her skin was almost white, paler than the weather worn statues in the Forum and her head was crushed above her right eye. I'd sobered in a heartbeat and screamed for the goat-herd to raise the alarm and get the local neighbours to bring help. His stupid questions only caused me to shout louder that there was a dead body in the ditch. I'd stood and stared at her for so long I couldn't remember much else, her empty eyes implored me to look away, which I couldn't do as my mouth gaped, my mind became as empty as the fog of the might and I was rooted to the spot. After some time the locals had come and we'd pulled her limp body from the ditch, men and women gathering in crowds to wail and shout at the death that happened on their doorstep.

"You want more?" Milo nudged me with his elbow as he took the empty bowl and woke me from my dreaded memories.

"No. No thank you" I replied quietly. Graccus gave me a strange look before standing, wiping his nose on an already encrusted sleeve and stating that we had better get back to our room as Scavolo would be in soon to check on us. I paid the bill and followed him in silence; the dead girls lifeless face still staring back at me from deep in my thoughts. I cursed Somnus as we walked back up the slope of the Clivus Capitolinus to the temple of Jupiter and considered how I could get hold of some wine to drink myself to a sleep in which the girl and Plaudits did not haunt me.

****

"All done?"

"Yes. I finished his last two as he had the shits from too much soup" I said to the slave who was collecting the scrolls and tablets to store them in the library where all records are kept for future use. It is one of the great developments of our modern society since the Kings had been deposed, that we create a record of every decision made by the laws of the twelve tables so that we can learn and apply equal measures to similar future situations. Gone are the days when the King would simply, quite literally, wipe the slate clean when one of his nobles paid the right fee to have charges against him or his clan dropped. The Republic is new, but men like my father are charting a way through the problems we face, and no man will ever hold that single power of kingship again, except in a time of war.

Graccus had complained of the food being too rich for him soon after we'd returned and had been consistently farting, complaining of gut ache and filling the small airless room we shared with fish odours to the point where I could barely breathe and I'd sent him home, agreeing to finish off his work. And to think, he was paid for this and I wasn't. I was shaking my head again before I stopped myself and let out a small chuckle in memory of my brothers actions the day before. The slave peered back at me as he was halfway through the door.

"It's alright, just laughing at Graccus." The slave smiled at my words, it's always good to see *someone else* with the shits.

"See you tomorrow, Master" he added, leaving.

I sat in silence, the candles flickering, for a long moment and considered what to do, whether to stop for a drink on the way home or to just steal some of mother's wine; she'd be none the

THE CASE OF MINERVA

wiser as she'd be past checking on the stock by now. It was heading towards late Tempus Pomeridianum, the sun would set in an hour or so. I was just about to leave when the curtain was pushed back and the brutal face of Scavolo peered at me with his usual look of distain.

"Doing his work again?"

The slave had clearly shared my comment. Bastards never keep anything to themselves.

"Happy to help out a fellow worker in need. I'm sure you did the same in the legions" I quipped.

He sneered. "Come with me, got something for you." His retreating form suggested this was an order, not a request and so I followed with a heavy sigh; I was even more like my mother than I thought. The temple was filled with the light from the low sun, which shone through the four large, open, double doors on each side of the square building. The heat of my small room was replaced with the cool of the evening, which flooded through the openings giving a fresh scent of Juniper mingled with the smoky aroma of wood fires from the houses below the Temple. A smell of incense drifted to my nostrils from two priests of Jupiter who sang as they burned offerings to the god on the central altar. There was an inner peace to the temple which I expected would soon be destroyed by the dressing down I'd be receiving from the tongue of Scavolo.

He was already halfway across the central opening and heading towards his office rooms that were next to the library adjacent to our small cupboard, so I quickened to close the gap. He by-passed his own room and entered my father's office, which immediately filled me with dread. I wondered what I had done and what they were going to blame me for this time. I slowed as my shoulders sagged. It was too late to stand and argue, and I was too tired to give a toss about anything they had to say. I'd already contemplated the marriage to what was no doubt a snotty-faced, bug-eyed child that they'd chosen for me and I knew I had to tighten my belt and suck up my anger as I really had only one other option – to leave and try to create a life for myself. But, deep down in my soul, I knew my life in my father's house was too comfortable to give up. I'd seen the beggars on the street and the bum-boys making a living in the alleyways and I didn't want to end up like that. I liked to think I was tough, winning a few wrestling matches with other soft-arsed Patrician boys of the same age, but in reality it was men like Scavolo who ran Rome, not a push-over like me. I had to endure in the fashion of my ancestors, so that was what I would do.

I entered the room and turned into the personification of a favoured son. "Father" I bowed in his presence, as a good son should. Scavolo was sitting as I remained standing, most inappropriate for a man of my blood. I stood taller to show that I was above such pettiness.

"Ah, Secundus." He spoke as if surprised to see me despite his dog having brought me to his feet at his call. "Sit" he ordered, with a wave towards a three-legged stool. I half expected it to collapse under my weight and both my interrogators to burst into fits of laughter as I crashed to the floor. I was disappointed when it held my weight as I flopped heavily onto the smooth wooden seat. "You have been here a few weeks now and started to get a feel for how things work in the courts" he said crossing his arms over his chest and looking across at me from behind a magnificent wooden desk with decorated legs carved with nymphs. I noted that the cherubs were playing with amphora flowing with the waters of life and a fat image of Bacchus leered at them. I dragged my eyes from their chubby legs and awaited my father's words. I glanced to Scavolo who was eyeing me like a hawk.

"Yes father" I replied, surprised at the question.

He nodded to Scavolo. So, here was the truth of it. My father couldn't even bring himself to pack me off himself, he had to get his henchman to tell me I was shit at the job and to push off. I sat stiffer, my jaw clenched, but trying to show that stoic face that I had been trained as a boy to deliver to any political enemy who raises concern about my personal actions, words or behaviour. It is our Roman way, to face danger dispassionately with a stern brow and a stiff jaw to give an aura of authority over those who challenge us. My brother and I had spent hours in such practice as children, my sibling, Sul, always ten steps ahead of my failing efforts, gaping mouth and fits of giggles. I was as shit at that as I had been in life in general.

"Dentatus has broken a leg" Scavolo said. "Prick." His dark eyes narrowed at my surprised look. "I need someone who knows a bit about the law to go with Fastus for the next few weeks and call for the plaintiffs to come to the Comitium." The process of law was simple. If you were accused of a crime or derogatory behaviour towards a fellow citizen you had to appear at the appointed time at the Comitium and have the claims against you called out in front of the people. The trumpeter Fastus had to go to the house of the accused and announce an accusation with several loud blasts, and then Dentatus would call out the names of the accuser and the potential crimes they had committed, as well as give a date for them to attend the Comitium to face the charges. Dentatus then, on the day of the case, repeated it at the Comitium for all to hear. Any citizen could come to listen to the cases and cast a vote and usually the agreement of the crowd resolved the issue. The man doing the calling had to have a good understanding of the law if he was questioned by those called to account for their actions, and I was cursed with a memory which could recall all manner of details after only a short reading or discussion and was arrogant enough to tell people why. It was why I had no friends; I was too keen to tell them they were as thick as the pile of shit that clogged the cloaca maxima on a summers day when they struggled to grasp basic concepts. I'd been a lonely child.

"Your father thinks you might be up to taking his place. I've told him you haven't got the balls for it, but he seems to think that your show at the Fuller's suggests you have a bit more spunk than I give you credit."

I glanced to my father, whose un-emotional face told me nothing. He'd clearly received top marks in his stoicism classes and my slack jaw and wide-eyed face showed that I'd never listened to the old Greek tutor he'd paid for as he dribbled on about Homeric Heroes and roles on the political ladder, which to his thinking were the only measure of success in life. Well, apart from dying a hero on the end of a spear in some pointless war.

"Well?" Scavolo asked in a bored voice, his look suggesting that I was too dim-witted to understand what he was asking.

I glanced to my father, his face remained impassive. Gods he was good at this; I needed to practice. "I'd be honoured," I said, standing and looking down my nose at Scavolo as the Centurion's mouth twisted into a half-smile, half-grimace that made him look like he'd trodden on a wet dog turd in bare feet. "I feel it would be a duty to the city, to this office and to my father. So I accept," I puffed out my chest.

"Right" said Scavolo, his eyes darting to my father and then back to me. "Just don't cock it up." He always had to have the last word. "Gallicinium tomorrow" by which he meant just after cock-crow. "Fastus has all the details. Don't be late" his head inclined to tell me to go. I nodded to my father, turned, and marched out of the door like a man who had been awarded a crown of bravery in a civic ceremony.

A job. An actual job.

Well, at least something more interesting than sitting in that dank room with that bore Graccus and his constant farting, pathetic stories about his pathetic family and then paying for his lunch every day. I set off home at a fast pace, my mouth curling upwards for the first time in weeks. I replayed the words, *your father thinks you might be up to it.* I nodded to myself as I walked. I'll show them how good I am at this job, that'll teach them to treat me like dirt, I thought. I'd strode down the Clivus and past the base Tarpeian rock where the traitors were hurled to their death before I looked up. I noticed I was standing at crossroad to the shrine of Janus and considered a devotion to the god for a new beginning. Yes, I'd show them all I was good for something, however much they thought I'd cock it up. I hadn't made a devotion to a god since my wife died, but this was a turning point. Maybe the gods were smiling on me now, and Janus, a new beginning, it was fortune that put me here outside his shrine and I dug into my purse with a happy heart. I pushed aside the heavy silver and dragged out a few coppers, with which I headed to the shrine and set out a bargain that I'd make this life better if Janus looked after me in my new role.

IV

It was past my normal lunchtime. My feet hurt, my belly ached and I was bored shitless.

Added to that, my throat stung from shouting out the stupid crimes that people were accused of by their neighbours or some other pathetic complainant with a grudge to bear. One idiot had cut down a tree that encroached on his land. What a prick. Everyone knows that you can only cut off the branch that encroaches onto your property and not the tree itself. He'd lose a good few Ases for that. The idiot shouted that he didn't know the law, but I'd shaken my head and told him it was his responsibility to know the twelve tables and that they were on public display for everyone to see. It was his fault and nobody else's. He'd called me a Patrician bastard and followed the trumpeter grumbling like a child caught stealing apples until I'd told him to fuck off and turn up at the Comitia at the appointed hour or we'd come and drag him from his home. Another had been heard cursing a neighbour after a fight. That was more serious. It is clear in the law that such action is inexcusable. When he was called, he'd claimed that the neighbour had cursed him first. Fastus and I shook our heads in despair at his utter stupidity. Surely, everyone knows that all cases involving witchcraft or cursing fall in favour of the first man to claim they had been cursed. Why are people so stupid? Do they not understand the law?

By Solis Ocasus, I was dead on my feet. Fastus said goodbye and told me I needed to be at the temple by cockcrow the next day. I groaned silently at my aching limbs and sat heavily on the steps of the Temple looking up at the wooden columns above painted with hunting scenes and joyous images of Jupiter in his many roles as deity of the sky, bringer of thunder and overlord of all the heavens. Being at the Temple suddenly reminded me of my bargain with Janus the night before on my way home. I cursed the copper coins I had lost to the god, who'd let me down, two-faced bastard. I let out a heavy sigh so long and slow I felt as empty as a used wine skin when I'd finished. I began to rub my aching feet, smelling the foul odours of unknown things I'd obviously stepped in during the day and was just considering which tavern I might be able to sneak into for a drink on my way home when I felt a presence next to me. I started as I realised that Scavolo stood right behind me, his cold face looking at me with contempt as he loomed over me like the chariot of Jupiter atop the temple behind him.

"Why are you still here?" he asked slowly.

I stopped rubbing my feet and wiped my hands on my tunic as I contemplated his question. I'd been taught to always stand and talk to those below me in social class, but for some reason I decided that sitting was a better option with the man-mountain who stood over me from the top step of the temple.

"I've just finished for the day. With Fastus" I garbled thinking he was complaining about my loitering on the steps. "I'm just about to head home and prepare for another excellent day in the judicial system helping the city…"

"Not that you prick" he cut me off as I was just getting up to speed with the speech that I would tell my family later this evening as I lied about what a great day I had had. "At your age, what are you, eighteen, nineteen?" he sneered as he spoke but didn't wait for an answer, flowing through my attempt to explain myself like a plough sheer through soft soil. "I'd killed twenty men, been part of four night attacks and won my first phalera for bravery. So why are you still here? Why don't you steal some of daddy's gold and fuck off on your own, save him some of the embarrassment you're going to give him over the coming years."

His words were so abusive I stood, his face lighting up at my anger and sudden aggression. "You can't speak to me like that," I stammered.

"Just did" he shrugged. "Don't tell me you haven't considered it. Soft-arsed kid like you?" he flicked his head in mock laughter and his teeth flashed as his lips parted in derision.

"I..." My words disappeared as I swallowed dryly. He laughed mirthlessly as he stared me down.

He was more than a head taller than me and for a split second I almost responded to his aggression, but I held myself in check. The bastard was goading me, I could see it in his eyes. He wanted me to lash out so that he could tell my father I'd struck him and have me removed. I wouldn't give him the satisfaction. I stepped back and sneered as I replied. "I like it here" I said, inclining in my head to the temple. "The gods have given me a new beginning and I'm going to take it. Janus and I have made a bargain. Don't get in my way Scavolo or the furies will come looking for you" I added cheerily invoking the age-old tradition of a plea-bargain with the gods turning on anyone who stood in the way of its completion.

The old bastard took a moment to show me his clenched teeth before his head rocked back in a mirthless snort of laughter. "The fucking gods shit on you from a height years ago lad. If you can't see it now, you never will. The only future you have is shagging that skinny bitch they're lining up for you and drinking yourself to an early death in boredom." He bowed with a flourish and turned away, still chuckling to himself.

Anger can be such a strange state.

I was boiling inside. My muscles were as tense as a bull having his balls chopped from his loins, and yet I could do nothing. I seethed. I felt like screaming at his retreating form, but something stopped me. Cowardice? I sat again, putting my head in my hands and closing my eyes. In a heartbeat I saw the dead girl's face looking back at me, then my dead wife staring at me and shaking her head in disappointment; she would have fitted in so well in the family.

Janus had shat on me and was laughing at my pathetic life with both faces, the bastard. I almost screamed. I needed a drink.

****

The roads were slippery, thanks to the army of animals that had deposited copious lumps of dung as they were herded from the Forum Boarium at the close of the market. I followed the trail of droppings towards the bridge to the fields where the shepherds and farmers would camp for the night before returning to the open marketplace again the next day to continue their trades. I knew a good, cheap, tavern by the bridge that would give me credit as I had little coin on me and my thirst needed quenching. I stopped at a corner and pissed in a terracotta pot, the face of Minerva displayed on the side. I wondered if it belonged to the Fuller, *her father*, as I emptied my bladder and remembered the angry face, the green dress, the noise and smell of the fullers yard. Then I heard music and wailing, the soft sounds of the flute followed by the hired plaudits from the funeral marchers paid to sing the virtues of the dead as they went to the heavens. I stood to the side and bowed my head as the procession progressed towards the bridge across the Tiber. Several people passed by as I hid in the shadows, their dark tunics pulled over their heads in sorrow so that none of them could see the light in homage to their dead family member. Usually it wasn't easy to make out men or women as they all dressed similarly for funerals and most Romans were of a similar build, but in this case three or four of the men were so tall that I was surprised and their shapes and heavy builds caught my eye. At that moment, I felt compelled to follow. I had no reason to do so, but I couldn't help myself.

At the funeral, I stood back in the long shadows of the trees so that I didn't intrude on this most personal of moments. The songs of Minerva, goddess of tradesmen, were sung as part of the dirge and I heard the words of songs to the gods that were sung at my wife's funeral come back to my ears. A tear slipped from my eyelids as the figure was lowered onto the funeral pyre by the four large men. I stood and felt pity for the family, for those who had loved whoever had died and was being cremated. I found myself wishing they'd had a happy and long life filled with music, laughter and fun. Memories of my wife's gasps for breath came to me as I watched the fire being lit, the torches flickering as the light of the day began to sink below the trees. It was a fitting scene for a funeral and I felt the urge to sit and weep but held back my tears as anger at the gods bubbled like the fire of a volcano waiting to erupt. I don't know how long I stood there, but it must have been some time because when I looked up once more there were only a few people remaining by the half burnt pyre, their shadows long and the members glowing red in the semi-darkness of the late evening.

Then I caught her eye.

A cold shock hit me and I knew it was the funeral of the girl, the fuller's daughter. How, I would never know. Why? It would haunt me forever. What had brought me here, to this moment? My jaw slackened as I realised that the girl's mother was looking directly at me, a calculating gleam in her eye. I turned quickly and scurried away, ashamed; frightened that she'd think I was intruding on their private moment. I hurried toward home, forgetting my need to drink and heading as fast as I could sensibly walk towards the road that would take me to my bed.

****

"You're wanted" said Graccus appearing at my shoulder with a hungry look at my half full bowl of soup. I realised that I hadn't spoken to him since I started my new job and felt somewhat abashed despite my initial pleasure to be out of his company. His reaction to my indifferent glance suggested he was pissed off with me. I looked at my bowl, then back at him as he stood above me, scowling with that drip of snot starting to build on his large nose. I slid the bowl across towards him and nodded for him to finish it off. His anger seemed to dissipate like a summer mist as he drew his arm across his nose before he started to slurp at the bowl that I'd offered him. Milo appeared like a fly around horseshit and beamed with that knowing 'second bowl' raise of the eyebrows that I knew so well. I shook my head slowly and let out a long hiss of breath; at least I didn't tut.

"Go on then" I said with a half-smile. Graccus grinned as he handed the already empty vessel to Milo almost as if the two of them had pre-arranged the meeting, which I wouldn't put past them. "Who wants me?" I asked.

"Scavolo."

"Shit."

I was rewarded with a lop-sided smile from my former colleague. "You coming back then? Cocked it up?" he suggested jauntily as another drip was forming at the tip of his nose.

I held my tongue. Clearly the bastards had been talking about me in my absence, and somehow the question of my inability to do anything properly had been shared with every man and his dog in the Temple. I pulled an As from my pouch and placed it on the tabletop as I got to my feet and ignored his question, giving it the disdain it deserved.

"What about bread?" asked the beggar who had taken half of my lunch and was now filling his belly with a second helping.

I was about to tell him where to shove the bread when Milo came to his rescue. "Don't worry Secundus. He's a regular so I'll let him have a few of the burnt crusts for free" at which I inclined my head and walked away feeling as if somehow I'd gotten a fantastic deal out of losing my lunch and paying for Graccus to stuff his guts once more. I hoped it gave him the shits.

****

"So, you been shagging her or what?"

Scavolo was full of questions, his face alight with intrigue and gossip as he stared at me from behind his desk, fingers interlocked as his hands rested on the tabletop. I noticed how empty his workspace was, no mountain of tablets or half-written scrolls, no task lists and job-plans, just clean empty space. However, on the desk sat a small pile of silver coins, at least a half years pay for a man like the ex-centurion whose narrowed eyes watched me as I squirmed under the ridiculous nature of what he asked. The silver burned into my memory as I turned a look back at the centurion and his statement, which had surprised me. The question had been prompted by my arrival, a nod to sit and his tipping out of the contents of a pouch, which he stated was brought to him as a gift to the temple by the Fullers wife. She had brought it herself and mentioned that she wished it known that Minerva had spoken to her in a dream and told her to make a gift to the Temple of Jupiter because a man from the temple would be the instrument of vengeance against the murderer of her child.

I blustered under his gaze, his comment stinging my ears. "I...I know nothing about it. What do you mean shagging her? Why do you think it's me? Any one of those pricks out there could be the object of her dream?" I was waving a loose hand at the pile of coins and starting to babble like an idiot, or worse still an accused man. "I saw her at the funeral... nothing else..." He was smiling at my red-faced anguish, his shiny head glinting in the light of the low sun that fell through the un-shuttered window to his right. "And what does that mean, her instrument of vengeance? It's got nothing to do with me Scavolo, you're barking at shadows."

He shifted forward, leaning on his elbows as his eyebrows met in the middle of his face. "So that's a no then. You're not shagging her?" he looked disappointed for a moment before sitting back.

"I couldn't believe it when I thought about it. Prick like you? Good-looker like her?" he scowled and shrugged and then his head leant to the side. "I've seen stranger things though." These last words were spoken with a faraway gleam in his eye as if the conversation was going to take a new turn before he seemed to remember I was in the room and the look of disgust returned. "So why did you follow them to the funeral? Guilty conscience?" he asked with a shrewd gleam.

"What?"

He shrugged.

"What!" I exclaimed more loudly, the implication suddenly dawning. "You think I had something to do with her death?" A messenger boy ran into the room just as I spoke, dropping a tablet on the desk before his eyes glanced to me with the look that told me he'd heard what was said. Fuck, that means everyone will know that Scavolo is blaming me for the death of the Fuller's daughter I thought as I turned my face back to my accuser, fear written in my eyes.

"Nah, we had your story checked out and anyway you haven't got the balls to kill anyone."

His reply stunned me. They'd *checked me out*! Had my father been included in *'they'*? I let out an exasperated hiss of breath before speaking again as I inclined my head to the pile of coins. "Why did she give you that lot? What else did she say? What's this about vengeance and who is her instrument of revenge?"

He looked at me for a long moment before answering my question, his gaze appraising rather than the usual rueful glare of disappointment that he and my father shared. "Funny that" he said slowly. "She was very secretive about that bit. Said something about the goddess coming to her in a dream but didn't add much more than that." His eyes rose as he waited for me to fill the silence and his face turned back to that statue-like gaze that the bastard used when accusing me of incompetence.

I didn't react to his question and silence. I was above such things.

Our stand-off stretched as my scowl grew deeper and his face remained impassive. *Bollocks,* even Scavolo was better at this Roman stoicness shit than I am despite my patrician breeding and long-suffering education. "I'll go and see her" I said, standing. "See what all this is about."

Scavolo shrugged and replied, "Why?"

I was dumbstruck. I didn't know. All I knew was that I couldn't sleep and her dead daughters face was staring back at me every night. "I don't know" I replied with a shaking head and a huff as I stared at the wall, gods I really am like my parents. "But something is telling me I need to."

The head man sat back in his chair and with steepled fingers touching his chin he watched me for a long moment as if he was calculating my next actions. "Right, if that's what you think will help, then go. But not before you've finished the day with Fastus you won't."

V

The trouble with work is that it leaves you mentally and physically drained. I'd walked up every one of the seven hills of Rome before we'd finished the afternoon, Scavolo sending messengers with more and more summons just as we believed we were done for the day. It was almost as if the bastard was trying to stop me going to find the Fullers wife. As we crossed Etruscan Street on our way back towards the forum for the third time that day Fastus turned to me and flicked his head in the direction of a group of men away to the right. "Isn't that that Fuller?" he said with narrowed eyes.

I looked up to hear shouts before I saw four men, two of them a head taller and twice as broad as the others coming to what appeared to be blows. A fight. We strolled over. It was always good to see someone get their head kicked-in in a street brawl, and by the size of two of these bruisers it would be a quick and enjoyable scrap. A small crowd had already gathered, the women shouting louder than the assembled men for a kick or punch to be thrown. I recognised the Fuller instantly and stood back with a smile as I wondered how he would handle himself, but then realised that it was three against one and I felt disappointed that it might be over quickly and a waste of our time.

"Where is he you little bastard" shouted the Fuller, dragging a scrawny youth about like a rag doll, the boys genitals flapping as his tunic, which was bunched in the fists of his attacker, rose to his chest to give the watching women a screaming fit of giggles. "We've looked everywhere. You said he'd be here."

Then my mouth dropped as Graccus, his nose dripping a

glistening globule of snot, and his torso writhing in the grip of the fuller turned his frightened face to the crowd and spotted me. As the Fuller twisted him around his voice screeched, "He's there" and an accusing finger pointed directly at me.

Every eye on the street turned in my direction and I felt Fastus melt away into the background as Graccus fell to the floor, discarded like a used rag. I was as rooted to the spot as Cyparissus, turned to a Cypress Tree by Apollo. My mouth fell open and I felt Fastus step further backwards, you can always count on your friends to leave you alone in your moment of need, as three thugs turned their heads toward me.

"Now, gentlemen" I started to say, trying to remain calm as the women folk squealed at the thought of a patrician in his shiny toga being on the receiving end of a good thrashing. All I could do was curse that bastard slave boy who'd listened to Scavolo's accusation that I had been involved in the death of his daughter and had clearly spread the tale across the city already. I cursed Janus and the loss of my coin once again, thinking that he was pissed at me for not giving the silver coins I had in my purse. You can't trust these bastard gods. They love you one moment and stamp on you the next.

The Fuller advanced like a one-man army his shoulders wide enough to block out the sun. He reached me in three athletic strides, muscles rippling, and then just as I expected a fist to land on my nose he fell to his knees and grabbed my ankle, his face looking up at mine as if I was his master and had caught him stealing the family gold. His two workers fell to one knee and their heads bent low, eyes averted. "Master, you must come with me. Minerva has spoken to my wife. We need you, master. Minerva has spoken. We need you. Come. Come" he implored, standing and beckoning me to follow, urgency in his movements. His words not only confused me but shocked me. I hoped that the smell of piss that drifted to my nostrils was from him and his men, and I'd not made a mess of myself. I drew in a deep breath and tried to ignore the fact that my heart was pounding like a thunderstorm behind my ribs.

"Of course, master Fuller. Of course I'll come if I can be of any use." I turned to Fastus, his face twisted in surprise at the sudden turn of events and I gave him my coldest glare at his betrayal. The crowds chattered like birds in the trees as we sliced our way through the throng who had gathered to see the fight, faces now turning away in boredom from the lack of activity. I noticed a strange smell and felt Graccus slip in beside me, his face eager for gossip. "Piss off" I hissed.

"I brought them to you, we'd been looking for ages. I should come too" he added. "To protect you."

This time I nearly did piss myself. Cheeky sod. If there was a fight the only use he'd be would be if the attackers tripped over him as he fainted in fear. His puppy-dog face beamed at me in expectation of a positive answer to his question. I shook my head in resignation and strode out behind the three men as they headed straight towards the Fullers yard. "Come on then" I replied after a few steps, though the gods only know why.

The yard stank as badly as I remembered and was still bustling with activity; the Fullers dance evident in the slopping noise coming from several cubicles. Business was obviously good. We were quickly ushered into the doorway that I had seen the mother appear from a few days before, her green dress and startling eyes still clear in my memory. The corridor we entered was long and thin and seemed to go on forever, passing locked doors to unknown rooms. Small windows ran along the wall to our left to let in light and we passed the open square where the family Lares, small busts and urns of Etruscan origin, sat in alcoves along the wall. It reminded me of our own room where the ancestors continued to look down on us with their painted faces and stern expressions. At least their urns didn't have passionless eyes which followed you around the room, these much more Etruscan in style with what looked like sealed jars and heavily painted black pots. Eventually we exited to a wide square garden filled with budding flowers and well-cropped sweet-pea hedges. I realised that the foul smell of the yard had completely disappeared and nodded my appreciation at the quality of terracotta statues that surrounded the tranquil space in which I now found myself. A slave, pretty and well attired in a white woollen dress, waved us across as her master called our arrival and I followed the Fuller, the other men heading in another direction, their job of finding me done. We were steered to a large square room with one window at the rear, which held a view of rooftops of the houses which ran to the Tiber behind which the Janiculum hill could be clearly seen looming in the far distance. The window had clearly been placed to maximise the view as this part of the Vicus Tuscus was on the highest part of the hill and it *was* impressive. *Piss must make money*, I thought as I looked with envy at the rich furniture, decorated drapes, and black and red Greek vases that adorned the room. I noticed a large statue of the goddess Minerva stared at me critically from the corner, her head tight in bunches of hair which were painted black, her dress a vibrant blue. The eyes stared back like two black dots which fixed me with their anger. I looked away quickly.

"I found him" proclaimed the Fuller in a flat tone as his wife turned a cool eye towards me. Her sweet lips parted as she smiled but her expression remained guarded.

"Secundus Merenda" she said as she rose, the familiarity making me wrinkle my nose and furrow my brow. "I knew you would come" she said cryptically. Graccus stepped on my heel as I came to a stop and I mumbled at the oaf. He retreated quickly. "Come sit, sit" she bent to move a soft chair as her husband stepped to her side and placed his hands behind his back to look down his nose at me. I bristled as I tried to copy my father's lead and took the stoic stance, blanking my face and breathing slowly as I sat on the proffered chair. Graccus stood beside me and placed his hands behind his back in mockery of the Fuller, his dark eyes searching the room as if he was my personal bodyguard and expected a vase of flowers to leap at me at any moment.

"A drink?"

I waved away the suggestion politely, just as my father would have done.

"I am Fucilla" said the mother, an image of her daughter flashing through my mind. "And my husband" at which he inclined his head "is Lucius of the Arturii tribe."

It was first name terms, they were trying to drag me into whatever plot or scheme to find their daughter's killer that they were building. I nodded respectfully as my father would have done. Was Janus playing with me? Had he come up with some scheme to lure me into having one of the Fuller's pots of piss poured over my head? I rued my decision to cut him from my silver and give him my base coins.

She looked at me with narrowed eyes. "I am the high priestess of Minerva" she announced as I let my chin dip in acknowledgement of the rank. It was a surprise but I tried not to let that show in my expression, though the curl of her lip suggested she saw this in my face and was laughing at my pathetic attempts to maintain my status and poise. "It is my role to ensure that the followers of the divine goddess honour her glory. I and my sisters tend to the Shrine on the Aventine as I am sure you are aware?" Again, I inclined my head; I was getting good at this and my lack of knowledge didn't deter me, although my brain flashed with images and words of studies with my tutor, things I'd forgotten as irrelevant came back in that moment and I compressed my lips at the thought. She smiled with the look of a predator that knows they are intimidating their prey. "Her support for the arts and crafts is well known and the five day festival was finished only recently" at which I saw a pained expression momentarily cross her face. Her tone turned heavy as she continued. "You will know that at the festival it is forbidden for any shedding of blood on the first day and this is followed by four days of games." It was true but had slipped my mind until that moment and I could hear the old Greek dribbling on about dates, festivals and Kalends as I listened to her talk. The festival system had been handed down from the time of the Kings and was steeped in tradition, with no animals slaughtered and no fighting or games which might spill blood, allowed on that first day; after that it was the usual drunken bloodbath. "So you can imagine our horror" at which she nodded her head towards her husband "at the loss of our own dear Lucilla." I'd never known the name of the girl, clearly named as a combination of both parents, very Etruscan, and as I watched the pain behind Fucilla's eyes I felt my heart quicken.

"My husband and his men have searched the streets for clues to what happened on that night" at which her sharp eyes narrowed by a margin that made me feel as if she was trying to read my thoughts. I remembered both Milo and Graccus telling me of the Fullers bashing heads to find an answer to his daughter's death, it had clearly been to no avail. "And nobody seems to have an answer. It is as if the goddess Nyx has taken her quickly in the night." An image of the broken skull I had seen on that fateful night hit my mind just as much as I was sure the Fuller had hit many heads in his fruitless search for information. "So we would ask you, Secundus. Tell us what you saw that night so that we can add your knowledge to that which we know" at which she glanced to her husband, who had shifted his stance and tightened his jaw.

So this was all they wanted, my story. I felt relief and decided that Janus wasn't the two-faced bastard I thought but the thought of the silver on Scavolo's desk also remained large in my mind. I'd better visit his shrine again and take a chicken to atone for my dismissive thoughts and lack of silver devoted to the god. I took a moment to reply, smelling the stale sweat of Graccus at my side. As I made to speak I remembered the words of my father when he was discussing a case in which the murderer had tried to cover his own tracks but in doing so had implicated himself as his tales of seeing different men grew wilder and wilder and made no sense at all. "I know little" I replied to evident frustration from the Fuller who turned his head to his wife and his teeth flashed as his lips tightened more than they had done so far. "I came across the goat herd, Ducus, and dropped into the ditch to find his missing animals. She" at which I stopped and looked into the deep wells of sorrow that were Fucilla's eyes "was on the far side of the ditch in the fog, halfway up the bank." My words dropped away and I connected to her sorrowful gaze and felt my mouth dry-up like a pond in summer.

"What else did you see?" asked the Fullers wife as she edged forwards on her chair with an intensity which surprised me. "What else can you remember? Any detail, anything of the smallest nature could help." She was almost begging, her husband glanced to her, his hand moving to her shoulder gently.

I looked to him, his strong jaw was lined with stubble and I saw dark shadows under his eyelids. It seemed that he hadn't slept much recently either. I placed my hands together and brought my fingertips to my mouth as I closed my eyes and remembered what I had done on that night, trying to search my dreams for any scrap of information. "I followed the Via Ostiensis along the flat land between the Aventine and Tiber" I said the words as I remembered my stumbling steps and rising bile from another night of drinking. "The roads were wet, it had rained" I looked up at my audience as I spoke and reddened at the concentration in their faces. Graccus wiped his nose as my gaze fell to him. I decided not to say how many times I'd stopped to thrust my fingers down my throat to empty my guts and reduce the inevitable hangover I knew I would be cursed with the next day. "I saw the face of Janus at the standing stone by the old wall of Romulus and I leant against it for comfort as I was too far into my cups to walk very fast or very far" I said in embarrassment. "A doorway was open on the right by the barbers, a light shone as a dog was let inside. Geese cackled on the river." I had closed my eyes now as the memories flooded back. I recalled how I'd felt the bile filling my throat and had to stop several times, pissing in an alleyway like a commoner as well as emptying my guts in a trail across the city; it wasn't my finest moment. "Two men passed me near the gate, the Trigemina. They moved away as I came close to them. I crossed to the other side wary of them too. It was misty and foggy so…" I shrugged as I spoke, to indicate that everyone is wary of people out in the early hours.

"As I approached the Boarium road I had to stop again, leaning on the old milestone next to the ditch." I didn't tell them that I'd leant against it to throw up once more, my guts aching as there seemed little left in my aching stomach but the retching continued unabated as Bacchus laughed at me for my stupidity. "I heard the goatherd Ducus calling for his missing animals. I could smell them too but it was thick fog" I added, looking up.

"Go on" urged the Fuller.

"I said I'd help him look for his animals and then…" I looked up once more. Meeting the eyes of Fucilla I could say no more about her dead child. I felt ashamed.

"What about the two men?" asked Graccus as every face turned to his. His gaze moved to each of us in turn as he continued, "could they have seen anything? Would you recognise them again?"

"Yes, I had not heard of this before" added Lucius, his eyes alight.

They were good questions and I screwed my eyes tight as I tried to recall the fleeting glimpses in the fog. "The first was" I shook my head. "Average height, dark cloak, long, almost to the floor. Good boots" I said suddenly as the curse of memory came back to me and I could see the image of the men in my mind's eye. "Yes, his boots were good, I didn't see his leg below his cloak so they must have come up above his ankles." It was a small piece of information, but good boots were not commonplace and might be easy to trace. "The other was fair haired to his shoulder, his right hand rested on a dagger at his belt and he was no taller than his fellow, but broader. No cloak, just a thick tunic with long sleeves."

"Why was one wearing a thick cloak and one just a tunic at such an early hour?" asked Graccus, his question annoying me as it broke into my recollections.

I was about to answer when the Fullers poke. "Would you recognise these men again?" he repeated Graccus' question more forcefully, his voice urgent as it was clearly information he had not gained from his own questioning.

"The man with the dagger" I leant my head to the side and then nodded slowly. "I watched him more closely than the other. I think I'd know him again, the other not so." The Fuller understood my words, I'd watched the threat I'd seen as any man would do.

After a moment of silence Fucilla sat back, bringing every eye to her movement. "You see Lucius, my dream was right. He can help, just as I said at the temple."

This caught my attention, and I recalled the silver on Scavolo's table once more and his words, his accusation. Something had brought us to this moment. Was it my deal with Janus? Had I been too hasty in my cursing him? I felt ashamed and decided I'd better make a larger devotion to the god of new beginnings. My glance back to Fucilla and I noted the silver rings on her fingers, the thin band of gold at her throat and the fine cloth that she wore. With all of their wealth it suddenly crossed my mind that they'd paid the bastard Scavolo to buy my time. Was that what this was, getting me to tell the tale I knew so that they could use it to bash more heads across the city in search of the man who murdered their child? I tightened my lips; I was not his slave and a bitter taste came to my mouth. The Fuller took my thoughts away as he replied.

"Master" it wasn't first name terms now and I caught the inflection of Etruscan in his voice which I had missed previously despite it being so obvious. "We visited your temple and spoke to your head man." The vision of Scavolo as *my* head man brought a small curl to my lips. "My wife had a vision, a mighty sword was wielded by a man who had seen death, seen our daughter as she lay in the filth of the ditch. The man worked at the Temple of Jupiter, it was clear in the dream. She saw Minerva striding beside him as he searched for Lucilla's killer. She saw him strike the killer, bringing him to justice. And it was *your face* she saw."

Graccus sniffed loudly as he inhaled, wiped his nose and stared at me with an expression which suggested I'd just kicked him in the balls. I could have thumped him if I hadn't been so startled at the words that the high-priestess of the Aventine cult of Minerva had seen *me* in a god-given dream and suggested that I would find the killer of her daughter. I swallowed so hard my throat hurt and I couldn't speak for a brief moment. After what seemed an age I turned to the priestess. "This is true?" I blustered the question as if I didn't believe the words of the man of the house, it was rude but I couldn't think of anything else to say. Her nod sanctioned it. I caught Graccus' wide eyes and awe-inspired gaze and understood the look on his face immediately. A goddess had appeared in a dream to the high priestess of the Aventine cult and I, Secundus Sulpicius Merenda, had been named within the dream. Well, not named as such but clearly linked to the god-given omen. Shit! This was big. It was no wonder Scavolo had so many questions and doubted her words. Had she mentioned my name or the details of the dream to him? He didn't appear to know of my part in the dream, so I guessed she hadn't; I hoped she hadn't. Was it just a dream? Had her catching my eyes at the funeral come back to her in her moment of need in the same way that her daughter's eyes came back to me in my dreams?

This was bad.

My heart started to hammer and my thoughts ran like dogs in the streets, yapping and yelping uncontrollably. Had Janus given me this new beginning? Had our bargain suddenly become greater than I could know or understand? The fear of what this meant hit me like a blast of cold air. I didn't want it, or any part of it. This was not the life I wanted. I instantly knew what my father would make of this knowledge and I almost broke my teeth as I clenched my jaw so tightly that my mouth ached.

Graccus sniffed. My mind came back to the moment.

"What else did the dream say? What do you mean bring the killer to justice?" I'd spoken the words before I realised that I might just have committed myself to this hunt and cursed at my stupidity.

"And what's the finders' fee?" said Graccus quickly, his crudeness turning heads.

"We paid a devotion to the temple" said the Fuller dismissively, his head twisting from his wife to Graccus, who now seemed to change from side-kick to manager of my future as his bottom lip thrust forwards in response and his head moved from side to side very slowly in mock surprise. He reminded me of Milo when he was bargaining with customers over the price of his soup at his store.

"We know nothing of such devotions. This man is not in the employ of the temple" he added with a hand waved in my direction, his voice rising with a strength I'd never heard from him before. I sat back and took my father's stoic lead, letting my social junior speak for me as it was beyond my standing as a patrician to be involved in such squabbles over payments but also considering that if he could earn back some of the coin I'd spent on his lunches for the past few weeks it would be a welcomed benefit.

Graccus didn't disappoint. "If you have agreed a devotion to the temple that is between you and the priests. My client is a free man with no hold at the temple beyond his desire to support the legal system in which his esteemed father is a part. His actions henceforth are not aligned to this work he does for the temple as he does this from his own good will, his own love of our new Republic and his personal sense of justice." He was making me sound less of the drunken fool and more like Cincinnatus who had famously dined out for years on his heroic service to the state as he saved the republic from its enemies before returning to his plough with no request for personal gain. "This search will detract him from his Herculean labours at the temple" he added, making the task appear mountainous. It was a good point, my labours in the dark room at the temple were Herculean in their boredom, and I glanced to Graccus with a new-found respect, he'd make a good lawyer with speeches like this. "And as his aide my time will need to be recompensed." He took a deep breath, snot dribbling on the end of that large nose which held all of our attention for a few seconds. "I would be happy to discuss terms" he finished by crossing his arms over his scrawny chest. I averted my eyes but nodded my head at his words.

Silence.

It had been a good bluff but clearly not good enough, or so I thought.

Then Fucilla, eyes brimming with tears took off a silver ring with an inlaid blue stone. It caught the light and I saw a dolphin dancing in the waves. It was old silver, I could tell. Solid, heavy and worth at least a year's pay to someone like Graccus. My mother had a box full of them which she never wore. I realised now just how much each one might mean to a mother who simply wanted to find the killer of her child. The eyes of the daughter came back to me, and I tightened my lips as I had a fleeting vision that this ring would have been hers, given on the day of her wedding. I couldn't bring myself to look at her, so I dropped my eyes as Graccus took the silver, sealing our bargain.

VI

One of the things that sets educated men apart from the rabble is that they can remember everything and write it down. The Fuller was clearly a clever man but not educated. Graccus had spent a long time transcribing every scrap of knowledge that Lucius had gained from his head-bashing trip around the streets of Rome onto several well-organised slates. And to top it all, the snot-faced lad had also written down my own memories. I was immensely impressed at his efficiency, something he certainly hadn't shown during our time in the dark room at the temple and I had a fleeting feeling that he'd played me well from the first day we'd met. Bastard.

I'd arrived at the temple an hour after sunrise the next day to see him finishing the last items on the slates and beaming at me like a new lover. It un-nerved me. I was about to comment on how impressed I was when our little world of joy was interrupted by Philus, one of the temple slaves, who had obviously been hiding in the shadows awaiting my arrival.

His overly sized nose and large eyes poked into our sanctuary to be followed by a flick of his chin toward the temple from where he'd appeared as he stared at both our happy faces with a leer that suggested the level of shit we were in was as deep as the Cloaca Maxima on the day after the summer festival. "Scavolo wants you" he announced. "Both of you" he smirked as he turned to Graccus and narrowed his eyes in disgust.

Bastard, I thought. He's obviously found out about our visit to the Fullers. I clenched my teeth. "Say nothing" I hissed to Graccus, who frowned.

Our feet slapped the stone floor as we passed across the temple, images of the gods looking down their noses at us and priests eyeing us suspiciously as they watched us walk by, lambs to the altar. Graccus had secreted the slates into a cloth bag which slapped at his hip as he walked. Every click of the slates seemed like a bell tolling our doom as we moved closer to Scavolo's room. As we entered we both got a shock.

"Father" I exclaimed, bowing quickly and trying not to be as surprised as I sounded. I hadn't seen him at home and assumed he was still abed. It certainly wasn't usual for him to be in the temple this early. I felt a thunderbolt coming and sucked in a deep breath as I bowed, Graccus bowing lower than I and averting his gaze.

"What's this rubbish I hear about you taking on a paid job" hammered my father within an instant. I turned to Scavolo, sitting in his chair whilst my father stood, the bastard. This time my father was happy to face me and stare me down, his anger above the pettiness of marrying me off to the bug-eyed skinny child bride I had not yet met.

"I have done no such thing" I replied, impressed with my cool response. I turned to Scavolo. "Has this come from your head man?" I asked with a glance in his direction, playing the calm stoic and feeling quite pleased with my initial gambit in the face of the enemy. I noticed that Graccus was still bent low, not yet daring to raise his head lest it be struck from his body like the snake-filled head of Medusa. Scavolo didn't reply, his face a picture of serenity; gods he was good at this shit.

My father let several heavy coins fall to the table. "Then what is this?" his voice thundered, moving from Vulcan to Jupiter in his fury.

I turned my head to Scavolo and then back to my father. "I believe that was given to your man as a devotion to the temple. It has nothing to do with me beyond the fact that the priestess of Minerva saw it fit to bestow it to the temple as she believes we might be able to find the man who killed her daughter" I answered quietly and in the third person trying to deflect the accusation. I was getting good at this. "It certainly hasn't been offered to me, father." I glanced to Scavolo, implying it had been offered elsewhere.

Scavolo rose from his seat like Neptune rising from the sea. "Then why did you visit the Fuller's house yesterday, and why are words coming to my ears that you have struck a bargain to find the killer of their daughter?"

My father's thick grey eyebrows crossed as much as his eyes at these words. I recognised the damage that such an act could do to his position in the hierarchy of Rome as well as to our families position in the social hierarchy and standing with his fellow judges and patricians if this news spread. Fuck! Janus had played me again. The image of his two faces both creased in laughter flashed in my thoughts. It wasn't the done-thing for patricians to take paid work, especially from the plebeian clans and even worse from freedmen Etruscans. I suddenly felt all my stoic training falling away like rain from the heavens and my mouth began to feel as dry as a sandal left out in the sun for a week. Had Scavolo been watching me? Was he following me? How did he know these things and what did he know about the details of the dream? Bastard. I turned back to my father to see in the expression on his face that his anger had reached the point where I could see him sewing the sack that would drown me in the Tiber himself as he tossed in the snake that would bite my neck and fill me with its poison. I was about to fall on my sword and beg for mercy under their ire when Graccus came to my rescue like Publius Horatius Cocles standing astride the Pons Sublicius in the face of the invading Etruscan army.

"Masters" he said, still bowing so low that his arse was almost showing under his high tunic. "Marcus Sulpicius Merenda, your pardon. It is I who has taken this contract. Not your son, sir" at which he bowed even lower so his nose left a snail like trail on the floor. "My colleague, Secundus Sulpicius Merenda, merely favoured me with his memories of the night, as did the Fuller and his wife. It was his suggestion that I took the case as we have discussed several cases as we transcribed them in our office, and he favoured me with his patronage. I have the details here." Lying bastard, the only thing I'd favoured him with was lunch, but the look on Scavolo's face was enough to snap my drooping mouth shut and return my stoic face. Graccus continued by pulling the slates from his bag as Scavolo, snarling like a bear facing a line of spears, leant across to take the bag from his outstretched hand. My hero continued in the face of the enemy. "I have agreed a fee, which I will earn in my own time to search for the killer. As I am the man that scribed the case I know it better than any other and I feel it would be a great service to the temple to help to solve this riddle" he said these words to Scavolo, who was reading the slates with a look of contempt. "And it was I that offered my services for a fee, not your son, sir. He is advising as he has a much clearer sense of the law than I." He stood now trying to reach his full height, which wasn't as impressive as his words but gave him a strength I had not seen before. "I would hope to be a lawyer one day, sir" he was now speaking to my father but still managing to avert his eyes, it didn't do for a plebeian to be bold in the face of a Quaestor. "And this could be the case which sets me on my path if mighty Jupiter's scales tip in my direction."

"What fee? Show me" snarled Scavolo, clearly not taken in by this story.

"Client privilege" replied Graccus, calmer than I expected and standing his ground impressively.

"Show us. It is important." My father's words were spoken with a quiet authority which resonated with everyone. I noted the vein in his temple that throbbed when he was in the full throes of his anger had receded, dissipating as he saw a way out of what had seemed a disaster; his son taking a paid role to investigate a murder was a problem, his helping a plebeian to rise in the world was patronage. His shrewd eyes glanced to me, then back to Graccus. I averted my gaze, but my chin rose as I turned a cold eye to Scavolo to show him that I was above his pettiness.

Graccus was about to argue, but I coughed lightly, a move which wasn't missed by my father as his jaw tensed at the hesitation in his employee but was followed by his furtive eyes roving between us. The smaller man pulled a string from around his neck on which was held the silver ring. My father took it and lifted it to the light.

"Etruscan" he nodded at the quality, turning the blue stone to the light to see the dolphin and appraising the image for a few seconds before handing it to Scavolo with a calculating look towards Graccus, who was glistening with sweat. I wondered how much Egyptian sand it would take to scrub him clean after today. But then my father turned to the wall as he spoke, and I knew a long lecture was coming. I settled my mind and relaxed a little as I waited for the words.

"It is not seemly for a man of the temple to do such work Graccus Porcius." It was formal names, so I suddenly felt that things were taking a turn for the worse despite the fact that Scavolo had taken the silver. It had been a heroic stand, but like so many Trojan Heroes our ending had been written and the orator was about to proclaim our doom. "This case is like so many others that cross our paths every day in the temple, gentlemen. There is no answer to these tragic events and there will be no murderer identified as nothing has been found and nobody has admitted to seeing or hearing anything which could give a clue to this death." He glanced to Scavolo at this, and he nodded his agreement at the evident waste of time any investigation would be. "It is a frivolity, a trick sent by Mercury. I cannot see how this will support your claim that you wish to be a lawyer and how it will benefit the temple, it will end in disappointment for everyone Porcius." By which my father meant it held no benefit for himself. It was the age old system of patronage, *how does what you do impact on how I look to my peers?* They were wise words and not missed by anyone in the room. "I see no future in this" he added with a cold glance towards me. It was a clear message to me and not to Graccus, his part in this was minor; he was only a pleb.

Graccus turned his face towards mine, his lips a thin line, and for the first time in my life I knew that I had the power to argue against my father's decision. He'd left enough rope for me to tie the ship to the dock or let it drift out to sea with all our hopes stashed neatly on the deck for the waves to destroy. It was another test; the bastard was giving me the chance to cock it up and show what a fool I was. I took a short breath and leant forward to lift one of the silver coins from the table. "There are at least five coins missing from this, father" I said, the implication clear as Scavolo ground his teeth. "But that is not the issue." I was thinking on my feet so played that dice roll with the hope that two sixes had landed and my father's mind was distracted as I gathered my wits. "The issue is that Graccus has contracted to complete his task. I was there, and I cannot lie that he did not do so. The ring is evidence and the twelve tables tell us that an oath and contract must be followed. He has written it down to seal the bargain." My father's legal mind was now piqued, and his eyes seemed to light up at the words.

"We can dismiss it" he waved a hand but his eyes were alight. It is all a game to him. "He should not have acted above his position at the temple, using our knowledge to further his own career. It would be easy to rebuff" he dismissed the case as easily as it would be to remove Graccus from his job at the temple. In a moment, the stakes had risen beyond a simple finder's fee to a whole life of being accused of usurping trust. Graccus' mouth gaped as wide as the Tiber in full flow as the words were spoken and he felt the weight of their implication. My father's eyes were now searching me, looking for the next move in the game, teasing me with this knowledge that I now had the power to save my conspirators credibility in Rome or crush it. His career, and his future were now on the scales of Jupiter that he had claimed may tip in his direction and I held the balancing weight.

"But there is the dream" I added. It was my second roll of the dice. I had hoped to play it later in my argument but as that had not yet fully formed it was all I could do under the scrutiny of the Quaestor with his dictatorial power and clever word-play. I turned to Scavolo, whose questioning gaze suggested that he had no knowledge of the words of the priestess, which is what I had hoped. My die were cast, my gambit was now to be revealed. Janus was back in my camp and his devotion was growing to a lamb.

"What dream?" both men said in unison.

I smiled, letting the words hang for a moment as Graccus turned a half-grin, half snot-dripping face to mine.

"The priestess told us that she had a dream. A dream that a man would find the killer of her child. And that man is Graccus Porcius."

****

It's strange how the gods affect us all. We live our lives buying affections from the various deities, bargaining for favour and changing allegiance when things go badly or sometimes doubling our devotions when they go well. Yet a dream from a goddess which names a man as the sword that will strike at her enemy trumps rational thought. My father had demanded evidence, to which I had given an interpretation of our meeting at the Fullers, and to which Graccus nodded in agreement, his nose wiped several times but his face betraying his unease. Scavolo had questioned every item we mentioned and demanded written proof, which Graccus had claimed he would gain from the priestess that very day. My father had looked at both Graccus, the man he had moments before been happy to cast to the sewers and to myself, the son who had been an absolute failure to him and almost, and I mean almost, smiled.

After that brief stand-off, where Scavolo had looked at Graccus with so much disbelief written in his face that I half-expected him to march off and ask the Fuller for proof of this dream himself, he had then dissected the slates with us, my father taking an active part in what had suddenly become a debate on the final acts of the girl, the men I had seen, the stories Lucius the Fuller had gained from his own search and every other scrap of information we knew from our discussion with the parents of the murdered girl, all of which were written on the slates in front of us. He was testing us, asking Graccus for thoughts, which he appraised in silence. After some time, Graccus was sent, with a slave in tow to ensure he actually went to the Fullers, to get a written statement from the priestess regarding the dream and we had been given three days in which to find the killer. To say I was in shock is an understatement. My father had even placed a hand on my shoulder as he'd left the room, a moment of affection that astonished me almost as much as my ability to lie to him that Graccus was the man chosen by Minerva.

As he left the room Scavolo had turned back to me and snarled "I don't believe a fucking word, but don't cock it up."

I expected no less, though I had reminded him that the ring he had secreted away belonged to Graccus. My father had said he could have it when he solved the case. We'd both turned knowing smiles to that.

VII

Milo placed the bowl on the counter and sniffed. "Cold today" he said, looking up at the clouds. "Storm coming." I couldn't agree more. What had I done? Three days to find a killer. Three days. I hadn't answered his comment so Milo, his black eyebrows busily rushing across his frowning forehead added, "What's up, Secundus. Girl problems?"

I tutted like my mother and grinned at the thought, "No such luck, work problems" I answered.

Milo scoffed, "work, you? Son of the boss? I heard you're kept like a prisoner to keep you out of the drinking dens across in the Subura, but surely it's not like a real job. Where's Graccus?" he added quickly, the accusation made without thought.

"He'll be here soon, better get a bowl ready" I added to his evident pleasure. I considered his words. Yes, I was the boss's son, and I knew it was just a prison without bars to keep me from further disgracing the family name, but something had changed at the Fullers. *The dream had named me.* The gods were giving me a sign that I had a place in the world, that I had a purpose. Was it my deal with Janus or was it Minerva now bestowing her gaze upon me? How I acted now could change my world forever. I cast my thoughts back to the words with Graccus as he prepared to leave for the Fuller's yard to get their statement.

"Why did you name *me*, Secundus" he whispered, wiping his nose on the back of his hand, which glistened un-invitingly.

"Did you not see that you would have been out on the streets if I had not done so. You would be no use to my father if I had said it was me that the priestess had named. I'd have that prick Scavolo at my side telling me what to do and you'd have been thrown to the crows." His face had moved through several emotions before his anger and shock had turned to understanding and then appreciation. The love-lorn look returned and I backed away with a dismissive hand gesture at his gratitude. In truth I wanted no part of any future in which I was beholden to petty gods who would as quickly kiss you as smite you and who knows if the priestess was just making up her stupid story regarding her dream to garner my help, I'd seen such pathetic stories before. Evidence, that's what my father needed, and so did I. Maybe we were more alike than I thought. When had the gods ever smiled on me? Certainly, the holes I'd fallen into recently were fuelled by Bacchus himself, but they'd given me nothing but trouble. I kept my lips tight as I considered all this trickery and foolery. Maybe it was Mercury trying to fool me as my father had suggested. It had certainly changed his attitude, his interest in the case and questioning of what we knew from our meeting with Lucius Arturii had given me a glimpse to the man of work that I never saw at home.

"Make the statement clear that the man who wrote of the death would find the killer. If nothing else we can both say that we did so and it's a good way to make a lie without showing that it is intended to be so. Get her to change the words, to name you as the man contracted to find the killer or make it ambiguous. I cannot be named in this Graccus. Explain the situation to her, so that it is clear; avoid naming me as the man in the dream. Something tells me that if I am named, things will go badly. Yes, tell her that." Graccus had agreed, saying he would do it and return as quickly as he could. It was basic, but I could think of nothing else at the time.

I took my spoon from my small bag and licked it before devouring the meaty stew. The bread was soft and served with flavoured oil which I also licked from the small terracotta bowl. I asked for more and Milo, to my surprise came and sat beside me as he delivered it, his eyes glancing into the street and back as he leant forward. "I have a man delivering wine this afternoon, I could sell you an amphora if you're interested. Good stuff from the north, not the crap from the vineyards over the river. I'm trusting you not to say where it came from though. Special service to a good customer" he added as his eyes narrowed. "Seeing as you're not allowed to go out, why not let Bacchus come to you" his raised eyebrows and nodding head stated conspiratorially.

I considered his words for a moment. If we were to find this killer I'd need a clear head, but a cheap amphora stolen from the vineyards of the Rutillii from the north, which is clearly what he was suggesting, was something I couldn't turn down. "How much?" I asked quietly, my own eyes searching the street quickly as I copied his own constantly moving gaze. Gods not only had I turned into a liar, I was receiving stolen goods now. I was becoming a real credit to my family.

His smile showed he'd landed his fish and we agreed a price after a short haggle in which I got an amphora of good wine for less than half the price of the wine merchant my father used. I ordered a second bowl of stew and sat back feeling happy with myself. I wondered if the devotion to Janus was coming through or whether I needed to make a devotion to Minerva, who had placed me in the priestess's dreams or whether it was all just bollocks and had nothing at all to do with the gods. That's the problem with the gods, you never know which one is smiling on you and which is testing you, and even if you do get lucky you never know if it is because of the god or just being in the right place at the right time. My mood turned glum as I tried to work out which god to give devotion to, or whether both needed my silver, or none, it was a truly theologian problem worthy of my Greek tutor and I had gained no ground when my inner contemplation was broken. Graccus returned, his downcast face giving me cause for concern. "What?" I asked as Milo dropped the bowl and some bread in front of him and they nodded to each other.

He whispered in reply, casting his gaze around the street as if every passer-by was suddenly interested in our conversation. "She wouldn't change the details" he said with foreboding. "She claimed that the words cannot be different to the dream lest the goddess feels we are taking her words and changing them."

I grimaced in response but remembered just how pious these religious types could be. "So, what did you do?"

He tightened his jaw and let out a deep breath. "I wrote the correct version but then quickly scribed the copy and changed it as you said. I gave her the first to read as I finished the copy. I made sure she only added their mark to the second and didn't get time to read it through. Scavolo has the copy now, I had to hand it to the slave when we left the Fullers, and don't worry he was too busy chatting up one of the Fullers female slaves to check anything."

I nodded, a smart move which could only cause problems if anyone asked to see both copies at the same time and a trick we'd seen lawyers, and thieves, use in everyday court cases. My depths of lawlessness were growing deeper by the minute. "We better find the killer quickly, and then we'd better destroy both contracts before anyone checks them." It was usual for contracts to be gathered together and reviewed once the details had been met so that everyone was clear on what had been delivered. Graccus slurped at his bowl as I sat in silence for a moment. Our discussions with Scavolo and my father had opened a staggering number of possibilities for our search and as Graccus continued to eat I was working through where to start our investigations.

I recalled my father's reaction to the revelation that Graccus was named in a divine dream. It had caused quite a change in both his and Scavolo's behaviour. The drip-nosed lad had been allowed to sit, Scavolo standing with his mouth agape; I grinned at the look on his face. Scavolo had demanded evidence and my father had asked for the details we had gathered, his enquiring mind turning to the facts as a good lawyer should.

"We know that the festival was late into the night when Lucilla, the dead girl, disappeared" I said to the room as I placed the first slate on the table and pointed to Graccus' neat words. "She'd been singing and dancing with her friends and had been watching the wrestling from the front row." I drew my finger to a point later in the notes and tapped the grey slate lightly. "Her father saw her with Arnth, the son of his brother, and two others."

Graccus took over the story. "The next thing that anyone can remember is the father of the boy who was betrothed to Lucilla, his name is Spurius Hastius, raising his voice with Lucius Arturius the Fuller. He was angry that the wedding between the girl and his son had been cancelled and wanted compensating for the time he and his family had lost due to the time they had been betrothed and his now needing to find a new bride." We all nodded at this, sometimes a change to a wedding contract could takes months to replace and all the remaining juicy contracts for half-decent dowries had already been claimed. I was suddenly aware of my own contract with the girl I'd not yet met and wondered just what terms my father had agreed. Graccus distracted my thoughts as he continued. "There was a scuffle as Hastius was clearly too far into his wine cup and he was dragged away by his family." My father was shaking his head and Scavolo narrowed his eyes at the thought.

"Idiot" my father said quietly, echoing my own thoughts. We all knew that a public brawl and reproach could land him in serious trouble if the Fuller decided to bring charges against him, and now that his daughter had been found murdered it was clear that a case could be brought. "Did the Fuller visit him?"

"Yes" I replied with a wave to one of the notes Graccus had made. "But let us follow the events as we heard them and in order so that we understand what has been found, then we will return to that point." My father appraised my words with a nod. "Two women said that they saw Lucilla arguing with a boy, but they didn't know who it was."

"Or wouldn't say" growled Scavolo.

I nodded. "From there nobody saw Lucilla again. She seems to have disappeared like a morning fog on the Tiber." We'd reached the third slate and I turned it toward me so that I could read what was inscribed. "When they realised she was missing people started to search for her, but the family were in several different locations by then. The Fuller and his brother searched for her in the Boarium, the mother and some of her friends searched the Forum and others went to the Subura and to the Field of Mars. The father came across some of her friends with a dancing group who were near the walls of the shops at the entrance to the Boarium, but nobody had seen the girl since shortly after the wrestling matches." I pointed to a statement and looked up at Scavolo as I spoke. "The Fuller questioned several people who said they had seen two men arguing and a boy running, but nobody could name them or describe them clearly as it was dark. There was little else of any value whatsoever"

Graccus wiped his nose before looking at the slate. "Just after the wrestling matches seems to be the last time she was seen." He continued on, "Another report said a couple were seen arguing in the shadows just before dawn over by the Argiletum. It was Lucius Arturius' brother that gave the account. He said that he'd kept out of the way in case it was a trick to rob him but they could have seen something or been implicated." I shrugged at the wise words as everyone knows that such trickery exists and is used to good effect, especially on visitors who come to the rescue and find a smack across the head and an empty purse as a reward.

Scavolo asked a number of questions at this. "Did the Fuller's brother get a description of the man and woman? When did they argue?" He interlocked his fingers and I could see he was thinking through what we'd said. "It seems that a good time point for this mystery is the wrestling match as Graccus said" he turned to my father, who agreed, his mind running through the timelines as much as mine and he kept glancing to Graccus with a shrewd look in his eye. "And were these sightings given to the Fuller on the night or afterwards when he searched for information?"

Graccus and I exchanged a look. "We didn't ask about any of that" I replied with a frown.

Scavolo's lips tensed and he nodded for the story to continue, disappointment written across his face. I took a moment to reflect on this, thinking that I needed to speak to Lucius' brother who had seen the man and woman arguing. The timeline was close to the murder, what might they have seen?

"The duck farmer and his boy were seen deep in conversation later that night and the father seemed angry at something, shouting at the lad. It could be nothing" Graccus added. "It might have just been anger at the earlier exchange with the Fuller."

"And this?" My father was clearly ahead of us and reading the fourth slate, our explanations too slow for his quick mind as he touched a section of writing on the slate.

"Yes, two men were seen hurrying away from the Boarium just before the dead girl was found. Secundus saw them" added Graccus, moving the fifth slate across to show my statement.

Scavolo nodded at the structured approach to the writing that Graccus had taken and said as much, to which my accomplice and I beamed. I couldn't remember a time when the man-mountain had ever given praise.

"Although the description given by Secundus is more detailed than this other one, so we cannot assume they are the same two men" stated Graccus. We all agreed with that. "Secundus then describes the finding of the body" We sat in silence for a moment before Scavolo asked about my father's earlier question. "Yes, he did visit Hastius, but the man turned him from his door. The Fullers brother" at which he bent to read his words "Larce, came to blows with one of his slaves at the gate."

"He's lucky he hasn't raised a case against him for damage to his property" said my father, meaning the damage to the slave, with a glance to Scavolo. The head man shrugged to suggest that no such complaint had been raised. He scratched his chin before adding, "And the findings of the search team?"

His question was to Scavolo, who had led the investigation through his small team who usually asked the main protagonists in a case for their statements and then made a decision, which my father ratified. In this case there was no clear evidence and so no further actions were to be taken by the state. "There was nothing" confirmed Scavolo. "Well nothing of any consequence. You scribed it Graccus, what were the main points?" He'd dodged the question quickly enough and gave Graccus a cold stare.

My friend pursed his lips. "There was little. She'd disappeared and with the exception of being seen with a boy shortly after the wrestling match nobody saw her again until Secundus found her. There was no evidence to convict anyone." He shrugged.

My mind flashed back to the scene and I saw her cold eyes staring at me. "Could anyone describe the boy?"

"No. And nobody came forwards despite the questioning."

Scavolo nodded at this. "There was no case, and so we closed it as unsolved, which is why the Fuller was so angry" he shrugged with a glance to me and I saw Lucius shaking his fists at me in my mind's eye. "But what can we do, we find several dead bodies by every Kalends, we cannot solve them all" he said, which was true. Life in Rome is harsh and muggings, gang fights, rapes of innocents and murders for property or riches are commonplace. Everyone grunted in response.

"If we could find that boy she was seen with after the wrestling."

I'd spoken softly before I realised everyone had turned to me. "If he was the last to see her, he might know in which direction she went" I ventured to their questioning looks.

My father took a deep breath and then asked me to explain what I saw when I found the girl. I went through my statement. When I'd finished he turned to the ex-centurion. "Scavolo, what did your man say about the body?" It was a question that raised my eyebrows. I'd never seen a report on a *body*, and didn't realise that they existed, but clearly they did as Scavolo left the room and returned within a hundred heartbeats with a wax tablet.

"It suggests she died from a blow to the skull on the right of her forehead. She wasn't molested" he said, his mouth turned down at the edges as he spoke. "Other than that, nothing. No major scratches, no bruising of any consequence. Nothing" he shrugged. "Novius has seen many a dead body and I remember he remarked that she was remarkably clean for a dead girl murdered and thrown in a ditch."

Something bothered me about this, but I couldn't reason what it was. "She wore no undergarments" I stated as my confused mind caught up with the statement, causing surprised looks. "When I found her, she had nothing on under her raised skirts" I said in response to their gazes as I flushed with embarrassment at my own words. "That is odd. Surely any self-respecting girl would wear undergarments, especially at a festival and late into the night." I remembered seeing her nakedness under her dress, white thighs and puff of dark hair over her groin. I bit my lip as an image of her reproaching eyes came back to me.

"Yes, that does seem strange" replied my father. "Although it is not uncommon for such things in the lower classes." It was a statement that many plebs ended the nights of festivals with a grope and a fleeting sexual encounter fuelled by wine and dancing.

Scavolo grunted. "Secundus is right, though. It is odd if she were not molested why would she be found with no undergarments?

It seems strange." He appraised me with a long look.

The question hung in the room for a moment before Graccus turned to the last slate and read the final additions from Lucius the Fuller that he had gained from his angry visits to his neighbours and friends who attended the festival. It was precious little, with reports of his daughter laughing and joking with friends and confirmation that a boy had been seen running away from the festival, but that nobody seemed to be chasing him and it was unclear if he was anything more than average height and average build with a heavy tunic to his knees, which almost every man at the festival was wearing.

That was the sum of our conversation before we had come to Milo's bar for lunch. My memories were exhausted from our conversations and my pondering had drawn a blank. I turned to my new partner and watched as he licked the bowl. "So, where do we start?"

"The duck farmer."

"Why?"

"Scavolo said he did it."

I laughed. Typical of the brute to have made his mind up so quickly. "Why? Did he say?"

"Money. He said that the Fuller had pulled his daughter from the wedding, and it was revenge against his loss."

There was some sense in this. Lucius had told us how the duck farmer, a man named Spurius Hastius, and his son, Aspius, had taken the cancellation of the contract very badly, even though he had written off the part-dowry. It had come to light that the son had fathered a child with another farmers daughter and Lucilla had made it clear she could not marry a man who would likely betray her if he couldn't keep his cock in his tunic. The Hastius clan refused to accept the decision and said that the contract must be honoured. It was very Etruscan to let the women have a voice, but with a priestess in the family and the Fuller's business being from the mother's side they'd added a clause in the contract that Hastius hadn't read, so Scavolo informed us, and there was not much that Hastius could do except complain, which he had done loudly and bitterly.

"What about the women who saw her with a man arguing just before she went missing?"

"They couldn't say if he was tall or short, fat or thin, old or young. No use at the Comitia" he shrugged in reply. I agreed with a frown. "You could look for those two men you saw coming from the Boarium? I'd be interested to know why one had a cloak and one didn't."

"My father thought it was just a slave taking a traveller to an inn that wasn't full because of the festival." It had been a good argument and one that neither Graccus nor I had considered. Scavolo, though, had said it could just as easily have been the murderers running from the scene, so we needed to check that loose stone too.

"There are several paths to follow Graccus" I said seriously, drumming my fingers. "Who was the running boy? Why was he running? Who was Lucilla arguing with? Who are the two men I saw? Where did Lucilla go after the wrestling match? Why did she wear nothing under her dress? Did she have a lover who she argued with and he turned on her?"

"And why were Hastius and his son arguing before they left the festival?" replied Graccus. "And the man and woman in the shadows arguing too?" he was shaking his head at the sudden list of questions to which we had no answer.

I rose and stretched before dropping a pair of bronze coins to the table and nodding to Milo. He raised his chin in response as he ladled stew for a man in a thick grey cloak, his oiled beard and greased hair making him out as a traveller. I looked to his feet, but he had thin-soled sandals over woollen socks without expensive boots. I was disappointed that the goddess had not brought one of my prey to my table immediately but waved it away as I'm not sure how this patronage thing works. "Right, where does the duck farmer live?" I said in a determined voice, "let's start there, I need a walk after that food".

VIII

Farmers are a notorious bunch. They never smile, they think everyone is out to steal their stock, their crops or their women, and they all own the biggest bloody dogs you've ever seen. These three had us pinned to a tree and were making enough noise to wake the Hydra; if only we had Iolaus to help us as Heracles had. These animals were cross-bred Laconian if I knew my beasts, large, small-headed animals with upright ears and a long neck.

"Hastius" I called in mild panic as the white teeth of the biggest dog snarled at me. "Hastius."

Nobody came, but at least the dogs were well trained and didn't actually eat us before anyone arrived to see what the commotion was. Graccus was half-up the tree hanging from a branch, and I stood with my back to the trunk, waving an official looking wax tablet bearing the seal of the temple at the dogs as if they had the intelligence to read the notice we'd brought with us and would quieten once they realised we were on temple business. After a few moments, in which one dog got so excited it started to try and mount one of the others, a bored looking boy appeared at the gate and gazed at us. He was pulling along a pair of dark-furred goats, black and orange, but was obviously having difficulty as they can be stubborn beasts and he grumbled under his breath as his eyes rose to meet us. As he tied the two goats to a tree with a thin string his brown eyes looked suspiciously at the two men cowering behind his dogs. His dark hair suggested he was of Sabine stock, and his command to quieten the dogs in the country tones of his forefathers confirmed this as the three beasts sat and dribbled with that mad look of an animal that was instantly friendly but could rip off your arm given the slightest wrong movement or a word from its master. The boy looked bored as he came to stand and look down his long, thin, nose at us as if men hanging from the tree at their gate was an everyday occurrence, which it probably was. His stance suggested some breeding as he was not concerned by my toga and he lifted his chin, showing a few days stubble and yellowing bags under his eyes. I spotted a horn handled knife at his belt, artfully crafted and no doubt sharpened daily.

"What do you want?" he called in an unfriendly tone from a few yards away, behind the dogs.

I lifted the tablet. In truth we'd decided to pretend that we were officially investigating the death of Lucilla on behalf of the temple, but the tablet contained nothing more than an official seal and a request to ask questions, which held no legal authority. We hoped nobody would know this fact. "We have some questions for Spurius Hastius regarding the girl Lucilla of the Arturii." I noted his eyes narrow marginally at this, his hand moving to his chest to wipe at something, or just a nervous movement? My father had told me that guilty men often had twitches or nervous ticks when questioned. Scavolo had agreed that you could never trust a nervous man. Graccus fell beside me, and one of the dogs stood and barked again, setting the rest into a crescendo of noise, but each dog looked at their master for the nod that would set them at our throats. My mouth dried and I tried to swallow but the movement stuck in my throat.

"Shush" shouted the boy, though he never took his eyes from mine. Impressively the dogs obeyed immediately. I noted the dirty hands and feet, he wore thin sandals with one leather strap around the ankle. His frame was bony, but he looked strong. "Is he expecting you?" he asked, "he's busy today" he added warily.

I raised the wax seal, showing the sign of the temple of Jupiter. He squinted, but I saw in his face that he recognised it; most people did if they paid their taxes and stored their gold and silver in the vaults beneath the temple floors. "Are you his heir" I used the phrase to give him credit above an ordinary son, though I had no idea if Hastius had more than one living child and the clothing of this boy didn't give him any standing based on looks alone. "We have some questions about Lucilla Arturii, did you know her?" The look of distain on his face suggested he might well be the jilted boy, so I pressed straight on with my questions. "Did you argue with her on the night of the festival? Was it you that was seen with her?"

"What do you mean? Who said it was me" he replied sharply but also in a guarded tone. The dogs sensed his anger and one of them stood and wagged its tail as it turned toward him pleading to be let loose to crunch on our juicy bones.

"Nothing? Nobody" I answered. "We just need to ask your father some questions" I replied keeping my eyes focused on his, the dogs forgotten as they were clearly trained well enough that they would only attack if given the command by their master. I'd stepped forwards slightly. "About the contract with the Fuller and whether it caused an argument at the festival. Is that what happened?" I was gambling, mixing questions and looking for an answer that would allow me to focus in on what I needed. My thoughts were jumping between the father and son, wondering if I could get two stories which might differ and might give me some clues to what happened that night if I pressed the boy before I spoke to his father.

His lips tightened and his hand flicked to his chest again, wiping at nothing I could see, whilst his gaze moved towards the house, visible some way down the track nestled within a ring of apple and plum trees, to the goats, which munched at the grass, and then back to me. I gazed beyond him, seeing that further along the road were the wicker fences where the ducks would be housed, their wings clipped to ensure they didn't fly away. The deep ruts from cart tracks told the tale of the commerce that the ducks brought; eggs, meat and feathers amongst three of the opportunities that the flocks brought to a clever businessman. I asked once more, hoping to catch the boy off his guard. "Were you the boy betrothed to her? Did you speak to her at the festival? We're looking for answers to her death, can you help us?"

Something seemed to flash behind his eyes at my words and I felt Graccus move beside me, which distracted him a little more. "If you don't have an appointment you need to leave. Send a message with your slave" he nodded towards a disgruntled Graccus. He was turning to leave, the dogs confused as they hadn't had a chance to eat us yet.

"If you were seen arguing with her you could be called to the Comitium" I ventured this as a last gambit. He came to a halt and looked back over his shoulder, unsure whether to speak or not but knowing that being accused could have serious repercussions to a wealthy family.

"I saw her, but we didn't argue" he replied coldly. "Little bitch." He turned to face us now, anger rising as his hand fell to his belt, fingering the handle of the knife. Graccus edged backwards slightly but I stood my ground. I wasn't going to let this pleb threaten me, dogs or no dogs.

I decided a different tact might work. "Did you see her argue with anyone?" I softened my voice to bring him into the conversation. "We heard that she was seen arguing with a young man."

He replied with a smirk. "She was happy to argue with anyone, just like her stupid father. I didn't see her after the wrestling matches had finished, and by then she was too drunk to talk to. Who knows who she crept off with into the shadows, it's nothing to do with me any longer." He stood his ground and crossed his arms over his chest, daring us to ask further questions.

"Did she spend time with anyone else?" asked Graccus. "A slave, a friend? Did *you* see anything else?"

He seemed to consider this for a moment before adding "that idiot Marcius was hanging around her like a dog in heat. Ask him." At this he turned again and called for the dogs to follow. The beasts lumbered after him playfully, belying the fact that they were about to rip our limbs off only a few moments earlier.

"Wait" called Graccus, his mind obviously clearer than my own as my anger at his turning away from me, his social superior, irked me. The boy glanced back but wasn't waiting around as he yanked at the goats. "Who is Marcius? What is his family name?" A great question, and one I would have kicked myself for not asking once I'd recovered my wits.

"Marcius Brocchus" he laughed. "You can't miss his family" he sneered. "Ask him where she went. He's her puppy dog now and he was with her most of the night."

At his departure I looked at Graccus and nodded. "Well, we have something new to explore now I guess. I wonder why this boy Marcius has not been mentioned so far?"

Graccus nodded as the boy disappeared into the farmyard. We stood for a moment, my mind thinking through what he had said as much as the way he'd said it. "He wasn't very friendly" I said without really speaking to anyone.

"Well, we did appear out of the blue and asked if he had been with the murdered girl on the night she was killed" said Graccus.

I looked to his wide eyed face and rolled my eyes. "Gods we need to get better at this don't we?" I laughed. "We might as well have just accused him there and then" I waved at the spot where he'd stood.

Graccus tapped his head and then wiped his wet nose. "We need to use our brains" he said as we set off back along the track towards the city. I gave him a long look as he walked ahead, thinking that if we're using his brain to solve this riddle we're doomed. Maybe telling my father that Graccus was the man in the dream had been a bad move. I needed to make a devotion to

Minerva, seek her advice.

****

We decided that we'd send a formal request to meet with Hastius rather than face his dogs again and I'd sent my partner to the Fullers to find out who Marcius was and where we might find him. The hunt had started and I decided to drop a coin in the well of Diana near the Quirinal as it was on my way back to the temple, it would be a good idea to keep her on our side too as the gods can be fickle and it's best to get them all on your side just in case your actions upset one of them. On my return I wandered along the corridor to our old room and was surprised to see two others sat in our seats.

"Who are you?" I exclaimed to their startled faces.

"Replacements" one of them replied, clearly happy to be scribbling away as his pile was larger than that of his colleague. "The work goes on even if you two are taking it easy strolling around the city and drinking wine, that's what Scavolo said" he answered at my frowning response to his words.

I stood for a moment with my mouth open and a stupid look on my face as they both glanced at me before bending their necks back to the work to suggest that my problems were nothing to do with them. I sighed, turned and wandered into the temple glancing around for someone who might know what was going on. The main room was busy, with people making devotions, the priests completing sacrifices at the altar and slaves dressed in dark brown tunics with iron neck rings cleaning and tidying as they were instructed to do. I'd stuck out my lip and thrust my hands on my hips in anger at having lost our room and was about to pay Scavolo a visit when I saw Philus sweeping dust by the rear of the altar. "Philus" I called as I stepped across to him. His face turned in my direction and he lifted his chin toward me as I approached. "Why has our room been taken? We're still on official business."

He greeted me with a calm smile, his head bowing slightly. "Come master" he said, propping his broom against the wall and striding out towards my father's office. I wondered if I was going to be given a bollocking and shook my head as I sighed and followed the slave. I noticed he had a slight limp on his left leg and carried his right arm at an odd angle at the elbow where a small lump was visible. I wondered if he'd had a fall as a child or whether he'd recently taken a beating. Either way despite these physical impediments he moved swiftly and to my surprise, as I had expected him to knock on the door, he walked straight past my father's room to a corridor beyond, into the shadows in the east of the temple. At a doorway I'd never seen before he stopped and bowed, an arm pushing open a heavy door which was carved with an elaborate hunting scene. "This is your new room, master. For you and Porcius while you do this task that Scavolo has set you" he raised his eyebrows expecting me to say something. I ignored him, stepping into the room and seeing two tables, two chairs and a large window which faced a covered courtyard. The room was light and airy and I noted a black pitcher with wine and three terracotta cups placed on a side table alongside a small bowl of fruit, grapes and figs, on which two flies were buzzing. I turned back to Philus, who stood by the door peering in, his teeth still showing through his parted lips and sneering mouth. "Well" I said, my surprise getting the better of me. I looked at the door, the carved dogs chasing deer and a rider in the final throes of launching a spear. "It looks like my devotion to Diana this morning has paid off." It was always good to suggest to the workers that you have the favour of the gods.

He didn't seem to make the connect if his blank stare is anything to go by. "Well Scavolo asked me to set it up for you" he shrugged. "For the next few days" he added with that smirk which was now annoying me. "And that came for you" he nodded into the corner of the room which was partly in shadow. "The man said you'd know who it was from." I peered into the semi-dark corner to see an amphora resting against the wall. It was the wine from Milo.

I smiled.

I thanked him and poured myself a cool drink, waving away the flies that now seemed to think I was a worthy meal and buzzing around my head. I took a slow sip, expecting it to be some cheap vinegar and my money to have been wasted, but my tongue sent a wave of fruity pleasure into my brain. This was good wine, my money was well spent. As I sat and contemplated this sudden change in fortune, I considered the impact that the dream had had on me. I suddenly had purpose and felt refreshed by this. I wondered what my mother and brother would make of this new direction when I met them later tonight; tutting and shaking of heads might not be appropriate. I smiled wryly. Taking a moment to look around the room I saw that my father had furnished it lightly, with a small cupboard on which sat wax tablets, slates and a box of stylus for writing. I noted that Graccus' tablets were stored on the left, neatly stacked. A second box which contained candles sat at their side. I nodded approval and picked up a slate and scratching stylus to write my notes from the meeting at the duck farmers, scribing the name Marcius Brocchus and leaving a gap for any further information we might get regarding the lad. I was about to write some thoughts so I didn't forget them later when I heard a commotion in the temple and stood, this was unusual. Shouting was followed by calls for the guard and I rushed out to see what was happening.

"There he is" called a voice as I appeared to see Philus and three other priests gesticulating with two men and a boy.

I stopped, seeing the boy from the duck farm with two other men, one clearly some sort of bodyguard as his shoulders were twice as broad as the boy at his side and his broken nose and twisted ears suggested he had plenty of experience in breaking heads for his paymaster. Philus, gods-bless him, stood like a rock, though more like a pebble in reality, in front of the mountain of muscle and was telling the arrivals to leave the temple at once or face the wrath of Jupiter for breaking his peace. It didn't wash with the man who was clearly the duck farmer Spurius Hastius as his red-faced anger turned towards me and shouted once again that I approach him or have to deal with the consequences. The muscle had crossed his arms over his chest and narrowed his eyes in my direction menacingly, and with a smirk at how small and weedy I looked. I could sense he saw an easy job at hand.

"You" called the red-faced father of the boy we'd met at the gate after a moment of pushing at Philus who remained a barrier to his entry. His hand shot out, a finger pointing accusingly at me. "Come here." He was clearly used to giving orders and my legs almost followed his command before I remembered my status and crossed my arms over my chest in defiance.

"Who are you?" I called. "What business do you have in the temple of Jupiter to be calling discord in front of the gods?" It was good gambit as the twelve tables were clear that the gods could not be dishonoured by mortals and causing an affray in any temple could levy a hefty fine, if not confiscation of lands. His finger continued to point but his son took a small step backwards looking uncomfortable. I was about to press my advantage when Scavolo appeared, striding across the temple like Achilles at Troy. Priests and acolytes parted before him and the faces of the newcomers all grew concerned at his arrival, including the hard-faced muscle, which pleased me.

"You lot, what's going on here?" called Scavolo, heads turning to his command. I noted the look of iron in his eyes, his shoulders flexing as he walked and his clean-shaven jaw clenched. At his side strode two of his former soldiers; men chosen as temple guards for their services and both of whom carried short but deadly wooden clubs. No metal weapons were allowed in the temple, although I knew there was a stash hidden in a box in my father's office just in case they were ever needed and the gods decided to magic them into place. The arrival of the temple head-man caused a sudden shift in the face of Hastius as he sidled to his right and half behind his own bodyguard. I hurried across the temple. I was not going to miss this encounter now that there had been a change in the wind and we were on favourable ground.

The brute, who must be Hastius' bodyguard, saluted to Scavolo, his hands rising in greeting to the others at the head man's side. "Salve, sir" he said, his voice surprisingly feminine in tone and deferential to Scavolo, who he obviously recognised along with the other two guards. I had expected the growl of a lion but got the twitter of a bird. "No trouble, sir. We need to speak to this man who has invaded my master's property and attempted to accost his son." His finger now pointed to me as all heads turned in my direction like geese at the gate turning to see an intruder. I was clearly too slow to adopt my stoic visage as Scavolo shook his head in disappointment at my slack-jawed stare. I tried to retain my dignity but felt the change in my poise was more like a slave bowing his head when found with his hands in the masters wine cupboard than that of a patrician of noble blood.

I rallied as best I could under Scavolo's disapproving glare. "I did no such thing" I responded coldly to the accusation. The boy couldn't look me in the face and hid behind the bodyguard.

"Not here" growled Scavolo walking past the small groups that had formed, anticipating trouble, and waving at us to follow. We arrived at his room quickly and placed ourselves standing, three of them and three of us, with Scavolo sitting. I glanced at him and marvelled at how easily he controlled situations despite holding no social graces, his position socially lower than at least three of the men in the room and yet he was obviously the man in charge.

"Spurius Hastius" he spoke quietly, seeing the steam that was almost coming from the ears of the leading plebeian. "What claim do you bring to the temple of Jupiter with your guard, who has raised a hand in anger within the sacred building?" It was as if a dark cloud had suddenly flashed a bolt of lightning into the room, increasing the tension with its inherent threat. It was another masterstroke from the head-man and one which struck Hastius like a blow from the hand of Jupiter himself.

"No, No, Scavolo. It wasn't like that. No threat was made." They obviously knew each other, which wasn't a surprise as the man who had made my last few weeks akin to a trip to Hades was one of Rome's most famous sons, his bettering of nine men at the siege of Satricum was legend. "There was no hand raised in anger." He turned to the guard for agreement, who shrugged and stuck out his bottom lip as he frowned but then nodded. "This man came to my home and accosted my son, questioning him about a death and accusing him of murder" he said forcefully.

Faces turned to me. I remembered my training and slowly shook my head as I placed my right hand into the fold of my tunic; very Greek. "Aspius?" I had looked directly into the eyes of the boy as I confirmed his name with a question. "Tell me what words you have spoken to accuse me of this crime to your father. Explain to us how I and Graccus Porcius, who were turned at your gate by three large dogs, had attempted to accost your person when we got no further than twenty steps from your property. Accosted?" I let that word sink in. "I'm sure your dogs would have said something about that if I had raised a word or a hand in anger." I let that sink in further as an image of Graccus squealing like a pig as he tried desperately to climb the tree came to my mind and I held back a smile. "I have written my account of the words I spoke and your answers in my notes, they are in the room along the corridor and can be checked against the testimony of Porcius when he arrives to see if our recollections match. No accusation was made, no laws were broken. We were simply asking for your memories of the night so that we can piece together when the murdered girl was last seen." It was good from a legal standpoint and I was pleased I'd taken a moment to write it down already. Scavolo was impressed, I could see by the gleam in his eye. My devotions to Janus, Diana and Minerva were paying out for sure and I sat back, confident in what I had said.

The father faced his son, a sudden flash of anger in his eyes as he realised he hadn't considered the legal aspects of his attack on the temple and myself and the words that I has accused his son. The twelve tables are clear on accusations and I know my tables, if for no other reason that my father and his friends had bored me and my brother to tears for years when I was a boy as they debated the laws and the implications of changing just one word in a sentence.

I faced my accuser. I could see the family likeness in them now. Both men were medium height and both had bored looking faces with heavy eyelids, the father was thick-browed with dark eyes and hard skinned hands, which were now flapping like his clipped ducks as they turned to his son. "Tell them what you told me" he demanded.

The boy squirmed as Scavolo, giving us all a lesson in creating tension, shifted noisily in his seat, placed his elbows on the table and leaned his chin onto his clasped hands whilst narrowing his eyes at the boy, a picture of concentration. It was unnerving and had the desired effect as the boy looked like he'd just shit his tunic.

"He came and accused me of arguing with the dead girl on the day she was found" he started to say.

"We" I corrected him.

"What?"

"We. I was with my colleague and fellow investigator Graccus Porcius" I said, raising our status as I did so but making the distinction in his words which would make them appear incorrect and cause doubt in his mind. Maybe I am actually good at this investigating lark I thought as I watched his face turn red at my interjection.

"You said he came with a slave" his father hissed. I almost laughed at this, Graccus was probably a social equal to the boy, though he did look and smell like a slug.

"He looked like a slave" blustered Aspius.

I jumped on him like Cronos on his father Uranus, my words striking like the adamantine sickle to castrate his hardly begun argument. "My first request to you was for an audience with your father, was it not?" My voice rose and I counted on my fingers in a slow and steady voice; gods that Greek training was inside me after all these years and my father's hard-earned gold had actually given me some skills I never knew I had. "My second was a question as to whether you were the heir of the property, and my third was whether you knew the dead girl." I turned to the father before I continued, not allowing the boy to speak. "His response suggested he was the jilted boy" at which the duck-farmers mouth tightened "and at that point I asked if he had argued with the girl on the night. No accusation was made, no reply was given" I finished with a cold look to the boy.

"Don't try and trick me lawyer" snarled Spurius Hastius as he rounded on me, causing Scavolo to raise his brows and turn his head slowly to me with a half-smile. The bastard was enjoying this.

"I'm no lawyer" I replied in shock at the accusation of such a lowly role. It brought a confused stare from Hastius and his son. The muscle glanced to Scavolo and his lips curled, he was enjoying it as much as my former boss.

Scavolo leant back in his seat and we all turned toward the sudden movement. His mastery of the situation was then raised to Homerian proportions as he stood and spoke as if he had been remiss in his role as Head of the temple. "Spurius Hastius, I must apologise for not introducing you when you arrived. I beg your forgiveness" he fawned with a slight bow and a gleam in his eye which suggested this moment was the highlight of his day so far. "Might I introduce you to Secundus Sulpicius Merenda, who has been asked by his father to look at this case on behalf of the cult of Minerva." The standing figure had not finished his words when the duck-farmer's mouth fell open as wide as the caverns in the Appian Hills. The boy's face turned in shock and seeing a beating coming he slid backwards away from his

Patres. The bodyguard turned an appraising eye to me and his grin suggested he really was enjoying this as much as Scavolo. Following this revelation I sucked in a slow breath and raised my chin to look down my nose at those below me in social status. My father would have been proud of me.

"You never said he was the Quaestors son, you idiot" hissed Hastius, clearly knowing my family name, before turning to me and bowing, his demeanour changing to a false smile as he changed tact. "My apologies to you Secundus Sulpicius Merenda and my best wishes to your father, I will send a half a dozen geese for the temple to beg your apologies." I was benevolent and waved away his apologies, glancing to Scavolo who was looking like he was going to piss himself with laughter. I decided to rise above the situation and act like the patrician I was, my father would have acted in the same way I was sure.

"No need, no need, I am sure Spurius Hastius" I gave him his full two names and a moment of relief before accepting his offer. "Although I am certain such a gift would be welcomed by the priests who suffer at our asking in the work of the gods." Scavolo was actually smiling. "Might we return to the *accusation*" I leant my head to the side as I spoke.

"No, sir, no accusation. A misunderstanding, sir. The boy is a fool. No accusation was made I am sure. It is as you say, a few questions and a misunderstanding" he was starting to sweat now.

At this Aspius flinched and I felt sorry for him as I knew what it was like to feel the ire of your father. He was about to turn on his son when I cut him off by stepping forward and holding out my hand to the boy. "Aspius, my apologies for not introducing myself to you at your gate, and not sending a messenger ahead as you suggested. Your dogs are extremely well trained, I commend their trainer." The boy was clearly slow as his mouth worked and his eyes widened but he stood as still as a tree in a heatwave. I pressed forwards, gripping the slowly rising hand. "And to you, sir. My apologies for causing confusion. I am on a three day timeline to review the case so had to dispense with formalities and made the error of coming to your home unannounced. Please forgive me." My hand was up, his grabbed it and gripped it like a beggar grasping bread.

Spurius was sharper than his son and responded with several seconds of jovial comments about misunderstandings and mistakes, dismissing my apologies with the falsest of smiles and shiftiest eyes I had seen in all my years. His son melted away like the mountain snow but I was not about to let this fish off my hook just yet as I laughed with him. In the background I could see Scavolo stood watching on crossing his arms over his chest like a mother overseeing her children.

As the tension eased I brought the subject back to the reason Hastius had appeared at the temple. "Might we ask a couple of questions I wished to ask earlier now, Spurius, if you have the time?" It was first name terms now, he couldn't get out of my questioning without appearing to turn me down, which he did not do.

"Yes, yes, of course, of course" he replied.

"Novius, fetch food for our guests" Scavolo said with a nod to the guards at his side. "And get us another two chairs" he added. "Drinks?" he asked, turning to a low table on which sat a Greek pitcher with a long handle, the scene etched into the black pot was two men in full Greek armour about to stride to battle. I had a feeling it was Patroclus and Achilles and was impressed by the quality. Four cups were poured and the wine was cool and grapey, clearly a good vintage. I wondered if he'd bought it from Milo or if it was a devotion that found its way to the head man's room. I asked Aspius if he had trained the dogs himself in an attempt to lighten the tension as we waited for the chairs to arrive, to which he rambled about a slave who was their keeper and had special skills. Scavolo seemed interested and asked if he could see these dogs as his own didn't listen to his commands despite several beatings. He'd turned a smiling face to mine as he said this; the bastard always had to appear superior. Hastius was overwhelmed with the thought that Scavolo might visit his humble farm and eagerly agreed a date for a visit. It was all far too nice and as the chairs arrived and we sat I changed the tone entirely.

"I'm sorry to have to ask" I said with a half-smile as I wasn't. "Could you tell me anything you remember on the night that Lucilla of the Arturii disappeared, anything at all?" It was an open question, no accusations, no leading comments. It'd taken me ages to consider what to ask first and I was proud of myself; Janus would be getting a silver coin for this new beginning, no more battered copper or iron gifts for him.

"There isn't much to say" started Hastius as he shook his head slowly. "I saw her at one point dancing with that idiot Marcius and then she was at the wrestling with all the other young men and women" he shrugged and wrung his hands as if cleaning them. It seemed very rehearsed and I was immediately suspicious. I noted the hard skin on his hands, callouses from working himself and I wondered why anyone would do that.

"You argued with the girl's father did you not?" It was Scavolo that asked the question.

If Hastius' instant reaction could have been more hostile there would have been fists, but he regrouped and sighed, masking the look of anger in his dark eyes that clearly marched in his thoughts. "Of course, you will know that they pulled out from their side of our bargain" he turned his face to both of ours as we listened and glanced meaningfully to his son. "I had made one last appeal to the head of the house, but she wouldn't listen. She is the boss there" he was shaking his head at the Etruscan tradition of giving women a voice in family matters. "So I appealed to the father one last time, man to man." It was a point that I hadn't heard in the fullers' tale. So Hastius had approached the woman of the house first before approaching

Lucius, why had they not said this. "As before, he declined to listen but that idiot brother started to shout and..." he shrugged and appeared embarrassed. His eyes then flicked to his son, who reddened. "Nothing has been raised to the court, I assume?" his fearful question to Scavolo who grunted that nothing had been received. This brought a moment of silence in which Hastius looked relieved.

"And you, Aspius. Did you see her that night, or speak to her?"

His dark orbs in his heavy eyelids shifted to his father for a moment and I saw fear behind them. I understood then that I needed to get the boy alone to hear the full story, but as that was unlikely I had to plough the field in front of me and try and remove every stone, however large they may seem.

"I saw her several times, dancing with her friends, and then talking to Arnth and later with Marcius. I didn't see anything else."

If the boy was trying to close a door I was going to use my newfound relationship with Janus to keep it open. "Did you speak to her after the wrestling?" I ventured. His eyes roved to Scavolo and then to mine before replying that he had not. "Did you see anyone else talking to her after the wrestling?"

Again a flicker of a look to his father. "I saw her with Marcius, standing in the shadow of the cloth shop by the crossroads at the Boarium. They seemed to be arguing" he added, his lips dropping at the thought.

"Did you hear what they said?" I asked, surprised at this new revelation as it didn't fit with his earlier statement. Could this be the man and woman arguing in the shadows?

"No, I was with my friends heading back for more wine and I only saw them for a moment."

Scavolo ploughed in with a question. "How did you know it was Marcius if you only glanced at them in the dark?"

"I'd know that idiot anywhere. Lumbering fool" he said with

hatred in his voice. Scavolo narrowed his eyes at this and the father turned a long look at his son.

I took a moment to understand what he was saying and how it fitted with what we knew so far. "Thank you Aspius" I said, seeing the relief in both the father and son at having appeared to find nothing of any consequence. "Did you see anyone running from the Boarium later that night?"

His reaction suggested not, his bottom lip out and head shaking as he replied that he hadn't seen anyone. I asked the same question to his father, who seemed to remember something for a moment but then shook his head.

"We have a report of an argument between two men" I said with a glance to Hastius. "This was after the scuffle with the Fuller so not related that we know of" I stated so that the duck farmer knew it was not an accusation. "Did you hear or see this?"

Hastius was shaking his head again and I could see his eyes darting around as his lids closed to a crack, thinking about how to answer the question. "Wait" he added. "I did see someone running from the festival." He turned to his son. "When you came to me just after the wrestling, maybe fifteen minutes after. We saw someone rushing beyond the pig pen at the far end of the square, we both looked and I commented."

Aspius seemed nervous as he nodded but didn't speak. The father continued. "I cannot be certain, but I would say that Marcius Brocchus was that man. I've seen him run before at the games, he's a good athlete" he added to explain his comment. "I'm sure now that it was him, your questions have brought it back to my mind" his thick eyebrows rose at this final suggestion and he gave me a firm stare which suggested he was certain in his assumption.

I sat back and nodded, a gap filled and a stone removed from my field but I had not missed the fact that the man had not answered my question so I dug my plough further into the soft soil of his mind. "And two men arguing?"

He took a second to return his thoughts and spoke quietly "I cannot recall any arguments beyond those of my own and the tricks Bacchus plays." It was an admission of his struggles with Lucius and the fact that he was likely embarrassed at his drunken behaviour.

"Thank you Spurius, and you Aspius, you have been a great help" I said to their relieved faces. Hastius was up on his feet and slurping the last of the fine wine before anyone could speak again, his son jumping up like a march hare in response.

"No problem at all Secundus" he replied jovially, first name terms once again and his hand held out to be shaken. I obliged, it was the patrician thing to do. The son offered a limp touch of a handshake, clearly happy to be let out of the noose that had appeared to hang around his neck. The men moved to the door, Scavolo thanking them for their support.

"Oh" I exclaimed. "One last question if I can be so rude" my thoughts still on the night of the murder. "We have reports of two men, one with a cloak and one without, hurrying from the Boarium shortly before dawn. Did you see them at all?"

"No" came the quick reply. "The family left the festival quite soon after the wrestling matches, it's a difficult trip in the dark back to the farm" he added.

I nodded my thanks and Scavolo led them from the room.

IX

Graccus was sniffing as he sat back and rubbed his stomach, Milo's garlic and lamb filled bread having been crammed into it moments before. I ordered watered wine to finish the meal as we'd expanded our lunchtime menu based on the fact that the Fuller was paying our expenses. Milo was happier than a pig in shit at our evident rise in status.

"So Scavolo thinks he's lying?" he asked. I nodded.

"Who's lying" asked Milo, leaning over and taking the empty bowls.

I tapped my nose. "Minerva's secret" I smiled, invoking the goddesses qualities of wisdom.

Milo gave me that all-knowing smile that echoed the look on the face of the statue of Mercury which sat in the temple on the Aventine Hill not far from my father's house. "Ah, you mean Hastius the duck-farmer."

"How the..." I was about to swear but he shrugged.

"I can see the temple right there" he lifted his chin to the enormous building behind us. "I see everyone who goes in and out and I have my sources." He tapped his own nose in mockery of my action. It was simple logic and he had clearly put two and two together. At least the story of Graccus' elevation hadn't appeared to have reached his ears as of yet. "I hear you've been moved to a new room and have three days to find the killer of the Fullers daughter" he added to my further frustration as my head shook and my lips tightened, which made his smile all the broader as his glance to Graccus made me suspicious that his source was closer to me than I might know. "So, who do you think did it? Not Hastius?" he asked with narrowing eyes.

"We can't say" responded Graccus as he sipped at the watered wine and winced at the sour taste.

Ignoring the facial expression Milo laughed and moved back to his ovens to serve a couple, a man and his wife, who had been standing looking at the food on offer. I looked at his boots, but they were cheap and had holes all along the toes where they'd been worn through.

After suggesting we moved back to our comfortable office I went through what Graccus had told me and we transcribed everything to a new slate. The Fuller had given the address of the boy Brocchus, and Larce, the brother of Lucius, had joined my partner on a trip to his house which lay out near the old tombs situated beyond the Subura. As this required transport on horseback Graccus had been sat behind the large frame of Larce for a few hours and was complaining about his backside constantly as he shifted in his seat while recounting his story. The boy had not been there, he was working in the fields and they had requested that he appeared at the temple before nightfall to answer questions. Graccus said his father had been angry and almost came to blows with Larce, the second man who had done so if Hastius was to be believed. I wondered if the Arturii brothers used their fists rather than their minds to resolve all of their problems as I remembered the fuller standing over me as I brought the death notice to his yard. Graccus agreed that Larce appeared to be quick to anger and said the Etruscan had quizzed him constantly on what we had found so far, despite it being only a few hours into our search, as they travelled to and from the Brocchus house.

I discussed what I'd learned from Hastius and his son Aspius and showed Graccus my notes. We possibly had our running boy and the person seen arguing with Lucilla in the shadows; it was Marcius Brocchus. It seemed too good to be true and Janus, Minerva and Diana were smiling on us and my purse was going to be lighter again before the end of the day. I considered adding it to the expenses but then decided that might not be the best idea I'd had that day.

"We need to find the two women and confirm if they saw the arguing man and woman at the same place mentioned by Aspius" he looked at the slate as he made his statement and I nodded at this; he was good.

I told him so but he shook his head and bent forward in a whisper. "We know that it is you that the goddess has mentioned, not me. Whatever I do is because of your patronage Secundus" he said with honesty and wiped his nose at the same time to destroy any answer I was going to give as the glistening line across his hand distracted me. I changed the conversation quickly, uncomfortable with any mention of the dream or divine support as my anger at losing my wife and son came back to me. I knew just how fickle the gods could be and was wary of their support or patronage in equal measure. I didn't want any association which might lead to servitude and suffrage. I'd seen the life my father led, long services at several temples, sacrificing animals till your hands were red with gore, arguing with plebs about minor infringements, reading endless scrolls till your eyes failed. It wasn't for me.

"I think the boy Aspius knows more." I was firm in my conviction but hesitation was clear in my tone. "But how do we get him on his own?"

"And will he open up?"

We heard footsteps coming to the door and looked up as Scavolo entered, shattering our peace. "Sitting on your arses, lazy bastards. I thought you'd be out there searching for clues." His admonishment caused Graccus to jump to his feet, but I remained sitting. "I've just come back from the Esquiline, trying to find that boy Brocchus."

This didn't wash with our old boss by the look on his face so I added quickly. "We're checking our notes and considering our strategy."

"Sitting and chatting like slaves at the river won't find the killer, goddess or no goddess" he said with a look at Graccus. "You're more than halfway through the day and you've got fuck all yet. I know. I've been in this game for a lot longer than you two pricks. You need to get out in the streets, ask questions, knock heads together and find those two men, cloak and boots." He waved a hand, "Novius has something for you as well, drop in on your way out. He's in the cellar." He left without another word, back to his usual charming self.

The cellar was cold and dark except for several light shafts from above which shot down like rays from Sol. We didn't know what to expect, but the cold and dark cellar didn't fill us with cheer. "Novius" I called into the half-light. "Where are you."

"Here, lads" said a voice further into the long room. "And keep your fucking voices down" came another reproach. What was it with these military types, always barking out orders but never explaining what they actually wanted.

Venturing further into the dimness of the cellar, Graccus kicked a loose flagstone and grumbled as I followed his lead and stumbled over the same object to the sudden detriment of my toe. I moved more deliberately after that. At the end of the room were two men, one was Novius the other we didn't recognise as he sat further back, cloaked by the darkness where the illumination of the candles didn't reach. "Grab a chair" said the guard waving vaguely towards a corner in which I couldn't make out a chair or anything else as my eyes hadn't yet adjusted to the poor light. "This is Sertor, an old tent-mate of mine. He has a tale that he'd like to tell us, don't you?" he said towards the figure in front of him.

As soon as the speaker started his tale I realised that it was Hastius' bodyguard. The man that had spoken like a bird and saluted the centurion and his two bruisers when he saw them above us only a few hours before sat in the chair with his face alive in the flickering candlelight. His name rang in my mind, Sertor, meaning protector, it was a good name considering his new job for the duck farmer. "Hastius was lying to you" he said, vindicating Scavolo's words. "He didn't leave with the family when they left the festival. He stayed behind, said they had a job to do. Aspius went with him."

My mouth dropped. It was a good job nobody could see me fail in my attempt to grow closer in my Roman virtues to both Scavolo and my father. "Why would he lie?" I asked the question before I thought it through, the consequences dawning on me almost immediately.

"That isn't all" added the figure in the blackness across from me. "Aspius didn't come home with him. I don't know why, but he came back later and was covered in mud and dirt."

Another addition to our slate and another series of questions to ask. A memory of the ditch and my own appearance flashed in my mind, the link clear. Had he been in the ditch with her. I could almost see the boy smashing a rock across her head as I thought about it.

"How do we get Aspius on his own?" asked Graccus, clearly further ahead in his thinking than I. "We won't get anything from the father, we need to talk to the boy" he added in explanation.

Sertor sat in silence for a moment. "He is at the bird sales tomorrow, on the field of Mars. I have to take him. His father has a relative visiting from Caisra so he will be busy for the sales in the afternoon. The head slave is going, you'll have to watch for him though, proper snake." The market for birds was very popular and a lot of the local farmers bought and sold there. It was a good chance to get to Aspius, if we could get him alone I felt sure that we could find answers to questions that his father's presence was clearly stopping him giving.

After a moment of silence Novius spoke. "Three silver coins" he whispered to my surprise. "That is the fee we agreed with Scavolo" he added after a few heartbeats as if my silence suggested it wasn't a good deal but the fact that Scavolo had agreed it meant it had to be paid.

"I don't understand" I replied, Graccus standing and placing a hand on Novius' shoulder.

"I'll get it" he said quickly. "Can you send payment to Sertor or do you want to wait. It might take a while to get that much money."

"I need to get back, I only popped out to get a stall for tomorrow's sales as we are trying to off-load a few of the older birds. I'll catch up with you tomorrow for the money Novius" said the brute as he stood and they clasped hands. "I'm trusting you to pay" he snarled threateningly into the darkness, though I guessed this was to me.

I hadn't gathered my wits properly by the time we'd returned to our room, Graccus already ahead of me and scribbling this new information on a slate. "Do you think they did it, just as Scavolo said?"

Wiping his nose Graccus answered that he didn't know how the mind of a murderer worked, but he could see Hastius being that man. I agreed. I could see them both smashing the poor girls head to a pulp and as I closed my eyes I saw her dead face looking back at me once more from behind my lids.

As we started to consider our next move a thought came to me. "We never found that man that Larce spoke to. He said that he saw a man and woman arguing. Do you have the slate?" He did, but it was a very basic report. "Can you find out if there are any other details? I'm sure this is important." Graccus said he would go to the house of Lucius and Fucilla later that day to get the information.

****

We decided to split up for the afternoon and meet again the following morning at the temple. Graccus was to visit the Fullers and ask for the names of the two women so that he could check out their stories as well as find out who had seen the arguing couple near dawn. I was going to search the inns along the Via Nova and Via Ostiensis to see if anyone recognised the two men, as Scavolo called them *cloak and no cloak*. Before departing we agreed that we should keep this latest news from Sertor to ourselves and not let anyone know what we had just heard. Novius had been paid, the last of my silver going for the information and not to the gods as I had planned; I hoped it wasn't a bad deal and the gods would forgive me. I told myself that any coins I had left in my purse at the end of the day would be used to buy at least one chicken to be given in offering to Minerva.

I'd dressed in a common tunic with a heavy woollen cloak as I guessed that my patrician status would clamp mouths shut as fast as a whore's legs to a man with the pox.

After several fruitless visits and sharp-tongued dismissals from hostelries along the roads it was the fifth inn that gave me hope, the rest having shaken their heads at my questions, one lady offering me a warm bed for an hour as I looked like I needed a lie down. I knew what that meant, and whilst her breasts were perky the pox scars on her neck and the way she scratched at her crotch suggested I'd be leaving with a few gifts I didn't really want. The innkeeper at the fifth venue was short, sour-faced and had the most frightening, red-rimmed eyes I'd ever seen. They gazed out of deep sockets like blood swirling in the pool at the bottom of a well. He had a face that looked like one of the masks that they wear in the Greek tragedy plays that come to Rome every now and that my father kept on the wall of his study, though I never knew why as he hated Greek plays. Despite his appearance his initial reaction was one of hope and my spirits rose that I would not receive another negative answer.

"Night of the festival you say" he looked at me shrewdly. I could see he was calculating a fee for the information.

I lifted the wax sealed tablet. "Official business" I said, secreting it away again quickly before his bloodshot orbs could get a proper look. He rubbed his chin and I noted the stubble and scars along the edge of his lower lip and across his forearm. His skin was loose and tanned like leather, he clearly spent a lot of his time outside, and there was a deep ridge across one of his collarbones that was visible under the low neck of his tunic which led to a slightly dropped right shoulder. An ex-soldier, I thought, or maybe a riding accident. I'd seen it before when men fell from horses and smashed the bones, which then set to create a lump on one side and a drooping shoulder. "I'm working with Scavolo" I added quickly.

My gamble worked, the man smiled as if I was his long lost brother and he set about making me sit and bringing me a cold glass of his best wine. It was disgusting but I sipped at it with thanks and returned his smile. It was amazing what the mention of Scavolo's name could do.

"Maximus" he said, offering a hand, which I shook gladly. His grip was iron. Here was a man who wouldn't drop his sword if it came to hand to hand fighting, I thought. I appraised him with renewed interest. His wiry frame belied the strength that he exuded under his baggy clothes. Scars radiated across his arms and I caught a glimpse of a lengthy white line on his thigh as he sat across from me. I wondered what was causing his eye complaint as he continued to blink continuously and his orbs seemed to grow redder and redder. After he'd rambled about Scavolo being the best warrior since Achilles I dragged the conversation back to the present. "I'm looking for anything you can tell me about the night of the festival of Minerva" I started.

"Is this about the Fullers girl?" he cut me off as soon as I'd started and my heart sank at another rebuff. "We already told what we know, but I heard there were people looking into it again" he replied to my questioning look.

"Yes" I replied. "I've been given three days to see if I can find the killer.

He appraised me with a slow stare and then rubbed at his eye, which unnerved me as it looked painful and I decided I'd better not shake that hand in case he passed on whatever problem he had to me. "Lucius came here the day after the death" he said. "With his brother, that idiot, forget his name" he looked at the table for a second as if he was trying to remember but then continued. "Asking questions and pushing the guests around" he was shaking his head. "They're a pair of pricks" he added. I agreed with a shrug. "But I told them to fuck off and they did." I guessed that even the two large Etruscans could see that the shorter man held some fighting skill so had done as they were told.

"I'm only looking for two men who were seen leaving the city in the early dawn. One wore a cloak and one didn't. One of them had expensive boots, the type that rise above the ankle."

"Riding boots" he answered at once. My widening eyes led him to continue. "They sound like riding boots. Let me check" at which he rose and disappeared into the inn shouting for someone. After a short while of further shouting he re-appeared with a man who I recognised immediately, it was no-cloak. His fair hair and blue eyes marked him as a Gallic slave immediately and I nodded at his intense stare in my direction. "Gallus" said the inn-keeper, "my boy" he confirmed as I nodded, seeing absolutely nothing about the boy that suggested he was any relation to the olive skinned, dark-haired man that stood over me with a series of slates in his hand. He looked through them mumbling 'festival' as he searched. "Ah, here" at which he raised a slate. He'd be good in the temple, I thought, assuming these were his guests listed so that their bills could be confirmed when they left. He saw my appraising look and replied. "Got to be organised these days, bloody taxes on land and now on additional income from three floors" at which he flicked a head at the roof above us, a three floored wooden inn could be expensive to run. He was right. As Rome had grown we'd seen an increase in land tax as well as some additional property measures added to the tributum, designed to cover the costs of war and state duties, for those that gained income from trades. It hadn't gone down well in the popular assemblies but the city needed defending from our enemies and who else was going to pay for the new walls and weapons if it wasn't the people themselves?

"Gallus, who was that Capuan you took to the stables on the night of the festival?"

"Marcus Opsius" he replied quickly to a nod from his father. "Horse trader." It made sense, many of the best horses came from the flatter lands which stretched from the marshes to the hills in the centre of the region. "He had to leave early because his horse was at the stables along the Latina because all the stables on the Ostiensis were full due to the festival" he explained. This too seemed plausible as the Latina was the best road to the south. I nodded my understanding.

"Sorry we couldn't help much" said the old man.

I looked to the boy, probably only a year or so younger than myself. "Did you see anyone else out on that morning?" I asked.

His lips protruded as he considered my question. "There was a man in the shadows at the gate" by which he meant the Trigemina where three roads crossed "and then I saw another soon after who looked in his cups. He was wary" he looked at me for a moment and then I saw recognition in his frown. "Was that you?" He was sharp and I smiled and tipped my head in response.

His father gave me a curious smile. "You're not blamed for the murder are you?" he asked, stiffening. It was a good question. If I was accused I might drag them to the court in my defence, which could cost him time and money as well as losing face with his clients if I was found guilty. The father and son shared a look which suggested they'd said too much and would shut like the gates of Troy if they thought for one moment that they'd be called to the Comitia.

I reassured him that I was not and moved on quickly as the fact that Gallus recognised me suggested he had good observational skills. "The man in the shadows" I asked. "Can you describe him?"

"Average height."

My face fell at what I expected to be the usual non-committal description of any thief in the night to avoid being dragged into court cases or disturb the local gangs who might come to silence any accusers. But then he rolled a double six and my devotion to Janus flew back into my mind, followed quickly by Diana and Minerva. This was getting costly.

"I'd say he was no more than fifteen summers with teeth like a horse. Looked like he'd been kicked by one too." I was about to thank him for this when he added more. "Wait. Not long after we saw you there was another boy, older and larger. He saw us coming and slid off into the streets to avoid us. I assumed he was a thief so kept a look out but never saw him again." He held up a hand to my raised eyebrows and opening mouth. "He had his hair tied back, like the Etruscans do" he said.

"What did he wear, was there anything else that marked him out?"

He started to shake his head. "Strong looking lad. I'd recognise him again if I saw him." This was good. "In fact, just behind him I saw a lady at the door of her house for a moment, probably out to empty a piss-pot, but she turned back as I approached. She wore a thick shawl. It was hard to be clear because of the fog though. They could have been together but I'm not sure."

He was about to continue but I spoke over him in my haste. "Would you be available to speak at the Comitium if the boy was found?" He nodded stiffly and I looked to his father as I was worried the boy might not be a citizen. If he isn't a direct blood family member the Patres of the house would have to vouch for him at the Comitium and his testament may not be as well received.

"Gallus is my son and a citizen under the laws, he can speak for himself" he said proudly and I nodded to them both in relief and with a warm smile. It was good news and meant that the boy could speak on his own behalf, which makes a big difference to the legality of his testimony should it be required.

I thanked them and said that I would mention Maximus to Scavolo when I next saw him, to which he beamed. "Tell him that my rates are reduced for ex-soldiers" he added quickly. "And a free jug of wine for any group of four." It made good business sense.

I stood to leave and Maximus walked me to the doorway. "I didn't get your name" he said as he raised a hand to me and I quickly placed mine on his shoulder in a friendly gesture to avoid the one that he'd dug into his eye socket and was no doubt going to offer in a handshake.

"My apologies" I said, suddenly nervous that I shouldn't say who I am as I'd dressed down and this would add even more suspicions to the question form his son. "Graccus, Graccus Porcius. I work at the temple of Jupiter." His eyes narrowed at this, clearly my ability to lie was in tune with my ability to act the stoic patrician. I smiled broadly and left, feeling an urge to wipe my hand across my nose.

This news opened so many new crossroads that my mind raced faster than the biting gnats that caught me every summer. I headed back to the temple filled with even more questions. At this rate we'd need to buy a mountain of slates to fill up every option we had found. Yet one thing was certain. I knew who the boy at the gate most likely was. All I had to do now was speak to him. Minerva and Janus needed my devotion.

X

Standing, I stretched my back. It was fast approaching hora undecima, not long till sunset, and I was tired. It had been a long day.

"Bastards not come yet" said Graccus tapping a tune with a single finger on the slate he had just finished. He didn't usually swear, he must have caught it from me.

On my return Graccus had told me that he had no luck finding the two women as the Fuller's brother Larce didn't have any names, just a street in which Lucius and his brother had questioned people. It didn't help and left us with another loose end to tie up. I hoped it wasn't a set-back as my information regarding the boy with the horse-like teeth was enough for both of us to smile and agree that Brocchus was our key suspect. He seemed to have been in the vicinity of the murder at the right time and clearly had some relationship with the girl. We discussed whether it might be a crime of passion, which most were if Scavolo was anyone to listen to. To be fair to the head man of the temple he had been doing this job for far longer than us and despite his abrupt nature he did get results.

I'd been through my report, and Graccus had written it down. He really was very good at this, I'd already decided that he could be the scribe and I'd do the talking. It fitted our skills and our status. I'd explained that I believed Marcius Brocchus was the boy at the gate. Brocchus was a common name for people who had large teeth, and I mentioned to Graccus that Aspius had said 'you can't miss his family', a clear reference to their appearance. He laughed at this and replied that the woman who had opened the door at the family home had prominent teeth too. It made sense and we were already congratulating ourselves on finding our man.

Brocchus was clearly someone we needed to talk to. Was he the running man? Why did he look like he'd been in a fight and why was he seen in the fog near the place where Lucilla was found murdered? We'd discussed various ideas, but none made much total sense. He seemed to have the opportunity to be the killer, being near the scene, but why would he do it? Lucilla was remarkably clean for a dead girl, that is what Novius had said, so if he'd fought with her we would expect to have seen signs of a fight. It wasn't clear so we'd scratched the name from the slate I had created and started a new one called 'Brocchus' and begun to sketch out any facts we knew already, with gaps where we needed his testimony to fill the blanks. The fact that the boy had not turned up added to our confusion. I considered a visit to his house, but it was a couple of hours walk at least and I knew that neither of us fancied a trip home in the dark. I had a growing concern that I should have spent my silver on assuaging the gods and not on Novius' man. I took a final mouthful of the wine, which suddenly appeared sour and stung my throat. My expression brought a glance from Graccus, which I waved away. "We'll go in the morning" I said, looking around the room and picking up a cup to which I added a measure of wine. "I'm going to pour a libation to Janus and Minerva and then go home." I stopped at the door, looking at the scene of the hunter, "and Diana" I added quickly, going back into the room and filling the cup to the brim.

****

I returned home later, by which time my belly thought my throat had been cut and growled at me as loudly as a rebuke from Scavolo and it was almost dark. I was therefore shocked to find my former boss was sat in my father's Lavatrina next to the kitchen where our family bathed every nine to ten days. I'd been summoned as soon as I stepped into the house.

My father sat in the first pool, big enough for two and as deep as his waist. The other smaller pool, designed for two but not really much larger than for a single occupant, held Scavolo.

"Jump in" called my father evidently delighted to see me.

I hadn't shared a pool with my father for a few years and so felt somewhat abashed as I returned to the small changing room and Betula, the kitchen slave, helped me undress. She brought wine and figs to the Lavatrina and told my father that more hot water would be a short while as the fires were only just getting the water to the correct heat. I dived into the figs more quickly than I dived into the water, Scavolo looking me up and down like I was a cheap street whore.

"Well, what a day" started my father after I'd poured wine into the cup he held out towards me. I filled Scavolo's as he leant forward and his penis flopped at me from the water's edge. I felt sick. "Tell me again Gaius" he said to Scavolo, "what the tablet said about this dream."

He relayed the information as I continued to devour the figs like Cronos eating his children, leaving a single fig, my Zeus hidden from their sight behind the wine pitcher for later. The story was every word Graccus had spoken to me earlier and I was relieved to see that both men seemed to have accepted it as the truth despite the holes I could see in the story as I knew the real version of events. Scavolo watched me with interest as I squirmed under his gaze whilst he spoke, standing to fill his cup a few times, his parts waving at me as he did so. He then stood and used a strigil to wipe away the dirt from his body. The scum on the water reminded me of Graccus' nose and I felt my belly start to ache at the figs I'd rammed down my throat.

"What do you make of him?" The question was to me and I had been stifling a heavy fart as my guts started to churn so hadn't really concentrated on the conversation. Scavolo handed the strigil to my father, who stood and scrubbed at his body as

Betula appeared and I started to answer the question. The fresh warm water from several smaller pans was brought in at the same time, the clever slave having split the water to speed up the heating process. I noticed her long leer at Scavolo, who happily stood and allowed the girl to pour the hot water over his head with a giggle.

The question had been asked of Graccus. What did I think of him? My estimation had increased enormously in the past day and I had to consider that they expected me to be as amazed about his part in the dream as they clearly were. "I am amazed" I said, because I was. "He had shown little real experience in the past weeks that I sat in that room with him. If anything I would have said he was lazy and bordering on stupid." Scavolo grunted agreement as he splashed water over his shoulders. "But since this news" I shook my head and looked up at the ceiling as if searching the heavens. "It has made a change in him for sure. The gods are clearly smiling on him. Today he has been Herculean in his search for the truth" I started to say but was cut off by Scavolo.

"How can he be favoured? He's never been out of that room and the only thing he seemed interested in these past weeks is scrounging lunch from you."

The accusation slapped me like the hot water that had been poured over his head and I felt my cheeks redden. "Maybe he has played us both well" I suggested. This brought a scowl from Scavolo but he dipped his head in agreement and let out a huff of air.

"Little pricks showed no skill beyond that then" he added, always having to have the last word, though he narrowed his eyes and gave me one of his long stares. "You were there when this dream was explained" he added. "What did the priestess say, was it just Porcius?"

I understood now what they were looking to do. Scavolo was playing the part my father had clearly asked of him. They wanted to know how they could turn advantage to my father and our family from this situation? If there was any sign that I had been included in this divine calling I could see my life turning to one in which I was inaugurated in the priesthood, had my balls waxed every week and spent the next thirty years overseeing festivals, burials, births and holidays. I had to find a way out of this conversation as quickly as I could. My father gazed at me expectantly, his deep desire to have a member of his family included in a divine dream radiating from him as much as the steam from the pool in which we stood. "It is exactly as you have said" I replied with a shake of my head. "I wish there were more, but I cannot lie in the sight of the goddess and her priestess" I added quickly, trying to close the door that they were furiously trying to prise open. I blustered on. "The change in him has been remarkable. His energy and enthusiasm has doubled" I said.

Scavolo still didn't seem convinced but I looked to my father, who was nodding with a resigned face before he turned to Scavolo. "Is his father coming tomorrow?"

"Yes, sir. All organised." Of course it was. Scavolo didn't cock things up. The head man was looking at me curiously as he spoke and I splashed myself with water to avoid his stare, picking up a strigil and standing to wipe away the sweat of the day.

"Good, good" my father spoke softly and I sensed little change in the conversation; I wasn't wrong. "Secundus, tell me what you have learned today and what part in this you have done and which part Graccus has done." They weren't letting this go.

They were testing me and there was nothing I could do but be cautious with every word I said. I suddenly felt as if my hours with my Greek tutor as a child had all been for this moment. My mind raced to Scavolo's words; *don't cock it up*. I kept to the facts and explained about Gracchus's trip to the Brocchus household, which had been fruitless and that the boy had not turned up at the temple at the appointed hour. I then noted that the two women had not been found as the Fuller could not give us any names, just a street which housed hundreds of people from where the information had come and that Graccus had spent some time tracking these women but to no avail. That part of our searching had been colder than left-over mutton. Scavolo ground his teeth at this and my father calmed him with a wave of his hand. I then reviewed what I had learned from my day, assessing the information from Sertor, that Scavolo had already imparted to my father based on their expressions and nods of agreement. I wondered why they had not paid the man three silver coins seeing as his information had clearly gone to them as quickly as it had been given to me.

"I visited the inns along the roads from the Boarium" I said, mentioning Maximus and his offer. Scavolo nodded at this and glanced to my father, who also inclined his chin and seemed to smile as the glance between the two men suggested they had further use for this knowledge. "His son Gallus was the man with no cloak" I said to Scavolo's wide eyes as I let out this information. I was pleased that it came as news to him, based on his seeming to know every other scrap of information we had gleaned. "And a horse trader named Opsius was the man with the boots." At these words both men seemed to share a private moment which peeked their interest even more. Then they both faced me with disappointed expressions, but I had saved the best till last and so rushed on. I grinned and Scavolo scowled in response, which un-nerved me as he stood at the same time and wiped his genitals with a cloth. "Here is the best of it" I was going to milk this. "Gallus saw a boy at the Trigemina gate, looking like he'd been in a fight." Scavolo stopped swiping his penis and looked at me, my father shifted in the pool. "From the description it is clear to me that it was Marcius Brocchus." My bathing buddies shared a look. "There's more" I added. "Along the road he saw another boy with his hair tied back in the Etruscan style, who rushed into the shadows as he approached.

He couldn't give me any further information but he said he would recognise the boy again if he saw him. And..." they were now concentrating on my words, "a woman was seen behind the Etruscan boy, though they may not have been together, she could have been emptying a piss pot from the house."

My father placed a hand on my shoulder. "You've done well, Secundus" he said quietly with a calm look on his face and a glance to Scavolo, who was also smiling. That un-nerved me more than his flashing genitals as he turned toward me. "Gaius, tomorrow send men to the Brocchus household, find this boy and bring him in for questioning." It was a command. "Tell Novius I want Hastius to come too. Make it clear that it is a summons. I'll question them myself."

I looked at him aghast. "Father" I said. "It is my investigation" I added.

His face turned back to the cold stone that I'd known for so many years. "You have stated that Porcius is the man named in this investigation, not yourself." I looked to Scavolo, who had also turned back into that fucking statue that I'd seen so many times; no emotion on his face, with the dead look that a fish gives when it's been hit on the head before it drops onto the slate to be sliced. It was my turn to grind my teeth. I'd sailed into their plan as surely as Odysseus into the Cyclops lare. "Porcius is my man, so I will lead" he added with finality.

"I..." I clamped my mouth shut, as my father's eyes rose in the expectation of my coming clean regarding the whole story and my part in the priestesses dream. "We are partners" I said desperately.

The centurion rose from his bath, naked and dripping with water. "If Porcius is the man named in this dream then we're fucked" he said. I gaped at him and he shook his head slowly. "You just said it yourself. If we don't step in he'll cock it up as sure as the Fabii were crushed at Cremera." The allusion to the great loss against the Veiians near the city of Fidenae wasn't lost on me and I sucked in my breath.

"I didn't say he was that shit" I added angrily, lighting up Scavolo's eyes.

"You just told us he had two jobs and none of them resulted in anything of any value. You said that his search brought nothing, not one scrap of useful insight or information, closed doors and barred gates. Nothing." It was critical but accurate. I bristled as I searched for a response but was beaten as Scavolo continued. "And yet your search found not only a potential new client for your father." I glanced between them at this statement and he responded to my furrowed brows. "We've been trying to get into the horse market for a while now but not found any potential leads and this could open new doors for your father" he explained to my questioning gaze. "But your investigations on your own have also found the best clue we've had to this case so far, two suspects near the body at the right time, you've found both men that nobody could find despite their days of searching. Tell me that isn't a coincidence and then tell me why this fucking dream didn't include you?" He was now leaning forward, his eyes boring into my own and a finger jabbing at my face.

My father tutted and shook his head.

XI

Graccus waved a hand in the blackness and I followed the direction, which led to a wall with a high window. He'd have to stand on my shoulders to reach it but it was the only way we could see to get into the house. It was hora secunda and the stars which told us the time were lighting our way so badly that I'd bashed my shins on tree roots more times than I could remember and my lower limbs ached.

We were criminals, reduced by the gods to breaking into a house to save my skin and cover our tracks. I felt shame, anger and depression filling my mind. Scavolo and father had quizzed me until my brain hurt, but I steadfastly refused to say that the dream included myself. The more they hammered me with questions, the more I repeated the lie and they grew more suspicious. Eventually I'd grown angry and left them in the Lavatrina and my mind raced with thoughts and my heart was drumming like the hooves of a horse in full flight.

On my way to Graccus' house I'd taken every last fig I could find in the kitchen and placed them on the shrine of Minerva as we ran across the city to get to the Fuller's yard. My accomplice in crime had been dragged from his bed by the door slave, who was sworn to silence with a promise of silver and an improved role within the household as soon as I told Graccus my tale of being in the Lavatrina with Scavolo and my father and that we needed to get the copy of the slate from the Fuller's this night or the whole story would be up. I was convinced that Scavolo would be at the Fullers door at dawn to check out my blustering denial that I was in any way connected to the divine dream. I'd held out like a last defence on a hilltop, Scavolo barking like a mad dog and my father ignoring my pleas. I'd retreated to my room and I left them plotting their next moves. It was gone midnight by my estimation when Scavolo left the house and I was instantly up and out as soon as I heard my father close the door to his room. I had to rescue this situation. If Minerva was with me, then now was the time for her to prove it.

Graccus, in contrast to Scavolo's view hours earlier, was not as shit as they thought and suggested that he could write a new copy and simply exchange it for the one that the priestess held, in this way when Scavolo asked to see it, it was in her house and he would read it and replace it without question. I thought it was a good plan, but I questioned how we could get into the house at this early hour, and we had no clue as to where the tablet would be kept. Again, his new status as an investigator rose in my estimation as he said that the tablet was kept in the Lararium, he'd seen them place it in a small alcove beside one of the family busts as he was leaving. As the Lararium was just off the Atrium and away from the main bedrooms I felt hope rise like the spring at the foot of the Vestal temple. I prayed to the Vestal fire that we would be successful and bargained a chicken's life for success upon our return as we headed out into the darkness with a new slate written and ready to replace the original.

Graccus was light, which I appreciated, until his large feet kicked at my ears several times and he stood on the top of my head putting my neck out momentarily, before dragging himself up to the window. I heard him scraping through the hole and sat back to wait. There was no way he could get me into the house without alerting the door guards, which every house had. We'd hoped that the guards would be the usual small boy who would shout and scream if he heard anything but would usually fall asleep by dark because nobody ever robbed a large Domus in Rome. Slums? Broken into every day. Inns and shops? Every week some idiot was trying their luck at the locks and coming up against a snarling dog or a sharp dagger from the door slave. But for some reason burglary on a large house was almost unheard of. The few slates and wax tablets I'd copied to vellum scrolls which claimed that a neighbour had climbed a fence at night to steal a silver ring or an expensive Greek pot flashed through my mind as I sat down to wait under the window but these were so few I felt we had a good chance of finding minimal, if any, security.

We also knew after her first refusal that the priestess would never exchange the document for us and I knew with the cold certainty of death that Scavolo would be here in a few hours to check the copy and to confirm what they had discussed with me in the Lavatrina, that Graccus could not be the man chosen by the goddess. This was the only way to get the slate and replace it so that he would find no evidence. A noise above my head worried me, but it must have been a squirrel in the trees as no more sound came. I swallowed dryly and rubbed my hands together. It wasn't cold, but it wasn't warm either. A good night to become a sneak thief I said to myself as I looked up at the stars and traced a few of the ancient heroes. *You were all thieves in the ancient stories too* I thought as I saw them staring down on me and Graccus with stern faces.

Time dragged past like a donkey over-laden with wool.

I must have dropped off as I jumped awake with a start hearing a clattering noise from inside the house. *Shit, he's cocked it up* I thought, panic rising in my mind as I gazed intently at the darker hole in the wall where the thief would appear. There was a moment of silence before a light became visible through the half-closed shutters in a window along the wall much higher than the one through which Graccus had entered. The light bobbed along the window, slightly open to the air for a breeze to run through the house, before disappearing completely and re-appearing as a small glow in the window above me. After what seemed like an age I heard a few raised voices and my panic neared new heights. I was about to abandon Graccus and run for home in despair when the noise abated and I heard a child-like crying before a voice was raised to silence the crier. It must have been the door slave! Whoever had gotten out of bed was blaming the door slave for whatever noise I'd heard. I hoped that Graccus was well hidden. Relief flooded through me. After a few minutes the light from the small window bobbed back into darkness, appearing in the other window along the wall from where it had started. I heard no more voices but felt that if I moved someone would see me so I silently sucked in my breath and slowly drew my knees to my chest in the darkness.

It was clear that whatever was happening inside Graccus had not been discovered; yet. After another endless wait I heard a slight scraping noise above me and turned to see a bare arse protruding through the window as Graccus' legs started to push into the space, followed by his torso and bunched up tunic. I stepped in as his legs dropped and he extended his arms. I grabbed his feet which were covered in some sort of slimy oil. I moaned about it but he ignored me. We knew that if he dropped and landed in a rut or on a tree root he could break an ankle so I gently eased him to the floor and whispered; "got it?" to which he seemed to nod.

"Go" he whispered. "Slowly" he raised his whisper a notch as I turned and instantly slipped on a broken branch, so much for the guiding hand of Minerva.

"What happened?" I asked once we'd gotten a good distance from the house and were enjoying the long downhill trip back towards the centre of the city, though we still moved slowly as it was almost pitch black in parts and we'd forgotten to bring a torch.

"When I got in I crawled across the atrium but I couldn't find the alcove" he said, his breath short as we were pushing along at a good pace up the hill on the widest part of the track. "The boy must have been asleep at the door as I couldn't hear anything or see anyone moving. So I moved around slowly because it's as dark as a cave in there. I eventually found the place where the alcove is and was searching about and caught my arm on one of the statues or urns or something. You must have heard it?" I said I had. "I tried to catch it but it slipped from my hand and landed on the floor with a crash like thunder. The bloody thing was full of some sort of oil. It went everywhere but I managed to get into a corner quickly as I heard the boy moving by the doorway." I rubbed at my hands which were still oily from his feet and nodded my understanding. "The lad must have been asleep because I heard a stool scrape back at that and then I saw the candlelight and I heard him coming. I crouched in the corner and hid behind a stool. I'm not lying if I tell you I was shitting myself." I laughed in response. "Did you hear the head slave bollock him?"

"I was so frightened you'd been caught that any sound from the house just made me hide deeper in the shadows" I replied, avoiding my thoughts of my judgement that he'd cocked it up.

He laughed. "Well, he got a clout around the head and he'll be paying for that broken statue for a long time." It was a sad fact of life that slaves tried, mostly unsuccessfully, to repay their cost to their master to gain their freedom. Such breakages would be added to that cost, and a family statue would not be cheap to replace, he might even lose his place in the home if they thought it was a bad omen. Poor lad, I gave him no more thought though – life is tough and he had to learn the hard way as did we all.

"I waited a bit longer to make sure they'd gone to bed, but it seems like an age.. You must have felt the same. And then I crept out and started searching again. I knew I'd found the slate because I could feel the temple seal on the front, so I replaced it with the copy I did and then came back out."

"You did a great job Graccus" I said with a glance over my shoulder, tripping on a stone as I did so and cursing under my breath.

"*We* did it Secundus. We seem to make a good team." I could feel his eyes turning to me, but ignored his look, I was above such emotional statements.

"Well, we need to be careful. If Minerva is truly watching over our deeds" which I doubted "then we may have tested her favour tonight. Tomorrow leaves us only two days in which to find our killer and my father and that prick Scavolo are already trying to take over the case by dragging Hastius in for questions and going to Brocchus' house in the morning to bring him in for questioning."

We agreed to be at the temple at dawn, which almost felt that we shouldn't bother going home, to plan the day and be ready for when Brocchus and Hastius were hauled in. Whatever my father said, this was still *my investigation*.

XII

My dreams collapsed in on me like a landslide in the hills devouring a section of forest. Initially the girl Lucilla had appeared, singing and dancing. I'd followed, like a puppy, until she stood at the ditch with Ducus laughing at her side as he pointed into the darkness below. In the ditch was a body, but not Lucilla's. It was Graccus, white like marble, his eyes turned upwards and his genitals flapping. His face turned to me and as he sniffed, slugs came from his nose, trailing silver threads behind them as an urn of oil poured over his head. My dream changed instantly to a dark alleyway in which a man with a horse's head galloped along at incredible speed. I was suddenly sat astride his back, fear coursing through me as he turned and twisted to unseat me. I screamed, but the noise was drowned by festival music as I saw Hastius clubbing at someone in the darkness, his mouth lathered with white foam in the madness that engulfed him. Graccus was then at my side and said *what goes through the mind of a killer* as we watched the terrible scene of butchery being enacted by the duck-farmer. Scavolo's laughter made me turn to his naked figure beside me, his teeth flashing and dazzling my sight before a vision of Minerva floated across the scene, lifting the dead girl from Hastius, who screamed in anger at losing his prey. A wax tablet, which was inscribed with one word, *veritas*, fell from Minerva's hand and Janus picked it up. Both of the two faces of the god looked me up and down and made me feel dizzy under his gaze. He pulled out his cock and swiped it with a cloth before leering at me and stretching his neck to shout to the heavens that he would castrate me for lying. Zeus came, blade in hand and his arm arched in a circle as he jumped on me.

I awoke drenched in more water from my nightly terror than when I'd been sat beside my father in the Lavatrina. My head pounded from lack of sleep, the wine and the figs. It was still dark, but not as dark as my dream or thoughts, and I sat up with a sigh. The dream ran through my mind replaying vividly against the stillness of the unlit room; parts of it making sense, others not so. Was it a divine dream from Minerva? I doubted it. It was just a nightmare. Or was Somnus trying to somehow give me clues to this case? Then I realised, this is the first night in as long as I can remember that I had not dreamt of my wife and child or the dead girl in the ditch. In truth I didn't know if it was any better than the dead girl's staring eyes. It shocked me and I felt remorse building as I stood and dressed, my head aching and my ears sore from Graccus' feet scraping at them with his ridiculously large feet and cheap sandals.

I slogged up the hill to the temple a short while later wrapped in a thick cloak against the cold morning. The temple candles were being replaced as I pushed open the door, Philus jumping at the noise as rarely did anyone appear so early. "Fuck!" he exclaimed as he was only a yard behind the door with the long taper which would light the candle he'd just replaced. I smiled at his surprise. "You are early master" he spoke quietly once he saw me but I saw suspicion in his eyes.

"Lots to do Philus. Is Graccus here yet?"

"No master" his eyes glinted as they narrowed. "Should he be?"

I could see the filthy traitor running to Scavolo with whatever I said, so cheerfully added "I didn't know if he'd finished the task I set him overnight." His eyes widened so large they appeared to shine like the moon in the light of the candle. I grinned as I walked away "Oh" I called over my shoulder, "where do we keep the chickens?"

Having opened the windows and lit several candles from one that was in the corridor I quickly marked the slate from the

Fullers with an X and hid it underneath the pile that was now building on the table in our room. I set my mind to thinking of a solution to our problem, to find a way to wrestle this case back from my father and Scavolo before they cocked it up. I grinned again, I was turning into Scavolo now with my thoughts of people cocking things up. I was just looking at the slate with Hastius' statement when Graccus appeared with two hot bread portions wrapped in a cloth. My stomach growled as soon as the smell of lamb and garlic hit my nose.

"From mother" he said, unwrapping them.

I took it with thanks. "Why was she up cooking so early?" I asked between bites as I crammed the food into my mouth ravenously.

"One of Scavolo's men appeared last night to request my father visit the temple at meridiem and so she was up before dawn preparing extra food as she thinks I might be asked to stay late and will need it" he explained happily.

I looked at him with concern. Gods they were feeding him up now, expecting great things from the son whom they'd plied with educated tutors and words such as *work hard in Rome and you will rise to greatness*. It was the age old desire of every plebeian family. What had I gotten him into? By deflecting the dream from myself to save the heartache of eventually letting my family's hopes and dreams fade to dust, I'd unwittingly passed the same ultimate fate to Graccus. "Do they know about the dream?" I asked quietly, rising to close the door.

"No. I said it was probably because I had been promoted and was working with the quaestors son on a legal case." His words were spoken quietly, as if he was concerned that he'd overstepped the mark by saying such a thing to his parents.

His round eyes were shining. Was Petulantia playing games with us now as well, the Greek goddess Hybris at her side? In truth it was correct, but the announcement that he was named within a divine dream would circulate around Rome like Achilles dragging the body of Hector; it would lead to no good. "Graccus, we need to discuss this. What do you think will happen when they find out that you are named in a dream from Minerva?"

He looked at me for a moment, his nose about to drip. Then in all seriousness he replied "I have decided that whatever is said I will not reply. In which case I have not confirmed or denied that I was involved in the dream and my words will not implicate me in any future challenges to their authenticity."

I looked at him incredulously and answered sharply. "It's written on the slate. I know it's ambiguous but we told my father and Scavolo it was you." I pointed to the table and his gaze followed my finger to the pile of slates.

"I've thought that through as well" came the smiling response. "It is just one case, one murder. When this is finished I will have gained notoriety for my part in resolving the case, with your support, and the dream will be mostly forgotten. However, it will earn me a junior role as a lawyer and, with your support" it was the second time he had said the phrase and I understood the claim to patronage that he was requesting, however informally, "I will be of value to the temple in my new role. Have we not proven our skills. I will be your right hand." My jaw slackened at this indication of his ignorance of the workings of divine support. Didn't he know that once a family is linked to a god it would be tributes, priesthoods and divinations until the gods were deposed from their heavenly thrones? Tedium beyond tedium, sacrifice beyond sacrifice. My father's arms stank of blood every night on his return from the temple. I don't want that. Of course Graccus didn't understand any of this, he is a Pleb. To his family it is one day at a time, not years of family tradition and honour. If only I had his simple life to contemplate and worry about, but I had a history and a clan which was bent on rising up the ladder to the top. My brother, a few years older than me was already on that slope. He was out most days doing some chore or other for his patron, long hours in which he hardly saw his wife, whom he'd only just married. That life was not for me. The cursus honorum was just that, a curse. A life of playing political games with your peers and trying to hide from your own failings behind bribes and corruption if you were no good at the games that the senate played. My father was good at it, I had to give him that credit. But I don't want it. I don't want that life. I thought about Minerva and her gift. Yes, it was interesting and had stopped my drinking and depression. Having something of purpose to do had filled my senses with joy and given me a new energy. I was grateful for not dreaming of Plaudita or the dead girl. But it was fleeting, just like the will of the gods. They'd drop me like a traitor from the Tarpeian rock if I didn't play their games. My thoughts had caused my face to contort into a morose gaze which Graccus caught. His startled face startled me as I blinked at his stupidity. Then I realised that my usual failure to remove all traces of expression from my face had caused him alarm. He knelt at my feet quickly and urgently. "Surely, Secundus, I have been of use? I did not mean to overstep my position" he was almost pleading and I felt the embarrassed redness flush across my face. He must have read my inner turmoil as dismissal of his request, a potential crushing blow to the future he had just described.

I stood and took his shoulders in my hands, raising him to his feet and looking directly into his frightened face. "Graccus, I could think of nobody better to whom I would give my support."

His relief spread across his face and he gripped me in the strongest hug I'd felt since I fought Septimus at the games two summers ago, that man was a bear.

"You two fucking lovers are in early" snapped Scavolo as he thrust open the door just as Graccus was mid-hug. I pushed him away quickly and he straightened his tunic, Scavolo's peering gaze looking him up and down with a sneer. "Which Incubus visited you to get you here so early?" he asked suspiciously.

"We only have two more days, Scavolo" I replied evenly. "Every hour is an hour in which we can find more information that will bring Graccus to the killer. We have work to do out there." I crossed my arms over my chest to suggest our conversation had finished.

"Better not send the sparrow out then when the hawk is needed" he laughed with a glance to Graccus, who was pinching his nose and sniffing. "What happened to your ear?" he added quickly.

I touched my left ear which had gotten the worst of Graccus' sandal in the night and realised it was quite swollen. "Fell out of bed after all that wine in the Lavatrina." It was a quick response and he grunted and grinned at my inability to hold my wine before turning to leave, then turned back again.

"I'll let you know when Brocchus gets here" he said sharply. Before I could ask anything else he qualified his statement. "Your father said you can join him at the questioning. Bring the sparrow" he laughed again and disappeared into the corridor still laughing at his own jest. Bastard.

****

Time has a habit of passing like a horse in flight when you need it to pass like a snail. A messenger had appeared at the temple just after dawn to say that Lucius had found the two women and they would be at the Fullers house within the hour. We agreed that I would take a horse, Graccus couldn't ride very well, and return as quickly as possible once I'd interrogated them. In truth the words of Scavolo were burning my ears as much as the bruising from the sparrow's kicks; *he had two jobs and none of them resulted in anything of any value.* I could feel my fear manifesting itself into a desire to make another devotion to Minerva and I made a mental note to do this as soon as I could manage to do so.

I was greeted by a slave, buxom and wide-hipped, wearing an off-white sleeveless Stola. Her throat, adorned with a black necklace of dyed bone, was as pale as the moon on a cold winter night and her gaze calculating but with a deep warmth. I smiled to her inclined head and tried not to stare at the pox scars or flea bites on her face, neck and shoulders. I guessed she must be the head woman as she was formal but relaxed in my company. After exchanging pleasantries and explaining who I was the horse was waved away to be cleaned and fed. She allowed me to follow her through to the same room I had visited on my previous attendance, the terracotta nymphs in the garden still smiling happily as I passed by. Three people greeted me, Lucius, Larce and a boy of probably fourteen or fifteen summers with unruly brown hair which fell to his shoulders. His appearance was that of the tribes from the North as opposed to the dark-haired and large Etruscans and my initial assumption was that he was a slave. He was a heavy-boned fellow with a thick chest and strong looking arms. I thought he might be a good wrestler as his stature suggested he either worked out a lot or he worked the fields to get those muscles. I half-smiled, he avoided my eyes.

"My son Arnth" said Larce, seeing my surprise at the boy as I greeted them and accepted the small cup of watered wine that was offered, which was sweet and aromatic, a plum vintage not unlike the amphora that I had opened from Milo and we kept in the room at the temple hidden under a sack cloth and away from prying eyes and thirsty mouths. I wondered if they bought their wine from him too. I gazed back at the lad quickly, brown-haired and brooding eyes with tense shoulders. Arnth, if my Etruscan was any good, meant storm clouds and I could see that in his face. His eyes never connected with my own and I assumed he was being deferential as I remembered Larce didn't look at me directly for some time either when we first met.

"Ah" I said to the boy. "I would appreciate a moment to get your story from the night of the festival" adding a tepid smile so as not to appear too friendly.

"Why?" came the instant retort from Larce, his harshness echoed in his eyes although that changed in an instant as he realised from my surprised face what he'd done. "Sorry, master" he added quickly as his son shifted on the spot, one hand gripping his tunic at the hip. "His words were written by your man Graccus" he stated with a small bow to explain his own reaction "is there something wrong with them?".

"No. I didn't mean to cause any upset" I smiled in response, turning to face the boy. I was back to my best patrician face, looking down on my subordinates. "It's just that we have some new information, and it has brought out memories which Lethe has chosen to hide in her waters." I was impressed with my answer, but clearly they did not know the Greek histories as they all stared back with blank expressions. There was no Etruscan similarity that I could remember from my lessons and so I explained. "She is the goddess of the river of forgetfulness, one of the five in the underworld. The new information might stir your memories, that is all." This seemed to calm them both, though the boy still seemed tense and something told me that if I made a move toward him he'd jump like a stallion let loose amongst the brood mares.

"What news is there, Secundus. Tell me" asked Lucius now urgent and on first name terms once more. It was a good trick to ease tension and I made a note to use it myself if the time came.

I hesitated, but then reminded myself that I am searching for his daughter's murderer and I had not yet reported anything of the findings from the day before, so I answered his pressing request. "Graccus and I found someone who placed Brocchus with Lucilla in the shop area just after the wrestling and the two men that were seen on the night of the festival also say they saw a boy matching his description hiding in the streets just before dawn and near where the body was found. Also…"

"Brocchus" snarled Larce cutting me off and causing us all to glance in his direction. "I'll gut the bastard and string his dead carcass to the nearest tree."

"Wait" I said quickly to his movement, one hand dragging his son with him as he was clearly heading off to meat out justice in the Etruscan style, fists and iron. I realised that I'd made a mistake and the gods were playing with me once again. I should not have mentioned the boy's name. I turned back to Lucius. "We also have another suspect coming to the temple today as his story does not add up either, so we should take no actions as nothing is confirmed." I was about to continue when the girl's father spoke loudly.

"Who?" snapped Lucius, his anger rising as quickly as his brother's had done.

I realised my second mistake in raising their hopes and bit my lip at my stupidity, was Janus twisting my words with double meaning? "I am not at liberty to say" I added quickly. "Remember that until his case is brought forward he cannot answer against it. We have facts that do not tie together, so we need to ask more questions, that is all that I can tell you for the moment. You must not act against anyone Lucius, or you Larce" I stared at them both and then to the boy, who looked away quickly. "I cannot stress this enough, the law states that unless you bring a case to justice you cannot exact a punishment."

His dark eyes brooded as he sat in silence. I decided to take a stab at the boy and turned to the younger Arturii, my voice calm and measured. "Arnth, you were with Lucilla on the night, at the wrestling." He nodded at this, obviously wary of my questions as his eyes roved to his father and uncle. "You sat with her, is that right?"

"Yes, with a few others too" he replied.

"Did she speak of anything in particular, had she fallen out with anyone?"

He shrugged. "She'd been dancing" he said slowly and then looked to me and added, "and her and Marcius Brocchus were together a lot. He's stupid enough to have upset her, but I don't know" he answered. "Ask her girlfriends, they'll know more than me."

I nodded. This was something I'd neglected to follow up on so far and I resolved to ask for names from Fucilla later. "Can you tell me what you saw on the night after the wrestling had finished?"

His eyes flicked to his father and then back to me, his fingers interlocking before he rubbed his hands and answered in a slow, deep voice. "Nothing until that idiot Hastius came complaining about us spreading lies about that dick Aspius." I sat with my eyes wide, waiting for more. He looked at me then away, abashed under my forceful gaze as the time stretched into silence.

"Take your time" I said, pushing him to speak. "Anything else?" He was shaking his head, fidgeting nervously, the lad was *clearly* a dimwit. "Did you see anyone near the cloth shop by the Boarium at any time?" I asked.

His eyes half-closed and I saw his lip twitch before he looked up and caught my eyes. "I think so." His voice didn't seem too certain and his eyes shifted left and right in thought. "If I'm not wrong it was" at which he sucked in a breath avoiding a curse. "Brocchus, I saw him lurking there in the shadows."

"Alone?"

His face twitched as he tried to remember. "I'm not sure. It was dark."

I nodded with an encouraging smile but it was another mention of the boy Brocchus in the right place to make him a suspect. "And later, did you see a boy running or two men arguing at all?"

Another glance to his left at his father before he answered. "I don't remember that" he said quietly. "Lots of people were running around, especially the younger kids."

I wanted to ask if he had seen Aspius or his father after the scuffle but then thought that would be too leading a question. Scavolo had given Graccus and I a short lesson in the art of asking questions and I knew enough of the law to understand the value of not giving away too much information for the speaker to simply tell me what I wanted to hear. However, it was another sighting of Brocchus in the shadows which was good enough for me. I nodded my thanks, seeing relief on all three faces as it was clear I had finished my questions.

"Does that help?" asked Lucius.

I continued to nod before turning back to the boy and asking another question. "What did you do after the wrestling?"

His mouth opened and closed for a moment. "We went dancing over by the olive trees" he shrugged. "Then" he shrugged again with a glance up at both me and his father "you know, just had fun."

His lips were tight now and I could see that he didn't want to tell us he'd no doubt been shagging one of the local girls. I hoped she'd used the oil and sponge lest another dimwit like this entered the world. "Oh to be young again" I laughed to ease the tension, although the lad wasn't that many years my junior. "And when the search started where did you go, to look for Lucilla?" I added as his gaze suggested he didn't understand my words.

He shrugged and fidgeted before answering, "we searched the Forum. That's where I was told to go."

I nodded. "By whom?"

He searched the ground for a moment before his eyes caught mine and then quickly darted away. "Mother" he shrugged. "She was telling everyone where to look."

I nodded slowly. Then I sat back on my chair as Larce glared at his son momentarily and I caught an air of anger in his face. Then I smiled and laughed lightly, changing the subject to give the lad a moment of respite as his dull brain seemed to be finding it hard to keep up. "I was out late myself that night, over the river at a party, as you know" I said with a gleam in my eye, although truth be told I had been so drunk I couldn't really remember much beyond some three-coined whore tugging on my dick so hard it nearly fell off and had pained me for two days after with a horrible red blister. I looked up at the three of them and put on my best virtuous face, the misery of my sore knob pushed to the back of my mind.

The arrival of the two women could not have been timelier as feet shifted uneasily for a short while during which I complemented the watered wine, earning a refill. Fucilla brought the ladies to the room, her face alight with expectation. She greeted me like an old friend, and in a surprising move gave me a small bundle which she said I must take to my office at the temple, bidding me to open it later as it was tied with string. She then introduced the two ladies; Aelia, named after the sun and Helen, named after the most beautiful woman to have ever lived but sadly not living up to such expectations. I didn't get their family names as I was too busy considering what questions to ask them. I sat, they stood, proper and fitting. I noted that Fucilla also sat, though behind me as she should, and all the men stood. It was a strange situation in many ways.

I thanked the two ladies for coming and offered them some of my hosts watered wine, which caused a stir, but I thought it would lighten the mood and get their tongues wagging. They were both dressed in heavy wool garments which flowed to the floor. One wore sandals and one bare-footed with a horrible black toe-nail that looked like it might fall off as the edges of the nail were inflamed and angry. I looked away quickly. They slurped their drinks and I smiled benevolently, even Scavolo would be impressed, I thought. "Ladies, might I beg of your memories. I understand you mentioned to Lucius and his brother that you had seen Lucilla and a boy arguing on the night of the festival just after the wrestling?" They were looking nervously to each other but nodded hesitantly. "Can you tell me what you saw please?" I tried to smile but this seemed to frighten them as they gave each other long stares which carried on for a few seconds.

I was about to ask the question once more when Helen started to speak and I noted that her teeth were perfect despite her lopsided mouth which seemed to curl on the top right of her lips, leaving a small gap when she pressed them together. "It's as we said before, we'd been dancing over by the fire with everyone else and then Aelia needed to pee" women always went in two's "so I went with her. We heard a noise over at the corner didn't we?" Aelia agreed, catching my eye before looking away quickly, it didn't look good to stare at your betters. Helen didn't agree with this and gawked at me, the slightly drooping right eye causing me to force myself not to stare at it and draw attention to the slightly enlarged eyelid which clearly held some medical problem. I nodded sagely and sat back in my chair to keep my distance as much as I could, you can't be too careful these days. "Well, it was Lucilla" at which she glanced to the dead girl's mother "and someone, but we don't know who, do we?" she added this to Aelia who looked down at the ground and mumbled that they didn't. I was reminded of a stage play and could almost see the girl redden with the shame of what was clearly a lie.

"Can you describe him at all?" They shook their heads in unison. "Was he taller or shorter than Lucilla?" They looked at each other.

"Taller" said Aelia. Helen nodded vigorously. I was reminded of my brother's shaking head.

I waited, but the silence began to stretch so I filled it myself. "Why was it that you could see Lucilla clearly but you could not see who she was with?" My question brought nervous looks from both girls and they seemed reluctant to answer. I waited a while longer as Helen started to grip her stola and wring it in her hands. I stood now and placed my hands behind my back like one of the good lawyers at the Comitia. "It just seems strange that the shadows were so deep that you could not see who she was with and yet you could see clearly that it was her. What was he wearing?" I asked. They glanced to each other again but didn't reply beyond a shrug. I stepped closer with a furrowed brow and a hard stare. They both stepped back raising their hands to their mouths as if I was about to chastise them or, worse still, hit them. I was reminded of Graccus' bruised ribs and flapping genitals and so I waved my hand slowly in a circle as if thinking of my next question and then rubbed at the back of my neck as I moved to position myself behind the chair. "At what distance were you from them?"

Helen again, clearly the voice of the pair. "About fifty paces, maybe sixty."

"You could see that he was taller than Lucilla but nothing more. Did you see his legs? Arms? Hair?" I looked at them both, their eyes fell straight to the floor. They answered that they could see nothing more than an outline. I smiled. "Before I ask again I would like to say something, which I hope will help. You might think that you are handing the branding iron to the juror by giving information which might implicate whoever you saw, but you must also know that any memories you have could also save that person from being accused. If he cannot give his side of the story and he is innocent..." I inclined my head slowly before shaking it dramatically. Their eyebrows rose at this. I circled slowly, walking quietly as my tutor had said one must do when confronting a difficult opponent to get him off guard. Once again I was amazed at how much of my lessons I'd actually remembered and started to think that my tutor had truly been half decent at his job rather than the dribbling, drunken old fool I remembered. "If the man you saw with Lucilla is innocent of her death we need to know what he saw. He might have been the last person to see her alive. She might have told him something that would give us a clue to who killed her." Aelia balled her fists and then flexed them, doing it again within a heartbeat as her eyes flicked to mine and then back to the floor. She is the key, she will break, I told myself as I glanced between them both. Helen answered that they had nothing else they could say and glanced to Fucilla and Lucius, reddening in shame at the perceived lack of provision of any good evidence.

"Thank you" I smiled with a heavy sigh as if I accepted everything they had said. The tension in the room dropped immediately and both ladies looked up, heads turning to each other and then back to Fucilla, who appeared saddened.

"Master" they both bobbed and bowed as they started to turn towards the door assuming that I had finished. Fucilla rose with them and Lucius touched her arm tenderly as she passed by him.

"Oh" I exclaimed lightly, halting them from their retreat. "One more thing." They turned and moved closer together, like two fighters taking a last stand. "Have you told them of the dream?" I asked Fucilla, who looked at me as if I had asked her to bare her chest. "I take that as a no." I rushed ahead, a desperate gamble but I had a feeling that they held a vital piece of information that could solve this case, I could sense it, and stepped forward between Fucilla and the women in a symbolic breaking of the bond between them, removing the safety that she had offered them. "The high priestess had a vision from Minerva." This got their attention. "She dreamt that divine Minerva came to her in a dream. In that dream the goddess said that I, Secundus Sulpicius Merenda, will find the killer of her daughter and bring him to justice. That, ladies is a fact that you cannot share with any living soul or the goddess will strip you and tear you limb from limb." It was dramatic but raised yelps as both women stood back from me with hands covering their mouths. Fucilla gasped and Lucius made a protective step towards her. Even the boy Arnth was impressed as he, too, moved closer to his father with wide eyes. I was pleased that the Fuller and his wife had not shared that information and that I had the desired effect on both of the women. These girls knew something and it was a desperate gamble, but it was one I felt Minerva was pushing me to make.

"You, Aelia. Know more than you are saying." I didn't mean to be too harsh but her eyes stared back at me in absolute fear and dread. To receive divine support, just as my father and Scavolo knew, was an incredible claim and everyone knew the consequences of ignoring those who claimed such support. The affirmation from Fucilla by way of a stern nod had sent squeaks through both girls as they huddled closer and stared hard at me as if I was a brazen monster sent from the depths of hell to rip their arms from their bodies. Aelia almost fell to the floor in a faint, her skin turning paler than the unpainted marble statues which adorned the Vestal Temple. "Who has paid for your silence?" I said loudly. "Tell me now in front of the high priestess of Minerva and if you do not lie, the goddess will spare you." I had no idea where the gamble had come from, maybe the goddess was actually talking through me, which I doubted.

"It was Spurius Hastius' son Aspius."

The answer was out almost before I could fix her with my hardest glare.

"He was with her. It was him" she cried, falling to her knees and covering her head with her hands as if I was about to beat her like a runaway slave. Helen backed away and screamed as if I'd stuck her with a knife before she fell to her knees too and started to wail about having to promise on their children's lives that they would never tell what they saw and were paid in silver coins for their silence. Her droopy eye quivered in fright as she stared transfixed at me. I was in awe at how the mention of divine prophecy had suddenly opened their hearts and mouths and led to this incredible change in behaviour. I stood over them like Jupiter holding court over the gods, arms crossed and judgemental.

They cried their pleas for mercy from Lucius as they cowered on the floor. The master of the house was screaming at them viciously, calling them lying bitches and advancing towards them like the Pontifex's Lictors about to administer a serious beating. I gaped as slaves rushed to the door at the commotion but were hurried away just as quickly and the doors firmly locked at their backs. Fucilla stared at me agog, her pretty face flashing the image of her dead daughter into my mind as I looked to her. Both kneeling women, hugged each other like babies in a crib, tears falling to the floor in puddles. I stood in silence for a long moment, shocked at their revelation, but also shocked at the impact of my gamble. Minerva really did seem to be speaking through me. I owed another libation.

"By Minerva's hand this will not be spoken of again unless this comes to court" I said to the women, turning to Lucius and his brother and staring them into agreement as well as their countenances had turned dark with anger. "If Hastius gets word that we know, he will not only come for these women, but he will send his son away and we will never know his story. You" at which I snarled at the sobbing pair strewn on the floor at my feet. "You will clean Minerva's shrine every day for three Kalends." To which they wailed agreement. "You will say nothing of today unless I summon you to the Comitium and you will give every coin of silver that you have not spent to the priestess in compensation. If you try and hide any, the goddess will know and she will rot your insides and make you barren before she turns you into old hags before your time." I added this in the hope that a curse would give them the impetus to pay the money. Fucilla nodded and in a whirlwind of movement had the crying women taken from the room and marched out of the house within moments.

Shit! My mind ran through what they'd told me. I was convinced it was Brocchus that had been seen arguing with Lucilla and I ran through their words again. Something was still nagging at my mind though. Other parts of the tale didn't seem to add up if this were true. Another path to follow? I was instantly distracted by noises and looked up to see Lucius standing with his brother, whispering, Arnth no longer in the room.

"Do nothing" I instructed them. "If you act in any way towards anything you have heard today you might frighten the killer and we'll never get to the conclusion of this mystery." My voice was loud and commanding, I really was turning into Scavolo. "Lucius, I need to get back to the temple, can you ask for my horse to be prepared please."

I met Fucilla at the door as I was leaving, my mind reeling through a thousand thoughts. She appeared with the bundle she had brought earlier, I'd forgotten it in the excitement and had left it in the room when we left. I apologised and thanked her. She was with three other women, the buxom slave, a fair headed taller woman who looked quite intimidating and a shorter Latin woman, thin as a pin, tanned skin and pretty-faced. "Secundus" the priestesses face was alight. "You really are going to find my daughter's killer. I know it" she leant forward and kissed my cheek, much to my surprise. "Minerva is with you" she said. "I told your man the same this morning" she smiled. At her kiss, my mind ran back to my dead wife, her soft lips and hot breath reminding me of my own loss and I felt a sadness fall over me as my horse was brought forwards. So, the bastard Scavolo had been to the house to check the slate. I wondered if he'd accepted the story. I'm not sure what Fucilla thought of my silence as I left the house, but as I considered what I had heard I realised I'd missed something and had further questions I needed to ask, If Aspius had lied about being with Lucilla then those that thought Brocchus was with her may also be wrong, or were there two separate meetings? I climbed aboard my horse and set off with even more questions circling in my mind.

XIII

Brocchus looked like he'd been through three rounds with Apollo in the bare knuckle boxing matches at the festival. I turned a shocked face to Scavolo, but then on closer inspection I saw that the bruising was a few days old and not inflicted in the time I'd been away. I could see the resemblance to the family name as his teeth protruded from a face wide at the jaw and narrow at the forehead. His dark hair was long and matted, as if he'd slept in a barn. Despite this he was wiry and whilst I could tell he was of average height for a grown man he was also tall for his age, which I guessed was sixteen. My father had not waited for me to start the questioning despite the protestations from Graccus to await my return and the lad was looking both frightened and resigned as I entered the large room. Light flooded in from my right and the boy had been placed to face the window so that he had to squint at the brightness of the rising sun.

I nodded to my father, who had stopped his questions as I entered, Scavolo standing by the window with his hands clasped across his groin looking bored. I'd obviously not missed much as I was greeted with "his mouth's closed tighter than an oyster fresh from the sea." Scavolo shifted, the denial of his interrogation skills clearly putting him out of sorts.

Graccus stood and wiped his nose on his sleeve. "He's refused to answer anything" he added as if I hadn't understood the metaphor my father had used.

I looked at the boy, who dropped his chin to his chest and something about the deadness in his eyes gripped me. I circled slowly and let out a slow breath as I looked down at him. "You loved her didn't you?" Everyone looked at me with furrowed brows, including Brocchus. Scavolo crossed his arms over his chest and his eyes widened slightly, then narrowed. "You and I both know what it's like to lose someone" I ventured, crouching on my haunches and facing him. His sad face looked to mine. "I lost my wife a few months ago. And my son" I let out a short breath before I stood and turned my back on him, circling the room. "She was the most wonderful person I've ever known" I said to the window. "When she laughed we fell around the floor together in fits of giggles that split my sides. When she cried we fell into each other's arms in sorrow and wouldn't move for hours until the smile came back to her face" I turned back to him. "Was it the same?"

He nodded. I saw my father turn to Scavolo, who didn't blink or move an inch as he feigned boredom, *he really is good at this shit*. I rubbed my chin thoughtfully. "We have information that you danced with her at the festival. Was she a good dancer?" He nodded again but didn't reply, I could sense his guard rising once more as his eyelids squeezed together tightly. I continued, moving away from the window so that he didn't have to stare into the sun. His gaze followed me. "Did my father ask you if you had met Lucilla at the shops after the wrestling?" He'd now closed his eyes and didn't respond. "I know it wasn't you" I said to which my father's stoic mask disappeared and he turned a questioning face to me. I ignored him. Brocchus looked up at this. I guessed that he felt he was being framed and couldn't get out of whatever scheme Scavolo and my father had decided to fit him into. "I know it was Aspius" I said, Graccus scribbling quickly and then staring up at us both. "Tell us what you saw on the night of the festival Marcius. We need to know."

His hands moved to his face and he started to sob, big deep breaths heaving at his chest as he cried out like a hired funeral actor.

Scavolo shook his head.

My father sighed and shook his head.

Graccus beamed at me.

I waved at them to sit back and let me lead the questions as I could see my father itching to continue with his own his questioning.

I waited till the boy sniffed, reminding me of my partner in trying to solve this crime. "When the wrestling was finished what did you do?"

His eyes remained fixed on a point on the floor but he spoke. "We left before the wrestling finished because Arnth was being stupid and annoying her." That was the first I'd heard that Arnth had annoyed Lucilla. "We danced, over in the olive grove. There was a big fire and music" he shrugged. Then he looked up at me and a small lift in the corner of his mouth suggested a smile. "Yes, she was a good dancer" he said, wiping the remains of a tear off his cheek. I returned a smile.

"When did you last see her?"

Something shifted in his demeanour and I sensed him closing again. I changed my question as he wasn't going to fall into my trap that quickly. "I know that she was seen with Aspius by the cloth shop, but I don't know what happened between dancing in the olive trees and that time. Help us, Marcius. Help us to understand what happened." His arms crossed over his chest and I saw his jaw tense. Something had happened, but what. I walked back across towards Scavolo, his head rising as I walked past, appraising me. My father was now back to his Roman best, sitting with a blank expression across his face.

"Why would Aspius want to talk to her?" I'd asked the question to the room rather than the boy. "Maybe it was his last chance to get her to marry him, a last plea. Was that it?" I rubbed my hands together as I walked along slowly. "No, that ship had sailed when he fathered a child with another girl. It must be something else. We'll never know" I said aloud.

"He claimed that it was a lie, the baby. Said it wasn't true. But she wouldn't listen and told him so. It was too late by then. We were in love, she didn't love him. If it wasn't for that bastard and his father..."

I waited but he didn't fill the silence he left hanging. It gave me precious seconds to think and to realise that he'd just told me he'd spoken to Lucilla, or at least knew what Aspius had said to her. Also he suggested they were in love. Was that why she wore no undergarments? I stared at his bruised face and remembered Scavolo's sneer when he thought I was shagging the Fuller's wife. I couldn't see Brocchus and Lucilla being a couple. It just didn't add up from what little I knew of them both.

"Was it the marriage? Is that why you were so angry?" I asked. He ignored me, back to his glum silence. I pulled a stool across towards him and sat close, looking intensely at his bruised face and wondering what had happened, but that was a question for later. "We know that you were near the Trigemina Gate close to dawn" I added as he flinched, glancing to me quickly at this news. "What happened between the dancing and dawn to put you there?"

"I was looking for her" he said. "I couldn't find her. She wouldn't have left without telling me."

"Did you get attacked by robbers?" I asked, raising my hand to his bruised face. His face flashed with anger but he showed no other response. "So, you have nothing you can tell me about Lucilla's whereabouts from when you last saw her dancing at the olive trees, nothing at all?" He was shaking his head and I dangled my fishing pole again. "Did you see her speaking to anyone else or find anyone who had seen her? Did you speak to anyone else about her movements?" He continued to shake his head and wipe tears from his face.

"So, how do you know what Aspius said to her?" I asked, my dice rolling again at his mixed story. Scavolo leant forwards at this, I could tell that he'd realised what was said just as well as I had done. I could see him narrow his eyes and close his arms over his chest from the corner of my eye. "Someone must have told you because they met at the shop quite some time after the dancing from what I have heard." I sat back crossing my arms over my chest and letting the silence fall between us as I studied him coldly.

"One of the girls told me."

"Which one, we'll speak to her."

"I don't remember."

"Describe her. What was she wearing? What colour was her hair, her eyes? Was she alone or with others?"

He shifted his position, looking at Scavolo as if he thought he might make a run for the door but instantly realising that he wouldn't get more than a few yards before the ex-centurion was on top of him, and probably punching him as hard as a hammer hitting a nail. He bent forward crying again, teeth grinding and mouth frothing as he rocked back and forth in the chair. I looked to Graccus, who raised his shoulders as he could offer nothing. Something was holding Brocchus back, something was stopping him from speaking. "Who hit you?" I asked the question forcefully enough for his gap-toothed wailing to stop in a noisy intake of breath. His face swivelled to look at me. "Was it Aspius? Did he do it after he found out about your relationship?" He didn't answer but continued to stare at me. "His father?" I suggested it as the only option that came to my mind. His sobs resumed as he clasped his stomach and rocked back and forth again, making me feel dizzy. I was angry now and could see why men like Scavolo just went straight to the kicking and thumping stage to get through this crap and find the answers they needed. I glanced to him, he was grinning, the bastard was enjoying this. I stood and turned to my father with a resigned look, and then back at Brocchus. "You better keep him somewhere safe, if the Arturii brothers find him they'll string him up" I said, watching for his reaction as a thought struck me. Why had he said Arnth was annoying Lucilla? Had I missed something there? The boy was certainly shifty enough when I questioned him.

Brocchus flinched and looked up, fear written in his movements. "What do you mean? Do they think I did it?" he snapped, suddenly standing, his head whirling in all directions as he realised what I had said about the Arturii brothers.

I sat, crossing my arms slowly as I looked up at him evenly.

"Answer me" he yelled, his spit landing on my face. I tried to ignore it, but one glob ran slowly onto my lips and I struggled to stop the feeling of it dripping onto my chin. Scavolo, moving like the wind, had Brocchus' arm twisted forcing him back to the chair before I could speak, giving me a chance to discretely wipe the spit away and return to my calm-faced demeanour. I didn't see my father but I was hoping he could see I was improving at this game.

"Why was Arnth annoying Lucilla?" I asked, leaning forwards. "This could be critical Marcius. Tell us, man. If you want to find her killer, tell us now." He stared at me, eyes full of hatred and fear, like a slave beaten for stealing food. I looked down at him as I stood.

His hand went to his mouth and wiped away a long wet line of spit. "He wanted her. The Northern bastard" he let out a long, guttural, cry which surprised us all. "He wanted to marry her, keep the business in the family, all the slaves know it and they told me."

"What?" said my father, Graccus and I in unison. Scavolo stood in silence like a statue, as usual.

He looked at all three of us as if we were idiots. "He's not his real son, he's adopted from his second marriage to that bitch. It was her idea, his mother." He wiped his face again, smearing tears, snot and froth across his already disgusting face. I waved at a cloth and Graccus threw it to him to clean himself. "He argued with her all night, kept asking her to make a union now that Aspius was discredited, pushing her to make a decision. She ran away to hide from him. He did this" at which his hand rose towards his face. We instantly understood who had given him the beating. "I told him I loved her, but he laughed and then the bastard lashed out." He buried his face in his hands again and sobbed bitterly for his lost love.

****

"How the fuck you did that I'll never know." Scavolo sipped at the wine in his cup, neat and un-watered. My father sipped at his watered wine and I stood with no drink. Scavolo's office was as clean as it always was, not a scroll or tablet in sight. Graccus appeared with two chairs and we sat.

"Impressive" said my father, his eyes alight before he turned a look of distain to Graccus. "Now tell us how you know Aspius Hastius was arguing with her in the shadows. The man will be here soon, as well as Porcius senior" he added with a glance at my partner, who grimaced under his withering look.

I explained what I'd found from my meeting at the fullers, and we also discussed the fact that Arnth had clearly lied to me in his suggestion that it was Brocchus he had seen with Lucilla and that at no time had any of them suggested that Arnth and Lucilla might be a union that was being considered. "I'll get the lads to bring the lad Arnth in for questions" said Scavolo.

"No" came the squeak of a voice that Graccus was suddenly using. He coughed quickly. "I think we should go to the Fullers and question some of the slaves and staff to see what we can find out before we confront Arnth. If Brocchus said anything he said that the slaves all knew about this. We should interrogate them as well, see what we can learn."

"What use is that?" scoffed the head man, taking another drink.

My mouth was parched as I watched his throat bob up and down with the cool liquid. My father took a long sip too and I licked my dry lips. "Graccus has reminded me that when we scribed the case there was a question about a family feud." I ignored the part in which it was Milo the street vendor that had raised this point as it had suddenly struck me like a bolt from the heavens. "Did your men find any evidence Scavolo?" He shrugged a no, which I knew as it would have been in the reports. "Then I think Graccus is right, if we ask some general questions about the night of the festival, who saw her when and what she was doing, we could add in some questions on this family feud about the business and then see where it leads."

My father looked into his cup for a long moment before speaking slowly, "we have three" he glanced up "no, four suspects." His lips pursed as he took a moment before continuing. "Aspius. Last seen pleading for her hand, which she rejected. He has motive. He then didn't return home so he has the opportunity. His father is the second suspect. They lied about returning home early and cannot account for their actions. Maybe they killed her together after the festival in anger at the slight to their family." He placed his cup on the table and I was racing ahead trying to work out what was coming next. "Brocchus" he said, which surprised me as I'd now discounted the lad. "I don't believe a word he has said." My creased brows indicated I needed more information on this deduction so he added, "he *looks* guilty and we don't know if she returned this love that he is claiming. How many times did he ignore our questions Secundus? He was playing for time, working out how he could implicate someone else. At no point did he account for any of his own actions. I don't trust him or anything he says. Look at him, clearly the gods have marked him. The lads got more tricks than a three-coin whore." I scratched my crotch at that painful memory. "Every time you questioned him he changed his story. All that weeping and crying like a fucking actor at a funeral, I don't know how you didn't just thrash his hide" he directed that last comment to Scavolo who was grinning again. "And now this northern lad, Arnth? Thunder cloud" he shook his head. It was a very literal translation but we all got the picture. "They're all quick to anger and quick to respond with a fist. What's not to say the bastard just took a club to her head if she turned him down. And why hasn't any of this Arturii family told you that there was a possibility of a union between the lad and the murdered girl? Someone had a reason to keep that from us." It was a point well-made and I bit my lip in anger at the statement. Was it Janus twisting the situation to confuse me again? Had I missed a libation?

Scavolo then added, "there's a fifth" at which we looked to him. "Larce Arturius. Known dickhead, speaks with this fists before his mouth and can't control his temper. He's hot-headed enough to be in with his lad on this or to have done it himself. What's to say that he didn't try to get the girl to agree to this proposal from his son and it all turned sour."

"But if they did it they'd lose the chance of a wedding and lose the prize." Graccus said what was working in my mind as he was clearly quicker than me.

Scavolo leant forward and tapped his forehead, which made us all frown. "Baby number two" he raised his hands at the simplicity of it. "I bet that fucker has already raised the suggestion that he marries that new-born. Get in early, take the prize as they say. Keep it in the family."

My mouth gaped at the simplicity of it, my father stared at me and I snapped it shut.

"You lot are new to this. I see angles you lot wouldn't have started to consider" Scavolo said, slurping his drink. My father clapped loudly, clearly enjoying the sport and lauding his man for his ingenuity.

We fell to silence at the complexity of the situation before my father spoke once more, his heavy eyes fixed on Graccus. "Well that was fun. Well done Secundus." I felt a sudden warmth so nodded at his words of praise. "So what do we do with you

Graccus Porcius" he said in a tone which concerned me. I looked to him, then to Scavolo, whose jaw was now tense and his face hardening. Something was wrong and the pit of my stomach started to ache with the familiarity that I'd be played and was about to hear the punchline to a bad joke in which the funny part involved me being pushed off a cliff.

Graccus' eyes shifted to me momentarily, then to Scavolo, then my father. He was about to speak when the head man produced an official slate displaying the temple seal and waved it at us, his teeth now shining like the stars in the heavens.

My arse clenched.

Graccus whimpered and squirmed in his seat.

My father looked serene, his face a picture of contentment.

****

Scavolo stood and circled the pair of us like Hector eyeing up Ajax outside the walls of Troy. "Nice try" he said as the tablet was held aloft before returning to his window and leaning against the wall.

"It's not his fault." I turned to my father, his face fixed in disappointment. "I made him change it" I said as Scavolo moved slightly and caught my glance. I ignored him, this was between me and my father. I stood. "I have the right to choose my own future and I do not want to spend my life in a temple pulling guts from sheep and pretending to read the will of the gods from a sliced liver." I started to circle, Scavolo all but forgotten. "This means nothing. It is one murder, one case to solve and then this stupid dream will be forgotten and we can all get back to our normal lives." I'd gone for the only thing that came to my mind, which was Graccus' pathetic defence he'd tried to push on me the previous day. "We can't even trust the priestess, who's to say she didn't make up this dream just to get someone from the temple to search for her daughter's killer. You know what they're like father, desperate for some sort of justice and desperate to get someone in authority to help them. She probably made the bloody thing up." I waved my arms in exasperation and turned to Scavolo who was grinning like the Greek mask of some god from a play that hung on the wall in my father's study. I was about to tell him what I thought of his stupid grin when my father spoke.

"Well" his voice was very calm, unlike my own. "That's changed our plans a bit" he added with a glance to Scavolo, who was beaming with excitement and joy.

Shit. I heard my own thoughts banging like an alarm bell. I'd well and truly put my foot in the piss pot.

My father smiled broadly.

Scavolo's grin was so wide it almost fell off the edge of his face.

I shook my head, Graccus groaned and put his face in his hands.

"I've given him my patronage" I blurted, pointing at the man I'd just condemned. My father glanced to him and then to Scavolo.

Standing, my father tightened his face into a half-scowl. "You are not the only one who can play games Secundus" at which he nodded to Scavolo, who opened the slate to show two empty sides. My mouth dropped, Graccus cursed and the fucking ex-centurion tilted his head and bowed.

"Fuck" I said, looking at Graccus. If only I'd started with his first defence and kept my stupid mouth shut.

"Fuck, indeed" replied my father, although his step was now light as he rubbed his hands in evident glee. "A good ruse Gaius and very well played." It was all a fucking game to him.

"Father..." He waved me to silence.

"Graccus Porcius, your father will be here soon. Please leave and prepare for his arrival, the grown-ups have some thinking to do before we greet him. Do not despair, your role at the temple remains."

Graccus was gone before I had time to think and Scavolo

sat in the chair I'd been in, another power play. I was being outmanoeuvred like Tarquinius Superbus at Lake Regillus just as I thought I had the victory.

I sank into Graccus' chair, defeated, my chin in my sweating palms.

My father looked down on me.

Scavolo looked down on me.

Then, in a moment of utter silence, my father gripped my shoulders and pulled me up to my feet. He hugged me, kissing my cheek softly and staring into my wide eyes with a faraway look.

Then, to my shock, Scavolo hugged me, kissing my cheek and nodding to me as if I had won a crown of honour for scaling the walls of an enemy city and beating twenty men to death with bare fists.

I nearly fell on the floor.

XIV

Porcius senior was the image of Graccus junior without the dripping nose. Yes he was older, but only just turning to grey, his jowls were flabbier and his waist-line larger from all the pork he no doubt ate, but undoubtedly they were two peas from the same pod. He'd been delighted to meet my father in person, to shake hands with the magnificent hero Scavolo, whom he'd cheered in the triumphs and seen at public ceremonies, he was delighted to be called to the temple.

 And then he'd shaken my hand without remark.

He'd brought two piglets as a gift to the temple, male and female. It was an extremely generous offering and one which Scavolo licked his lips at because it offered the option of breeding and eating, something akin to his own heart I was sure. Graccus had sat in the corner fidgeting, trying to catch my eye for any sign or indication of what had been spoken about since he'd been asked to leave the grown-ups to discuss the future, which meant my father and his head man telling me what they would do. I ignored him, I couldn't look him in the face.

Porcius had spent some time telling us how his family had grown their own crops and held large tracts of oak forests to feed the pigs which created the best flavoured pork in the region, my mouth watering as he spoke. I realised I'd not eaten for what seemed like an age and my belly started to growl slowly, which I stifled with a cough. When the strips of cooked chicken and liver, fruit, nuts and eggs arrived I struggled to wait while Porcius filled a small bowl before I dived in like Salacia diving into the spring fountains. I wasn't listening to the pig farmer conversing happily with Scavolo, who seemed to know a lot about farming techniques and livestock management as my head was filled with the words my father had used once they had stopped kissing me.

This could get you a tribuneship and put the family in the running for Consul.

Scavolo had said, *this is your moment; don't cock it up.*

It was exactly what I didn't want. Scavolo had listed the military tribunes across the city and the dates for elections coming at the close of the year. That was their plan, to push me up the Cursus Honorum on the back of this pathetic dream. I didn't want it. It appalled me that they'd already discussed my future, chosen a path for me and started to plan my every step to achieving the greatest role that a Roman Political career could give me. My father had counted the cost to buy support, which factions and individuals were rising and which falling. They'd both stated that they should look to those who supported Minerva or her temples to find funds to support my *new life*. Scavolo had made a list, the bastard. They reviewed my brothers role, where he could initially advance to let me fall into the space he left behind, filling his shoes and buying favours from those who rose with him. They'd confirmed their plan with eager eyes and quick strokes of their styli and had slapped their wax tablets shut like a chapter on my life being sealed. I hadn't been asked for a view or to add any input to my future, it was done, I would fit in or fuck off.

"So" my father had raised his voice, waking me from my glum memories but also to try and stop Porcius chattering away like a washer-woman at the river. I could see where Graccus got his ability to bore me to tears with inane noise and I glanced to the boy, who was sitting in the corner with the exact look on his face that I guessed I'd used when my father and Scavolo were deciding my future before his father had arrived. I decided that I could not let my friend, *fuck me I was calling him my friend now,* go to the dogs. I bit my lip as anger started to bubble inside. I realised in an instant what a total fool I was. Realisation of my position in the world was starting to dawn on me like an ice cold day in winter. None of my drinking buddies had appeared at my door since I stopped buying them drinks. None of the girls who'd whispered sweet nothings in my ear as they took hold of my penis in one hand and my purse in the other had come to find me and check how I was doing since my wife had died. I'd not been invited to a single party or event since my father locked me in that cupboard with Graccus. *He was my only friend* and whatever level of friendship we had had been dictated by my pretentious attitude to him and his status. He was as much a victim in this as was I. As I looked to him I realised that he had accepted everything I had asked of him with the willingness of a family dog and despite the shitty situation we now found ourselves in he still wished to follow me. He'd climbed into a house to steal the slate that could incriminate both of us and done it willingly. He'd stood by me like one of Scavolo's soldiers, spear in hand and shield raised. I looked again at his forlorn features and realised that neither my father nor Scavolo had mentioned him once in their discussion. I bit my lip and started to consider *our part* in this future that was being planned for me by the *grown-ups*.

"On to why I asked you to come today" my father started to say, Porcius' ingratiating smile broadening in the hope of some small measure of quaestorial support as he waved to Graccus to rise and come stand beside him. Scavolo grinned. Something was coming and I had a feeling that I wouldn't like it.

"Yes" I rushed in, stepping in front of my father to cut him off and getting a scowl from Scavolo who physically flinched as I did so. I was thinking on my feet and hoping not to step in the piss pot as I did so. "Graccus and I are working on a murder case" I said, placing a hand on his shoulder, a level of familiarity that widened his father's eyes and made my parent scowl. "He has done exceptional work and I commend you and your family for raising such a well-educated and intelligent young man." Whilst

I could bluster all day Porcius' eyes kept glancing to my father as clearly he hadn't understood who I was or what part I played in this meeting and he was awaiting an official sanction, not small talk from a boy. To his credit he nodded and turned a smile to Graccus, who looked about as happy as a young female slave sold to the brothel house. I placed my hands behind my back, looking for a way to grab hold of this conversation and making a mental note to offer a goose to Mercury if he could get me through this negotiation. Gods, this business was going to cost me an arm and leg. I could sense that my father was itching to bring the conversation back to his own course so I rushed in like Patroclus against Euphorbos, hoping that Apollo would not remove my wits as a thought had struck me. "You clearly have an excellent knowledge of local business" he was nodding but with a confused frown. "Tell us, how is the cattle business growing? Will it have a good future?" I stopped in front of him, hiding my father from his view and staring directly at Porcius.

"Cattle will always be good business" he shrugged. "But I have few so I know little in reality." He answered with a confused frown.

"But has it grown? Is it on the decline?" I asked with a glance to Graccus, whose narrowed eyes showed he was trying to get up to speed with what I was thinking.

"A year ago one cow was worth three pigs, a bull four. Now" his head moved slowly from side to side. "I would say it is one cow to four. For a bull it is more like five, but only where the bull has proven breeding capability" he looked confused.

"And duck farming. Is it a growing industry or failing? Are there any concerns regarding this business that you would consider would be of interest if, say I had a wish to invest heavily in it today?"

Suddenly my father and Graccus were alive with movement, both turning to Porcius with interest as they realised what I was doing and why I was asking these strange questions. Scavolo looked non-plussed and sipped his drink with a calculating gaze.

"I wouldn't waste your silver" he replied instantly. "There was a recent sickness in the flocks and they have decreased by a half at least. From what I heard the sickness has killed several slaves too. Bad business right now if you ask me and any money invested won't come back for four or five years at least, if not longer. The gods have clearly shown their disinterest in them. Have you been offered options?" He was interested now. "Eggs is the only constant money-earner" he added, his eyes glancing up as his ringed finger tapped his lips. "But you have the transportation problems of getting them fresh to the market" he was starting to warm to his task and I could see another long diatribe coming so stepped in to cut him off before he explained all the mechanics of carting and distribution, which I have absolutely no interest in.

"So a declining business" I nodded, seeing my father dip his head too.

Graccus jumped in, his face alight with some revelation. "Father, you mentioned to me recently that there had been some trouble with contracts between some of the farmers. Was there a dispute related to the Hastii family?" It was a gambit to mention the name, but one that I hoped would pay off.

His face fell for a moment at the mention of the name. He looked to my father and spoke directly to him. "Sir, I cannot be named in any gossip against my fellow farmers" he said in a serious tone.

My father answered. "This is more of an information gathering discussion" he smiled. "Anything spoken of today will not be used in any proceedings but we may investigate it should it lead us to consider doing so. Your name will not be mentioned, I can assure you of that."

It was the assurance he needed. "You won't have seen the disputes as we have a committee that deal with our own problems first." Scavolo grunted acknowledgement. We all knew that the plebeians had small assemblies where they worked together to confirm their local judicial arrangements before bringing them to the formal justice system for scribing or judgement if needed. It worked, so the Senate never bothered to change it. "Hastius has raised complaints against two of his neighbours, claiming damages to land and that the sickness came from a flock of chickens which border his own." He shrugged. "There was no proof so it was dismissed. He is an angry man" he added this with a look to Scavolo.

"And the problem with the river?" Graccus added.

"Oh, of course, the river" he said jovially. "There is a small water course which crosses his land and from which he draws water. It has all but dried up because Ristarius Appianus has taken a channel to feed his cattle. He has claimed compensation as his lake has declined to half of its former size as a consequence." He raised his hands before his shoulders rose and fell again.

"The counter argument is that he has lost half his flock to the sickness so there is no loss?" said Graccus. "But he has raised a further complaint against Appianus."

"Yes, but that cannot go forward as Appianus is now sick and his advocate is also sick. They are counter claiming that the sickness from Hastius' birds has been passed to them."

"Difficult" said my father, rubbing his chin.

"So the man has his back to the river and cannot swim" said Scavolo to the room at large, but mostly to his boss. They exchanged a look, which I understood. Another cut to the sword arm for Hastius' defence when we get to speak to him. Sickness, failing businesses, problems with water supply. It was all adding up.

"What of his family?" I asked. "He has one son?"

"He has a son and a daughter, she is only a baby. His son is a dimwit" he shrugged and shook his head. "He works on the farm. They don't even have a tutor for him" which he addressed to my father as one parent to another in an exasperated tone. It caused a curl of the lip but no other response. I felt the weight of disappointment in that flicker of his mouth.

"He was betrothed to the Fuller's daughter?" I asked. Graccus sniffed and wiped his nose on his sleeve. Even Scavolo grimaced as he did it.

"Yes, poor girl" his head dipped. "It was a bad match and one that the Arturii rued as soon as they found out about the sickness and reduction of the flock. It was clear that Hastius was trying to get a good dowry and a claim to their business. The contract was written with the Etruscan clause that the girl could decline if she wished to do so, but Hastius never read it. He argued, of course, but he had no legal claim so it was cancelled by the Arturii." He looked to Scavolo who nodded because that had been confirmed through the proper processes.

"He must have been angry" I said quietly.

"By the gods he was" replied Porcius with eyes widening. "At the festival he was like a boar protecting his herd."

"You were at the festival?" I said with such surprise in my voice that everyone turned to me, then to Graccus, who looked as shocked as I was, and then back to Porcius.

"Of course" he said raising both of his shoulders, evidently as surprised as we were that this hadn't been considered. I stared pointedly at Graccus who raised his hands as if he hadn't known this fact.

"What happened?" I asked, scowling at Graccus as I did so.

"I was standing talking to Lucius and his head man about some options for wood, I have several forests in which the pigs roam and am increasing my stocks to sell firewood" he added to confirm his meaning, with another shrug to accompany his words. "And Hastius came rushing over with his son and two of his clan, shouting that the contract should not be closed as the lies about his son fathering a child were unfounded and the Arturii had broken their oath. He accused Lucilla of spreading the lies herself to get out of the contract, saying that a woman had been spreading gossip at the shrine. That oaf Larce and his wife started shouting back at Hastius and his men and then Lucius and one of the other men started pushing each other. The Etruscan women are as hot-headed as the men and started shoving as well, you know what they're like. Larce squared up to one of the Hastii men and then…" he shrugged, it was a habit that was starting to piss me off. Graccus sniffed again too, that was pissing me off as well. I let the silence stretch so Graccus' father filled it once more, the man could talk for sure. "Well, Fucilla Arturius sent him packing soon after that with a few choice words about the gods pissing on his flocks. They can swear those foreign women" he added with a shake of the head as he shrugged again. I grimaced then tried to set my face back to its stoic best.

"What did she say?" I asked.

"That the girl had no confidence in the boy and had changed her mind because he couldn't keep his cock in his tunic, it was in the contract and if he didn't have the wits to read it then that's his problem as he was clearly as stupid as his son."

My mind flashed back to my own comments to all the idiots across the city about their lack of understanding of the twelve tables when I'd helped Fastus; she was right. I shook my head and looked to my father, wondering if I had missed anything. He was smiling back at me, which was unnerving to say the least.

"Why didn't you tell us of this before?" The question from Scavolo was directly to Graccus. I could feel the tension now between my father, his head man and the boy, my friend.

"He was away buying new thatch. Idiot nearly burnt the house down" replied his father with a glare and a shake of his head. I remembered Graccus showing me his patchwork of bruises, amongst other things. "We didn't discuss it after that" he shrugged again and I felt like placing two large stones on his shoulders to keep them still. I was shaking my head at the words, which Graccus saw and his face fell, misunderstanding my thoughts.

My father looked to me to see if I had any further questions, I didn't and quickly shook my head. Then he looked to Scavolo, the man nodding purposefully in a manner which suggested they had agreed something before the meeting. I felt that sudden dread that Porcius' son was about to learn his fate. I felt powerless, which of course I was and had just decided that any devotion I was going to give to Mercury could fuck right off when the ex-centurion began to make the speech he'd arranged with my father.

"Thank you Porcius" he said, moving seamlessly from his position at the side of the room out of view and taking full command. My father stepped back to allow Scavolo the opportunity to lead the conversation. "It has been an honour to meet you." He glanced to me before continuing. "Despite evidence to the contrary, Marcus Sulpicius didn't ask you to come today to question you regarding the festival or the local farming situation" at which I received a glare from Porcius as if I'd somehow tricked him into declaring information which he shouldn't have given to us. "We asked you to come to discuss your son and his position in the Temple." Graccus' head dropped at the words and I turned a protective glower on Scavolo. "As we have mentioned, the boy has done decent work for us and has supported our investigations." We all waited for the 'but' to come next "and is a credit to you." This got a nod of recognition and a wary movement of the mouth. "But..." there it was, the bastard. "Things have changed recently and" his eyes connected to mine "Secundus Sulpicius Merenda has offered your son patronage" at which my head shot up, Graccus' head shot up and Porcius' face fixed like a fucking statue. Even he was better at this shit that I was, bastard. "Which of course the Quaestores must sanction." He'd moved swiftly from family names to status, another lesson in diplomacy and the art of conversation from Scavolo. I bit my lip, then, realising I had failed my tutor again, quickly fixed my face into my best bored expression as my lesser, Scavolo, dealt with the contract of patronage. I still had so much to learn.

Porcius' lips twitched, I was pleased he wasn't as good as I had given him credit. Graccus was almost hopping from foot to foot, quickly wiping his nose on his sleeve once more, causing my father to peer at him with distaste.

"Secundus" I noted we were back to first names again "has suggested" which I hadn't "that three carts of firewood and one piglet per year to support the family of his father, would suffice for protection and guidance for your family in supporting your sons career. Of course the salutatio for Graccus Porcius" back to formal names to show his status as below my own "will be in the form of working here at the temple supporting the valuable work that he does to help his patron. In this respect we would expect such work to be paid in the form of fifteen Ases per Kalends to your son plus any bonus by agreement as and when that should that occur and to be written at the time." It was a good opening offer and Graccus was trying his best not to shout in glee. Porcius senior, on the other hand was a thinker and had nodded slowly, considering the offer, although his eyes were bursting with pride and his chest rose and fell like a man weeping with joy at the birth of a healthy son. Scavolo, though, continued before the pig farmer could answer, which surprised us all. "The Quaestores would extend personal support for the Porcius clan in any requests to the Senate or law courts and give protection and guidance." At this Porcius' mouth dropped. Ha, he was as shit as I was. I was grinning inside but held my fixed face, I was better than him. "The offer for salutatio is that the Quaestores will purchase one Jugera of land for development of the swine herd that is given to Secundus as salutatio, which you will manage on his behalf. This herd will earn commission for Secundus such that he can fund his place in society." My face slackened, my mouth opened wide and I turned abruptly to my father, his eyes warning me to get my stupid expression back to where it had been. I stiffened and did so. Scavolo scowled at my failings in the stoic Roman way before he continued. "You will bear all costs of management of the land and slaves, the feeding and rearing of the animals. You may claim any additional costs from profits by agreement. For this you will account for forty percent of all profits to Secundus, paid each three Kalends and you will retain the rest for yourself. I will personally set up the contract with your head man.

"You must know something first before you consider our offer" Scavolo then said with a flourish as he turned quickly to face my father, who grinned and placed a hand on my left shoulder, before the head man faced Graccus and said, "tell your father about the Priestess of Minerva's dream and the goddesses words with regard to Secundus Sulpicius Merenda."

****

I was in a state of shock. Porcius had kissed me on the cheek, water dripping from his eyes.

My father had kissed me on the cheek. It was becoming a habit.

Scavolo had given me his fiercest scowl and then kissed me on the cheek.

Graccus had kissed me on the cheek and left a cold wet patch where his nose had touched me. I fought the urge to wipe my face.

Then they had all left the room. Was it the kiss of death? I didn't know. I felt numb. It was not what I had expected, although to be honest I don't know what I expected. I'd gone from a drunken waste of time to a landowner with two clients in the space of a few moments. I needed a drink.

My thoughts were broken by Scavolo, who marched back into the room noisily. "Didn't expect that did you?" he stated it rather than asked. "Timing lad" he said, tapping his nose again like he had done when revealing his cheap trick with the slate. "It's all in the timing. You said it yourself." My incredulity clearly showing in my dumbstruck features as he continued to give me the benefit of his wisdom. "When you said that it could just be a lie, or it was just one dream about one death and would soon be forgotten." It wasn't exactly what I'd said but I understood what he meant. Spreading the message would give it a life of its own and now that it had wings, just like those on the feet of Mercury, it would spread quickly. Porcius would twist it to fit his own family and no doubt gain his own clients from the lower orders in doing so. My father would milk it like a herd of goats and no doubt Scavolo had already worked out how he could profit from my *luck*. I groaned and shook my head at what had they done.

"Right, I've got a lot to do to get your farm and lands sorted. My fee is here" at which he handed me a tablet that he had already prepared. I was shocked at the speed at which he'd moved to outflank me, the bastard. "Your father's signed it, so just scribble next to his seal" he said dismissively to make it clear that it didn't matter what I said or did, this was my father's plan. "That move with the management of the lands was a good one I must say" he added with a smile at his own words. My vacant look made him continue, explaining in slow sentences so that my thick brain would understand. "Your father has been considering it for years but never had a decent farm manager, they're sewn up tighter than a sack full of unwanted dogs" he said, alluding to the practice of dropping unwanted puppies in the Tiber in a sack to drown. "We've checked out Porcius and the guy has an excellent reputation and everything he touches seems to turn to gold, just like Midas in those old Greek stories. He has contracts out to Veii and all the way to Herculaneum." He looked at me and shook his head. "Maybe this story of the goddesses patronage *is true*" he scratched his crotch absentmindedly, reminding me of Graccus. "But I doubt it. That bitch will be using her position to get what she wants just like you said" he added with a look of disgust "as well as using your fathers position to get to you because you found her daughter and have a position which can support her." It was exactly what everyone else was doing, I thought. Using the story to get what they wanted. What do I want? I was about to speak when the head man turned on his heel and, reminding me to sign the tablet with a stabbing finger, was gone.

****

The wine was sour and after a few cups I'd fallen asleep at the desk, waking with a stiff neck and a bitter taste filling my mouth. Someone had been in, refilled the wine and added a small bowl of nuts and fruit alongside a fresh bowl of water and a cloth. It was half-way through day two and we didn't really have much certainty as to what had happened to the girl, with too many people still in the running as the killer. I rubbed my face and decided to take a piss, lifting the lid of the pot in the corner and releasing my flow with a sigh.

"About time you woke up." Scavolo made me jump with his sudden arrival and his overly loud words. "And you can get that wiped up as well" he added with a flick of his chin as I'd missed the pot and splashed the floor because he'd made me jump mid-stream. I grimaced. He took my seat and a handful of nuts. "Hastius is here, you're needed." His words were spoken as Graccus appeared and stood at the doorway to keep out of Scavolo's vision. Scavolo helped himself to another handful of nuts before he departed, ordering me to clean up the piss from the floor lest it start to stink and to be in my father's room within the next five minutes.

"Hastius is pissed off and looks like he's here for a fight."

I could sense the tension radiating from Graccus' voice but we had to stick to our plan. My partner was going to the bird sales to try and prise some information from the younger Hastius. I splashed some water on my face and ran wet fingers through my hair. "Go quickly and see if you can get anything out of Aspius.

Take Philus" I said suddenly. "He can take notes, we need two people to hear what he says or it won't stand as evidence. Keep it light-hearted and tell him we have Brocchus here" he was nodding at my words "and suggest that we think he has a lot to answer for. Let him think you're his friend but find out why he didn't go home that night and if he saw anything. Let him know you know he didn't go home if he doesn't open up." It was a gamble as I was reminded of Scavolo's words and I was giving the sparrow an important task. I held back the feeling I had that Graccus would cock it up and slapped him on the shoulder. That's what new friends do.

"I understand" he nodded and left swiftly, eager to press on with his duties. I followed him out into the cool corridor and turned towards my father's office, thinking through what might happen when Hastius was backed into a corner. Scavolo was leaning against the wall when I arrived, the room, to my surprise, empty.

"They're doing a tour of the temple to soften the bastard up a bit." He sounded bored. "He'll be telling your father about his friends in high places" he added. I nodded, knowing what he meant, it's all about who you know and who your patron is. "We've checked him out, don't worry" he said this as if I was. I hadn't even thought about it and realised I still had so much to learn. Scavolo moved to the doorway and peered out before turning back to me. "Let your father do all the talking. Don't be as eager to step across him as you did earlier." Obviously they'd spoken about it. I was angry and it must have shown in my face as his lip curled. "You don't know how these bastards work, lad. Keep your mouth shut and ask permission to speak. If you cut your father off with Hastius he will see it as an affront. This time we need to be more formal and choose our words wisely. You know enough about the laws to know that we cannot accuse him directly." It was a good point. I was playing in a game where I didn't really understand the rules. I let my head dip in understanding. "Good. You're there" his face pointed me to a seat to the left of my father's chair. "Oh, we're not mentioning the priestess and her dream to him." My brows raised at this. "There's too much between them. It'll be a distraction we don't need at this time and if he gets wind of it he'll close up like a phalanx against a cavalry charge."

My place was set and my role understood. I sat silently and waited.

Hastius' false smile greeted my introduction when he entered the room. Scavolo stepped forward as we all sat. He nodded to his betters and then to Hastius and the two men he'd brought to be his advocates should they be needed. "Thank you for coming Spurius Hastius" started the temple head man. "I am sorry that we have interrupted your day. We find ourselves in the position that we need to recheck some of your previous statements relating to the night of the festival of Minerva." Hastius' frown and slight inflection of the head suggested he could continue, the bored expression hardly changing at the words. Scavolo opened a tablet and looked at it for a moment. "You left early on the night of the festival, with your family as you wished to return home due to the long trip to your farm." This got a cursory nod. Scavolo rubbed a finger on his lower lip as he narrowed his eyes before picking up a second tablet. "This report says that you didn't return home with your family" he was now looking directly into the face of Spurius Hastius "and that you returned a while later."

Hastius' face remained calm and he didn't answer, just shrugged.

Frustration evident in his response to this, Scavolo asked "why was that when you told us you left early to return to your home?"

Hastius sat straighter and looked to me and then my father before he replied. "Am I being accused of something?" He was now looking to his advocates, both of whom glared at Scavolo and crossed their arms across their chests to show their defiance.

"I am checking all aspects of the case and no accusations have been made, Spurius. You know I must follow all aspects that do not match." First name terms and a half-smile.

The duck farmer seemed angered as he realised someone had informed on him before he let out a sigh and spoke slowly, as if explaining to a child. "I told you the family left early to return home. I didn't say that I had returned home with them." He seemed happy with this response.

Scavolo placed the tablet on the desk, his face stern. "We can play games all day Spurius, but you were asked to account for your time so that we could use any information to find the killer of the Fullers daughter. Why didn't you tell us the truth?"

"Should I tell you all my business dealings?" he challenged, turning his face to my father. "I have nothing to hide and told no lie as I answered your questions accurately" he added. "And I saw nothing more than I have already explained to you."

"And what business is conducted in the dead of night?" asked Scavolo.

"I do not need to answer that question as it is irrelevant to this investigation. I saw nothing as I have said."

"You must see that if you cannot account for your time it raises questions. Bring me a written statement from whoever you met. If you and he were in the city then maybe he saw something if you did not." It was a logical argument.

Hastius remained relaxed under the scrutiny of Scavolo. "I will consider your request but the person I met did not leave their house. I will, of course, confirm with them if they wish to make a statement and bring this to you."

I wondered if he was meeting a woman and as Scavolo lifted his chin and half-closed his eyes I could see he was thinking the same. I waited for the head-man to ask the question that was now burning in my thoughts but he didn't, turning a glance to my father who simply interlocked his fingers and continued to smile back at Hastius. A moment of silence was followed by the head-man who seemed resigned to having nothing else to ask as he shuffled the tablets and said "well, thank you for coming to speak to us. I look forward to your friends confirmation…"

I coughed lightly. Heads turned to me, Hastius with evident frustration.

"Please" said my father with a dip towards Hastius. "My son is leading the investigation, as you know. Please indulge me if he has some more questions."

This brought a begrudging acceptance. "Might I ask in which part of the city you attended your meeting" I started with a simple gambit, hoping to lull him into my trap.

He shrugged as if this was not important. "On the slopes of the Caelian" he replied, meaning he would have travelled along the Via Latina from the Forum Boarium and no doubt passed the stables where Marcus Opsius had kept his horse. If I needed to, I might be able to find one of the stable hands to confirm if he saw Hastius pass by. It was better than nothing.

"Thank you." I nodded in appreciation. "And might I ask if your advocates were with you?" I turned to the men behind him. "They might have seem something which you did not?" I added to their hard-faced stares.

"No" came the quick response. "Only my head slave, Justinus was with me."

I had what I wanted. Now I had my fish on a hook I needed to know how to get him in my net. I thanked him again and turned to Scavolo, whose face suggested that he was trying to understand what I was getting at. I raised my hands to show that I had no more questions. He turned to my father, who had sat silently throughout the whole encounter.

"Thank you" said the Quaestores. "I'm sorry to have called you here for such a short discussion. You know how it is Spurius" first name terms again and a smile "we have to turn over every stone."

Hastius stood once my father had done so, as was befitting the situation, and said that he was glad to help with anything as he and his family had nothing to hide. I smiled at that. As the men turned to make their way out of the room I said "gentlemen, I'm so sorry. I have one more small question?" Hastius turned an angry face to me.

"Yes." He'd almost snapped the word at me.

"Did your family make it home safely? They saw nobody on the roads? We had reports of a boy hiding in the shadows at about the time they would have left?"

"No, they didn't remark that they had seen anything." He was turning to leave again.

"And Aspius, did he see anything on the trip home?"

He turned back to face me, his brow creased in confusion. "As I said, nobody saw anything on the trip back to the farm." It was a curt answer, his exasperation at my repetition clear in the tone of his voice.

"But he didn't return home with the family" I replied softly. His jaw tightened and his left eye closed slightly at the words, the lid trembling faintly.

"You are mistaken" he said sharply.

"Ah, then I apologise" I replied. "Yet, our report says that Aspius returned home in the early hours of the following morning and was covered in dirt and mud. Maybe I can visit your farm and speak to him." I wasn't going to say that Graccus was already chasing the boy down on the Field of Mars.

"Who made this report?" he was snappy again but I wasn't letting my catch go.

"You know that we cannot answer that unless it is used in court as evidence. Much the same as you have no need to give us the name of the business partner with whom you met."

Scavolo was grinning. My father was grinning. Hastius was grimacing.

"Whoever it was is a liar" he was turning puce at the neck as his anger was building. "Aspius is away for weeks, he has business to deal with and won't be returning. He left at dawn." A clear lie, but not one I was going to argue against as I knew better but didn't want to let him know. The boy would certainly disappear as soon as Hastius could get to him. "We had nothing to do with this" he added loudly staring at Scavolo and then turning his cold stare to me. "Those fucking Arturii are lying bastards. If they've fed you pig swill about my family then you'd better be prepared to back it up with solid evidence."

"No accusations are being made Spurius." My father was back to his calm and respectful self, his hand placed on Hastius' arm. "We just need to check all the reports with everyone. The truth will come out and I am certain that your family will be blameless as you say, but we must check, it is our role to do so for the good of the Republic."

Hastius let out a huff but nodded sharply. "You are a trusted man Merenda" he said to my father before turning to Scavolo. "As are you. Don't let those bastard Estruscans trick you with their words. They'll turn us all against each other in the end."

I was about to speak when my father laughed jovially and stepped across the room to lead the duck farmer out at a leisurely pace, discussing the merits of a multi-cultural society in which every man could grow his place in society under the patronage of the gods.

I noted that I had not been included in the list of *trusted men* and Hastius had not even said goodbye to me personally, clearly seeing me as an underling and a nobody. I hoped Graccus would return with enough evidence to have the boy sewn in a sack with a monkey and a dog and I ground my teeth at the thought that I could throw in the snake that would sink its teeth into his soft flesh.

XV

Kicking my heels used to be the easiest thing to do. I'd spent years lounging around and doing nothing and felt that I had become quite adept at it. But since that damned goddess had named me in her dream I couldn't sit still and had the itch to keep moving like a dog with fleas. Having written up my notes I dressed in a dark blue tunic, short-sleeved and knee length as it was a hot day and headed out to pour more libations that I owed to the gods for their support. I then continued to walk to the Fuller's yard where I had several questions that still needed answers. With Graccus out on his mission I'd decided that rather than sit around and wait for him I would speak to the slaves myself and try to get a handle on the issue of the family feud, time was running out on our second day and I felt the pressure pushing me towards an inevitable cliff like a traitor to the Tarpeian Rock. I knew that any evidence given to me by a slave couldn't be used, well not without whipping his back raw, but I hoped it would give me enough of a clue to at least create a hypothesis, as the Greeks called it, and to guide my actions. We still had at least three good leads to follow up; where did Aspius go, why did Arnth lie and what about Brocchus, I still wasn't sure whether to believe him or not despite Scavolo's accusations.

On arrival I was told that Fucilla and Lucius were out for the day, the buxom female head-slave suggesting I return at a later time. She was older, maybe in her forties with deep brown eyes, lined as if she smiled regularly, although her face was stern at my arrival. I asked for Larce but was told that he was with the master as were the majority of the family. "I would like to ask some of the people who attended the festival some questions to see if they saw anything or heard anything that may be of use to my investigations. I am happy for you to attend with me. This is crucial to the investigation and time is short" I impressed upon her. She seemed nervous. "I am sure that the goddess Minerva sent me here for a reason" I added, seeing her look up at me at the mention of the goddess' name. I'd gambled that the whole house knew of the dream. It worked, I was in and being shown around within a heartbeat. Her name was Tertia and she proudly informed me that she had bought her freedom and served as a paid member of staff, to which I complemented her. It was a big thing for a slave to buy their freedom, especially a female, although the Etruscans had some strange ideas about the roles of women in society. As she showed me into the domus she said that there were several families in the extended household and many of them lived in the yard or the rear of the house and that most had visited the festival on the night of the mistress' daughter disappearing.

"Can I start with asking some questions of yourself?" I began as we entered a courtyard which was open to the sky and had doorways ranged around the perimeter. Tracks where people walked frequently stretched across the hard-packed earth emphasising a few spots of greenery around the edges of an otherwise well-kept space. She nodded her agreement. "Were you at the festival?" She replied that she was, but also quickly added that she had seen nothing. It was a quick reply which immediately put me on my guard. "When the family realised that Lucilla was missing, what did they do?" I changed the questioning style to deflect from herself, thinking that I could come back to her own movements soon.

"The master has told you this already" she replied guardedly. It was true, he'd told me that the family had split up and started searching for the missing girl, but I didn't have anyone else's version of what happened that night so I pressed on with my questions.

"Yes but tell me from your perspective so that I get a different view. It will all help. Did you search for her?" I'd brought it back to her own movements quickly and was pleased with my quick thinking, thinking I better get another libation for Minerva for guiding my thoughts.

"Yes. I went with Fucilla and the women. And then when we met with Boronia she suggested we split into three groups."

"Boronia?"

"The wife of my masters brother." I nodded that she continue as a memory of a taller lady flashed in my mind to associate her to the name and I now realised she must be Larce's wife and Arnth's mother. "She had been to the wagons to fetch clothes as it was turning cold. We searched the Forum, asking people if they'd seen her, but nobody had so we went towards the shops." Tears were forming in her eyes as she remembered what they had done that night and realised the conclusion at which it would inevitably arrive. It made me think of the dead girl and her beautiful face as she lay in the ditch, a vision of her lifeless form returned to my mind. "We couldn't find her there, though it was very busy and so then we headed towards the Temple of Vesta. Fucilla thought she might have gone there to make a devotion."

It was a good suggestion, many of the girls who were looking for husbands prayed at the temple or dropped copper and silver into the small well, sometimes with a votive request to find the right man with the right breeding to make the right match. "That's quite a walk though, for a girl on her own" I said.

She shrugged. "We didn't know what else to do, the mistress was distraught. Fucilla said she may have met others and gone with them."

"Who had Lucilla been with, which girls?"

"There were several of them dancing and singing and then she seemed upset by something."

"Go on" I prompted as she hesitated. She seemed nervous again.

THE CASE OF MINERVA

She looked at the floor. "That boy Aspius upset her. Boronia and Fucilla argued about him, they often did. It was a bad match."

I agreed but wondered what arguments had happened and what this meant.

"Were there any others at the temple? Did you find any evidence she had been there?"

"No, we hadn't reached the spot because we stopped and asked every group if they had seen here. Then Boronia and her son found us and told us that there was news and a body had been found over by the gate to the city by the duck farmer."

I nodded at this. It must have been heart-wrenching for Fucilla to be searching for her missing daughter and be told that a body had been found. I felt my jaw clench at the memory of my wife dying and the feeling of hopelessness that had jolted through every fibre of my body like a thunderclap from Jupiter. "Did anyone hear or see anything either at the time or since the festival that you think might be useful in my search?" She paused thoughtfully, then shook her head. "Are any of the girls she danced with in the house today?" She confirmed they were and beckoned for me to follow her. We moved through the large kitchen and back towards the Fuller's yard where the smell of piss began to fill my nostrils once again. I was introduced to two young girls who were drying clothes on a wicker frame which they turned with a rope, the slow spin helping to dry the clothes more quickly in the light which streamed unimpeded into this corner of the yard as the surrounding buildings were single storey.

I nodded to them as I was introduced and then asked, "when Lucilla left the olive grove, was she with Marcius Brocchus?" They said that he was following her around like a puppy and gave each other a knowing look. My interest was piqued by their glances to one another. "What? Is there something I need to know?" I asked. They suddenly looked fearful, as if they'd said something they shouldn't. "Don't worry, I know that they were close" I said with what I felt was a pleasing smile and a friendly tone but they looked at me as if I'd spoken a different language and my words were confusing to them.

"Close?" repeated one the girls with a questioning glance to the other. "I think Brocchus would like to think so, but she didn't really like him very much." She looked to Tertia, who was nodding in agreement.

I was confused. "So Brocchus and Lucilla were not close?"

"Not really. He was always hanging around, bringing her flowers and things since her engagement to Aspius was called off. I think he felt that if Aspius was out of the picture he had a good chance with her. His father owns one of the carting and wagon businesses that deliver our pots. He drives the carts." It was news to me and in direct conflict with the story Brocchus had given us. Was my father right? Could the boy be trusted? Had he lied so convincingly that he'd taken me in with is play-acting and continual sobbing and wailing? I tightened my lips before asking another question. "When was the last time you saw Marcius Brocchus on the night of the festival?"

One of the girls looked to the other. "When Boronia sent him away from the olive grove. He was being a pest and getting in the way. I think he was very drunk" she added.

I rubbed my lips at this news. "Was that before or after Arnth upset her?" It was another roll of the dice to see if I got an answer which might fill a gap in my own interpretation of the movements on the night and the girls seemed to be happy chatting so I had rushed it into the conversation.

"Arnth didn't upset her did he?" said one girl to the head woman. She looked at me with an inquisitive frown.

"I'm sorry, we have a report that Arnth had upset Lucilla at the wrestling" I shrugged to suggest that I was simply repeating what knowledge I had been given from others but all the time now I was realising that Brocchus had fed me a line and I'd grasped it like a hungry fish.

"No, that was Brocchus being an idiot" said the other girl. "Arnth and Lucilla didn't argue that I know of." She was looking to the others again for confirmation of her words and they both appeared to agree.

So, Brocchus had played me well, the bastard. It seemed my father's gut instinct was correct after all and I was a fool to dismiss his and Scavolo's assessment so quickly. Had Arnth beaten him or was that a lie too? Things were starting to get more and more complex. They had nothing else of interest to add to their story, so I thanked them both for their time. I was then taken to a small boy who stank as if he'd been standing in the piss pot for hours, which he probably had. His name was Rupio and his front teeth were missing which led to him speaking with a slight whistling sound as he answered my questions. He told me he'd spent some of the evening playing chase with the girls, including Lucilla. They'd all splashed water from a water trough and laughed and joked, splashing about until one of the older women had shouted at them and they'd all run off to get changed into dry clothes. With all the stories of weddings, family fall-outs and the fact that she'd been murdered it was easy to forget that the girl was still a child when she was taken from them and that such activities probably happened all across the festival in pockets of close family units.

"Lucilla was fast" he laughed, whistling through his broken teeth as he did so. "She was so beautiful. I miss her."

It was a simple statement but tugged at my heart as his earnest round face looked up at mine. I felt like patting his head but the smell of piss that permeated from him put me off and instead I took a small step backwards as I realised I'd bent to listen to his words and was directly above him. "Did you see her at all after that?"

He seemed to consider this for a moment and then said, "Only after the fight."

"The fight?"

He turned bright red and then looked fearfully back at Tertia who was also showing signs of surprise.

She repeated my question to his wide eyes and then flicked her head towards me to give permission to answer. "Will I get into trouble with the master?" he asked her directly.

"No" we both replied together, glancing to one another. This was my investigation and I didn't need Tertia stepping in and taking control of the questioning, the boy needed to answer to me.

"The master's son Arnth chased that boy with the big teeth and they had a fight. Arnth smacked him around the face and he ran off crying. Arnth said he should leave Lucilla alone. She called Arnth an idiot and went off after him, the boy with the teeth."

It was clear that to the slaves that any member of the owners family was classed as the *master*. "Brocchus?" I replied to his description.

"That's it" he said. "He didn't fight back at all." At this his brows creased and his mouth turned down in disgust at the lack of fight from Brocchus.

I was excited by this news. "So Lucilla was there when the fight happened? When and where was this?"

He looked at Tertia once more and her eager face pressed him to continue. "We were playing chase over by the fire in the olive grove, to warm up after the water fight. It was when that group started to leave, the duck farmer and his people. All the carts were leaving and then I saw someone running and Arnth catching him, Lucilla came rushing over, but she was wearing a shawl so I didn't recognise her at first until she started shouting. I didn't recognise her at first. She didn't look the same because everyone had changed clothes after the water fight." I stared at Tertia, she stared back.

"Why didn't you say this before?" The question was from the woman at my side. She'd taken control once again and beaten me to the asking. I was getting irritable at her interjections but decided not to react as the answer would come from the boy whoever asked the question. It was Minerva testing my patience for sure.

"I wasn't asked" he replied genuinely with a resigned expression. "Nobody speaks to me unless they have to. I do the early morning shift so I get up before cock-crow and there's usually nobody around except a couple of us, and then I have to go to bed early so I can get up on time. I don't see anyone unless I'm working too slowly or my cloth isn't clean enough and then I get a smack for it. I keep my head down" he said this as if it was just a matter of fact; do the job well enough and be ignored, mess it up and get a smack across the head for it. I looked at him, a boy of about ten or eleven summers. His dark hair was thin, almost shoulder length and his complexion was ruddy, with a healthy sheen, although that could just be the effect of the piss on his skin. His face was clean but he had small red marks lining his neck where his tunic sat, likely fleas or fly bites, and his feet were wrapped in thick cloth to protect them between tasks as they softened when stepping up and down in urine-filled vats all day long and could lead to problems – a slave was expensive so you had to look after them. Memories of slaves in my father's household flashed across my mind, people I saw daily but even now remained nameless. It was the same in the temple, I don't know anyone other than Philus and maybe two others. Half of the priests are just ghosts who drift in and out as I go about my duties with my head down just like this boy Rupio.

"Can you describe the shawl, what colour was it? How long was it?" I was interested now, it was something new, something I could start to work with.

"Blue and brown I think. It was hard to see in the firelight. It was long though, went to her knees" he glanced up at me, "to keep her warm" he explained as if I didn't understand.

"And what happened to her wet clothes?"

He shrugged. "Someone probably brought them back later, we left them on a cart."

I looked to Tertia who responded. "Yes, there were a lot of wet clothes from the children and we always take spares to the festivals in case they get wet or cold. They were washed and dried the next morning as usual."

So, Lucilla had changed clothes during the evening. I wondered if some of the people whom I'd spoken to before might recollect seeing her if I informed them of this fact, but I realised I didn't have the time to go back over every individual to review their stories. I was subconsciously biting my fingernails as I was thinking and then having been brought back to the present by the pain of drawing blood I realised I'd been silent for a few moments and the slave boy was looking at me expectantly. I thanked him and gave him a copper coin, which brought a look of delight to his face. He shoved it hastily into a hole in his belt as he continually thanked me. Tertia patted his head and I reminded myself not to shake her hand when I left as we continued around the yard.

I had started to get a theory as to why Lucilla wore no undergarments, but I needed more proof than that of the Fullers slave boy, maybe one of the others could give me the information which would help solve this part of the mystery. I also had to consider where this shawl was as I had no memory of the garment from when I found the girl in the ditch. If she was wearing it when she ran after Brocchus, where was it now? It could be vital.

"Did anyone come and ask if a shawl had been handed in on the night?" I asked.

Tertia considered this for a moment and was slowly moving her head to suggest that nobody had before she said that if there was it would have been with the door slaves who collected all cloaks and other garments which were returned or lost. It took us a few minutes to reach the door.

"Boy" she said to the door slave somewhat curtly, there was clearly a hierarchy and he was at the bottom of the pile. The sad figure standing before us looked as if he hadn't eaten in a month, sunken eyes and rigid cheek bones on a skeletal thin neck. His shoulders were no better, stick-like collar bones pushing through a threadbare brown woollen tunic which hung loosely like a rag hanging on a washing line. I stepped back a little, it wasn't unheard of for people to keep their slaves at work even if they had marsh fever or some other dreadful plague and I certainly didn't want to catch anything from this lad as he looked as close to death as I could imagine anyone looking. "On the night of the festival were there any clothes handed in at the door" asked Tertia to his broad-nosed face.

Despite his startling appearance he answered cheerfully and pointed towards the kitchen. "Yes there were quite a few cloaks and other items, they were handed to the kitchen."

"Was there a blue and brown shawl?" I asked.

His lips pushed out as he narrowed his eyes in thought. "No, sir. I don't think there was. There was a big pile of wet clothes, hats and cloaks, heavy ones which had been taken in case of bad weather but it was a nice evening. I don't remember a shawl." His tones were of the Samnites and I considered that he must be a recent acquisition from the current war on the border lands, a captive likely sold to this household explaining his starved appearance due to brutal treatment in the slave camps or the slave-traders yards which dotted the port area at the two bridges of the Pons Cestius and Tiber Island crossing. He seemed happy enough with his lot now and is clearly trusted enough to man the doorway, although I felt that Lucius should dress him better as the first impression any visitor would get was of a scrawny, under-nourished and sickly household which to my mind wouldn't be good for business.

I was nodding, Tertia shaking her head and shrugging as if we'd come to the end of the trail. His eager eyes glanced between us and I asked "did you notice anyone wearing a blue and brown shawl? Maybe they came home later than the others?" It was a gamble, but with Minerva supporting my questions I was hopeful.

He rubbed his chin slowly with his right hand, long fingers pinching the flesh. "People were coming home at all different times, some early, some late" his shoulders rose and fell as he spoke. I understood what he was saying and tightened my lips, resigned to nothing which would help, but he continued. "Blue and brown" he spoke as if something had occurred to him and then he looked back towards the door as if some of his memories were coming back to his mind. "The mistress has a blue and brown shawl" he said.

Tertia's jaw dropped as I looked to her. "She probably does, maybe she loaned it to Lucilla on the night?"

I nodded, placing that in my 'to ask later' thoughts as I thanked the door slave from my position as far away as I could stand and far enough away that I didn't have to breath the same air as he, lest I catch anything; you can never be too careful. He seemed happy enough at my thanks and sat back on his rough wooden bench to stare at the back of the closed door once more.

After four or five more interrogations nobody else had any revelations or recollections which added to my notes for the night of the festival and so I thanked Tertia and, avoiding the hand that had ruffled Rupio's hair, I touched her on the shoulder in a friendly gesture. I was half a step through the door when Larce appeared, chatting animatedly with whom I assumed was his wife Boronia. I smiled to greet him and got a scowl in return.

"Secundus Merenda" he bowed at my greeting and gave Tertia a harsh glance which presaged a strong conversation after I'd left with regard to her allowing me in the house. His wife stared at me for a long moment, a look of distaste written in her features.

"Larce" I said cheerfully, hoping that a friendly tone would warm them to my questions. "I came to speak to yourself and

Lucius, so the goddess is smiling on me and has brought us together." I saw his eyes flick to his wife, whose expression suggested she believed that as much as I did. "Might I have a very short moment of your time?" He didn't seem happy about this but consented. "You too, please" I added to his wife as she turned to leave.

"Why do you need to speak to me?" she asked defensively.

I raised my hands, palms toward them both, "nothing specific but if you have any information which can help to find the killer it would be valuable. Boronia isn't it?" I was looking between them both now as I inclined my head towards her. She seemed genuinely shocked that I knew her name.

Larce nodded and placed a hand on her forearm. "Come" he was moving inside. "We can spare a moment, but we have returned to fetch a basket of food which was forgotten. We cannot be long."

I followed them to a small room off the kitchen and was ushered to a low bench which sat along a wall. They sat opposite. Larce leant his elbows on his knees and flicked his head for me to ask my questions. Boronia crossed her arms over her substantial chest and dropped her chin, not giving me any eye contact. "I understand that when Lucilla was found to be missing the family set off in different groups to search for her. Can you tell me who was there and where they searched?"

Larce frowned. "People went in all directions" he answered, sitting back with a turn to face his wife. "I went with Lucius. We started in the Forum and then headed along the Jugarius towards the docks at the port." He looked to his wife, who didn't move a muscle and seemed incapable of speaking. "The women went to old shops and then the temple of Vesta" he was looking to her again. She nodded. "Some stayed at the carts because we thought she might have returned there. A slave was sent home to check if she'd returned" he added. I didn't know that fact and nodded as it was a sensible suggestion.

"And where did you search, Boronia?"

She looked as if I'd slapped her across the face. I waited as she seemed to take a few moments to catch up with my question. "I'd been to the wagons to take the wet clothes" she answered. "And then I searched the forum. There were a lot of people." She finished, glancing once to me and then to her husband.

I nodded, expecting more. "Where were the wagons?" I asked out of interest.

"We had two. They were near the fish market" she answered.

I considered this. The fish market was no more than a few minutes' walk from the forum so would not have taken long. "Did you go alone? Did you see anyone running or anyone hiding in the shadows?"

She turned her face to me for a moment and I could see in her glance that she was thinking through what she'd seen. It was the first time I seemed to have gotten anything from her short answers and non-committal approach to the questions I asked. She was shaking her head. "And I understand you met with the women later in the forum?" she nodded but didn't expand. She was as closed as her son. Maybe she didn't speak Latin very well as she was clearly from the northern areas where I knew few people spoke our language. I considered that maybe I'd been too harsh on her and turned to Larce who held his gaze on his wife with a frown. "Was Arnth with you when you searched?" The question seemed to surprise him.

"No" he sat back with a perplexed look. "He was with the children" he glanced to Boronia who nodded at this.

I nodded, but that didn't add up. "Arnth was seen to have chased Marcius Brocchus and hit him." At this Boronia bristled and turned an angry face toward me. I raised my eyebrows. "It is what I have heard" I countered to her angry expression.

"He has done nothing" came the stern-faced response. "That boy Brocchus is an idiot and if he got a smack then he deserved it."

"I agree" I said, seeing that I'd touched a raw nerve. Larce watched me intently as I turned back to him. "And did Arnth search with you?" he shook his head and turned to his wife. She stared back at her husband but didn't answer. I waited in silence.

"He was with the others" shrugged Larce. "We had all split into groups and I don't know who went with who" he added in a tone which suggested he was speaking the truth.

I was nodding. "And who brought the news that a body had been found?" I knew who I'd been told it was, so sat back to await their version of events.

Larce's eyes glanced to Boronia, who seemed to struggle with the question. "People came from the Boarium to tell us that a body had been found" he was shaking his head. "It was foggy and I could not tell you who first brought the news." Boronia's head movements suggested she was agreeing with this.

"And how did you find out Boronia?"

Her lips tightened before she answered. "I heard it from a man who came running into the forum and was telling people."

I nodded slowly. "And Arnth was with you at this time?"

Her eyes flashed toward me and then to Larce. "Yes" she replied after a moment. "Were you alone, just the two of you?" Her eyes narrowed in suspicion at my words, searching me as if I were trying to trick her. She shrugged. I frowned. "Can you describe the man who brought the news?"

"He was a boy" she said. "Shorter than you but not by much." She shrugged again.

"Would you recognise him again if you saw him?"

She seemed on firmer ground now and nodded, "I think so. But it was foggy" she replied.

I nodded to this and sat for a moment trying to gather my thoughts. It was the opportunity Larce needed. "We have to get back to the others" he said, standing. I followed his lead, as did

Boronia. I thanked them both and they disappeared to leave me alone in the small room. I had some information but parts of what they told me were not adding up. I ran through what I'd heard at the house in the last hour or so and realised that several gaps needed filling. After a few moments I headed towards the door and found Tertia stood waiting for me.

"Has Larce left?" I asked. She nodded and I shook my head. I had an important question I'd forgotten to ask. I looked to Tertia. "Were you with Fucilla when Boronia and Arnth brought the news that a body had been found?"

"Yes" she replied with a furrowed brows.

"Did Boronia have the clothes she'd returned to the wagons to collect?"

She looked to me with a calculating gaze. "No, I don't think she did. But she could have given them out or left them where we had been sitting earlier."

I agreed with this. "And" I had to be careful now as I was unsure if I was treading on dangerous ground. "What exactly did she say when she announced the finding of a body?"

Tertia looked at me quizzically. "She said that a body had been found in the ditch by the Trigemina gate, that someone had shouted it out in the forum, calling for help."

It wasn't exactly what Boronia had said but it was close enough. I thanked her and headed for the door, Tertia following. I'd learned quite a lot from this visit and my mouth widened into a great smile as I left. There was more to this family than met the eye. The lack of detail from Larce worried me as did his wife's defensive stance, especially relating to her son. I decided I'd drop a copper coin into the spring of Juturna for good news on the way back to the temple. I also hoped that Graccus had positive news from his visits.

XVI

"I can't believe it. Bastard."

It was Novius who gave me the news that Brocchus had escaped from the room they'd put him in. He'd managed to pull a plank from an old doorway that led to the street at the back of the storeroom they'd placed him in and had somehow managed to squirm through the gaps that he made. Idiots. They should have placed him somewhere more secure. Scavolo and two of his men had gone out searching but I guessed they'd never find him. My wine tasted sour as I considered the fact that we might have held the killer and now he'd escaped, my father and Scavolo's confirmation that he was *the killing type* ringing in my ears. I looked at the red liquid in my cup and winced. How had it turned so quickly? Had Milo sold me some second rate vinegar? Was Minerva turning against me after all this time? Had I missed a libation?

Novius apologised again, which was odd coming from the old soldier. I grunted and then offered him some of the wine, which he accepted. "Tell me" I had just thought of something. "You saw the girl when they brought her body here didn't you?" He nodded in reply, rolling the wine around his mouth with a disappointed look on his face. "What do you think killed her?"

He puffed out his cheeks and let out a stream of air. "I've seen a lot of dead bodies Secundus" he started on first name terms, which I accepted as we were obviously working buddies now. "Hers was strange in that it was so clean and perfect almost everywhere. There was a large indent on her right temple where she'd been clobbered" he lifted a hand to his own forehead just above and behind the right eye socket. "Just here" he then looked at me and laughed mirthlessly. "You know, you saw it too."

"I did, but it was foggy and dark and to be honest" I swallowed some more of the sour wine "I didn't want to look at it."

His head moved in acknowledgement. "Yeah, awful when you first see that sort of thing. But there was very little blood, well nothing much. Whatever hit her crushed her skull without really breaking the skin. Like a club or a heavy stone" he lifted a finger to stop any further questions. "But it must have been a smooth club or stone because there were no jagged edges or other cuts beyond the place where the impact happened. I guessed it was just a single blow to the head." He leant his head to the right and then stood. "Just a minute" he said and strode from the room, returning momentarily with a handful of assorted clubs, sticks and heavy objects. "Nah, not like this" he placed a flat-headed, heavy looking, wooden club on the table, followed by another, then another as he appraised each one. He lifted a thick oak club with a heavy end set in a ball which had been smoothed out over many years. It was the length of my forearm but had enough weight to be deadly. "This sort of thing could have done it" he said. I looked at it and felt a tingle as I remembered the girls face, her eyes looking up at me and the deep red patch over the eye. I realised at that moment that the swelling had occurred and the in-dent that Novius spoke of was under that large swelling I had seen. I closed my eyes for a second.

"Stand" he said to my surprised look. "Here" he was placing me next to the window and picked up the club. "If she was hit here" he was placing the end of the implement next to my head, I flinched slightly, "then the man who hit her was left handed." He made a slow swing with the club to show what he meant, then tried with his right hand and I instantly understood what he was saying as the natural hit was to the left side of my head. His bottom lip wrapped over his top and he stepped to the side.

"Although" he rocked back and forwards and then stood behind me and made another slow swing which came over my right shoulder. "This could have been the strike" he shrugged. "I'm not sure though."

I was interested in this. All I could remember were her eyes and the patch of hair between her legs. "Did you undress her?" I asked, not sure what role he played in checking the bodies when they came in.

"Not really. Scavolo asked us to check if she'd been sexually assaulted, there's usually bruising and blood" he replied quickly. "Otherwise, we just check them over to see if there are any marks or anything which suggests how people died, you know. A dagger wound or strangled. It was clear she'd been struck to the head and she was gone, poor little thing." He was giving me a strange look as he answered. "Scavolo sometimes asks us to check anything which looks odd, like bruising or burn marks from a rope." He rubbed his cheek, the bristles rasping on his hand. "I looked at her arms and shoulders, knees" he raised his shoulders as he spoke. "There was nothing out of the ordinary that I can remember, no scrapes or cuts. It was one clean blow which bashed her brains in" he said with a slow shrug as if such a things was an everyday happening.

I picked up the club and felt it's weight. "Do you think she was hit with something like this?"

"Probably."

I remembered where I'd found her. "What if she fell into the ditch? She could have fallen onto the grass and slid down the steep slope? Was she covered in mud or dirt?" I thought about the shawl. What if she were wearing it and it had been removed? His lips protruded and his fingers rubbed over them as he grunted that it was possible. I looked at him and I searched my memory for anything I could remember from that night, the dense fog, Ducus and his dog, the goats bleating. I had a strange feeling I'd forgotten something important but I couldn't put my mind to what it was and assumed it was just my drunken thoughts of the morning playing tricks on me.

"Why wasn't she covered in mud" I said absentmindedly. "I was after I went into the ditch and she was on the other side."

"Maybe someone threw her over the ditch."

It was possible. The girl was quite slight and I considered my memory of her. I could certainly have lifted her body and thrown her to avoid stepping into the muck which ran along the bottom. It would certainly have hidden the body in the fog.

"I'm going to go and look in the ditch" I said to his raised eyebrows. "To see if I can find a club or a shawl."

****

People avoided me as I strode towards the river. Not because I was menacing, but because I stank of the filth that filled the ditch. I'd been up and down the shit-filled trench and found nothing but a few animal bones and various shards of broken pottery. No shawl, no club. A waste of time. Upon reaching my destination the water of the river welcomed me like a mother snuggling a baby to her breast and I swam fully-clothed as I tried desperately to remove the dirt and the smell. It didn't work. I might be cleaner but the smell lingered like one of Graccus' farts in our small airless room.

Now, as I strode back toward the temple, people avoided me because I stank *and* was soaking wet, leaving a dripping trail as I walked. I was making a name for myself for all the wrong reasons. At least the flies that had followed me on my trip to the water had found something else to feast on, but my arms and legs evidenced their attentions as they were dotted with nasty bites and red stings. I looked every bit like the slaves I'd interrogated earlier and I ground my teeth in anger at the time I'd wasted. Children laughed and I growled back at them as I trudged up the long slope of the Clivus Capitolinus, the road to the temple of Jupiter atop the hill. The gradient was steep enough to raise my heart rate and I panted slightly as I reached the apex of the road and turned to see Jupiter and his Quadriga on the temple looking across at me with what looked like a smirk. It wasn't as bad as the look that Scavolo gave me as I approached the steps and saw his looming figure eyeing me with disgust. He wrinkled his nose and motioned for me to go around to the back to the animal entrance with a jerk of his thumb.

"Did you find him?" I asked of Scavolo and Novius, who appeared together as the door opened.

"No. The bastard's disappeared" scowled my former boss whose anger at having lost Brocchus was clear. "But we'll find him" he spoke with an assurance which suggested he always got his man and I didn't doubt him.

I entered and was thrown a cloth to wipe myself and a clean tunic. I discarded my soaking attire as Novius lifted his chin. "Find anything?"

"Nothing" I sighed rubbing my legs vigorously. "Maybe whoever did it ran off with the club." I shook my head at the time I'd wasted and brushed at an arm full of red spots.

"Ah you're here." My father arrived like the main actor on a stage, his head high and a beaming smile until he saw the state of his prize son and his face danced with revulsion just as Scavolo had done. He shrugged away the desire to ask why I looked such a state and spoke quickly. "We've solved it then, that bastard Brocchus. I told you it was him. Have you sent the men?" he was addressing Scavolo as my jaw fell slack at his statement.

"Yes. They should be at the house by now and I've told them to strip the place if they have to. If the family get in the way we'll drag them in too, they must have known" he replied casually.

My head turned from man to man as questions formed in my mind overtaken quickly by the dawning of what their words meant. A vision of an army of Scavolo's men trampling over the Brocchus household in the name of the twelve tables ran through my mind. I was appalled at this sudden turn in events.

"Had to be him" said the head man at my incredulous look. "Why else would the prick run" he stated. "Had to be a guilty conscience."

"Seen too many like him." My father was shaking his head slowly, both Novius and Scavolo mimicking his movements and agreeing that Brocchus was the killer and they'd found their man.

"What?"

"You saw him. Had to be guilty. They're all the same, looked like a criminal from the moment I saw him. Never trusted a word he said." My disapproving parent's bottom lip protruded from his beard as he patted my former boss on the shoulder to suggest that Scavolo had solved the case quickly and the job was well done. "Got any of that good wine?" he asked. Novius picked up his ears at this.

Scavolo grinned. "Lots" he replied with a grin.

I followed like a sheep tracing the tracks of the flock as my father extolled the reasons why the ugly and poor were forced by the gods to be criminals. He quickly switched to explaining to me as if I was a child, I suppose I am in his eyes, how in his experience the guilty always give themselves away with their actions. People can lie, he said, but when the pressure builds on them and the weight of evidence is closing in on them they will always run like a coward on a battlefield. Scavolo agreed, turning a sneer towards me. I stood taller at his jibe, facing him with what I thought was a formidable glare and strong stance.

Scavolo had a large silver jug on the table in his room, an image of a water carrier pressed into the side, and poured the wine into terracotta cups, mine adorned with full bunches of grapes. It tasted suspiciously like the wine I used to have in my office and

I swirled it around my mouth bitterly as the full-bodied taste slipped down my throat to remove the acid vinegar of that I had left behind in my own room. Novius gave me a sideways look as he slurped at his cup, clearly noting that the temple head man had better tastes than me. Bastard.

"So" it was my austere father's look toward me first and then to his employees that caught my attention as much as the pitch and tone of his word. "What to do next" he said as if this whole episode was now finished with. "Have you sent for the priestess?" Scavolo nodded, his dark eyes glancing to me with a curl of his lip. "Good, good. Then we need to consider the punishment and how we can work this to an advantage for the boy." He was talking as if I wasn't stood next to him. "At what point do we let out the story about the dream to affirm that which we told Porcius? He must be spreading the tale as much as he's spreading the muck his pigs make." He laughed at his own jest, Scavolo and Novius following suit as I stared at them all like a dimwit, mouth agape and all pretence at ever having been schooled in stoic behaviour gone forever.

"The priestess must tell the tale" said Novius, turning into a conspirator and slackening my jaw even more at how quickly my new-found friend had joined in with the others in deciding my future and agreeing a plan which I would have to accept or be damned.

"Yes" appraised my parent pursing his lips in a gesture of agreement.

"Secundus, you must speak to her." It was an order. "Get her to agree to come to a party at the house. She'll be here tomorrow?" It was a question to Scavolo, who inclined his head at the words to show that he had sent a message to bring them to the temple as noted just seconds before. My father then turned to Scavolo and raised his cup as he added "get a few amphora of this, it's rather good" to which he upended the cup and saluted the vintage before nodding to me with finality and turning towards the door. "Four days" he instructed to the men at his heel. "That should give the story enough legs to bring a few senators and even a consul to the door." At his words he seemed to stop and consider something before nodding to Scavolo. "Do you still drink with that old rogue Callus?"

"I've not seen him for a while, but yes I am sure I can do." Scavolo was grinning, clearly something in both their minds linking up whatever plan my father had just thought about.

"Then let's discuss it later" he was motioning to leave.

He had it all planned. I stood for a moment and watched the three of them leaving but then I called out. "Wait." They turned with curious looks on their faces. "We have no proof it was him, Brocchus. How can you condemn him so quickly?" It was a fragile argument but I felt compelled to make it.

"He did it" said Scavolo assuredly. "His flight proves it" he shrugged. "If he wasn't guilty he'd have stayed and argued his case" he added to Novius and my father's bobbing heads.

"What about Hastius?" I said. "And the Etruscan boy Arnth; he clearly lied too." Six eyes looked at me as if I had lost my mind. "I don't think he did it." I crossed my arms like the petulant child my father knew I was before feeling suddenly very self-conscious under their gazes and uncrossing them, placing them on my hips and then dangling them uselessly at my side. Whilst I did this dance of stupidity my father was shaking his head, Scavolo tightened his lips and then bared his teeth as his head dropped and shook slowly and Novius sighed. I felt like I was back at home undergoing another bout of family torture. I was about to launch into a long argument about dispensing justice according to the law of the twelve tables when Graccus appeared, his eye bruised to a brilliant red and a swelling on the side of his face that looked like he'd been hit with a hammer.

****

I climbed into the bath that Betula had spent the last half an hour since our small group had returned to my parents' home preparing for me. I had listened to my father telling the whole household that I, and by extension he, had been granted the favour of the gods. The story had sounded magnificent through his voice, my mother had sipped wine and cried tears of joy, my brother glared at me from behind his fixed visage (the money spent on his training had clearly been worth it) and the slaves clapped with joy at the news that the gods were favouring their masters household. After some time of questions and answers my father had gone to his study to prepare the party, due in four days, and write to the list of important guests he had lined up to invite. Scavolo had left for his own home and my mother had filled another glass of wine and kissed me on both cheeks with brim-filled tears in her eyes before she flounced off with her chamber slaves to drink some more wine in her own rooms.

The weight of the day's events pressed on me like the darkness outside as I considered all that had happened in what had been a very long day. I recounted what Graccus told us in order to try and add it to my memories and find some links which might disprove Scavolo's assurance of Brocchus' guilt. Graccus and Philus had caught up with Aspius Hastius in the Forum and confronted him as soon as they could get him alone, which had taken some time. Initially the boy had been angry and dismissive, but they pressed and pressed until he'd told them that he had been with his father at a business meeting with a client and that if they wished to know any more they should speak to his father. The boy had denied everything else they asked and shut up tighter than the treasury in the temple of Jupiter Optimus Maximus. When confronted with his lies about his movements on the night, his answer was that we had heard his words incorrectly. They'd followed him asking more and more questions until a horse had lashed out as they came too close to its rear-end and my friend had taken a kick to the head which had laid him flat for over an hour. Philus had thought him dead and after drenching him in water and slapping his face several times tried to drag his limp corpse through the Forum before the boy awoke with a headache from the gods and bruising to match.

Scavolo and Novius, soldiers to the core, had burst into laughter at the fate of my friend, saying that they wished they'd been there to see Graccus kicked by a donkey and being dragged from the Forum half-dead, my father soon followed their merriment as Graccus groaned and had to lay down, drooling from the corner of his mouth. Eventually Philus left the scene after an order to bring us food and Graccus was sent home to sleep off his pains, one of the temple slaves sent with him to ensure his safe arrival. We'd returned home in the fading light with a retinue of temple slaves and staff as my father busied himself giving orders to one of his scribes who wrote them diligently as we strode downhill. Scavolo walked at my heel and hummed a marching tune, which really grated my nerves all the way to the door. Bastard.

The Lavatrina was steamy, just as I liked it. My mind continued to run over the events of the day as I slumped in the hot waters. I was getting morose by the time I'd reflected on all the twisting and turning events that had happened and my brain hurt from thinking. Had the god and goddess given up on me? If I was the chosen one, the person to solve this case, why was it all still a mystery to me. I couldn't see how Brocchus was so clearly guilty, as everyone else was so convinced he was, just because he'd run. I put my head in my hands as I slipped under the hot water. The day had started well. I'd gained a lot of insight into what had occurred on the night of the festival and the last movements of the girl Lucilla. The more I thought about it the more I was convinced it was not Brocchus who had been her murderer, but I had no clue why I thought this and if he wasn't the killer I didn't know who it was. I needed to speak to the other two boys involved and I also needed sleep. I rubbed my face in the hot water and used a wet towel to wipe my body as I stood half in and half out of the bath. The door opened and I expected to see my father as I turned toward the doorway, but instead my older brother stood there, his frame blocking the entrance and an oil lamp in his hand. I turned a friendly smile and was greeted with a glare of anger.

"Hello brother" I ventured warily as I sat back in the heat of the bath, a cold draught rushing into the room and prickling at my warm skin.

He entered, closing the door slowly and deliberately behind him before sitting on a stool by the shuttered window to my right. His dark eyes reminded me of my father's as did the shape of his brows and forehead. Placing the lamp on a ledge he crossed his arms and tilted his head to look down his nose at me from his elevated position. I could feel the tension in the small room start to rise and I grew more concerned as he took an age to speak. "What's the deal then little brother?" He couldn't sound angrier if he tried. "You get land, clients and free meat just because some pissed-up pleb makes up some cock-and-bull story about a dream and I've worked my hands to the bone for the family and get fuck all. What scheme have you got going?"

I snapped my mouth shut. I had no response.

"Yeah, that's right. Nothing to say as usual."

He stood, his arms now crossed so tightly the veins in his forearms and hands showed, pulsing slightly. His breath sounded harsh as he breathed heavily through his nostrils, which flared like the horses he rode. He leant down toward me and the white glint of his teeth flashed in the light of his oil lamp. "I don't like it Secundus, and I know you better than anyone. If you've somehow planned this with your drinking mates to find a way to get yourself out of the shit hole you're in I'll fucking kill you myself."

"What?" I splashed around as I tried to get out of the water but was pushed back by my brother from his position of height. "You think I've planned this shit?" His glaring eyes suggested he did.

"Fuck me, give me some credit." I was exasperated enough that my words narrowed his eyes. "I didn't ask for this crap, Sul." It was what we called him at home. "If I had I'd have chosen something different. I've been up since cock-crow for two days now and hardly slept. Do think I'd do this to myself?"

He continued to scowl but replied. "You better not be lying to me little brother." He was jutting his chin out as his words bounced around the small room.

"Why would I lie? Look at me" I raised my arms and shook my head. "I have nothing to gain from this. Lands?" I was shaking my head. "Father has them all tied up, I'm just a name on a document, nothing else. You know what he's like, look how he got Scavolo to get you into your role in Siculus' office" I said. Siculus was a Senator who had a string of people working for him during his year of office. It had been a good role for my brother on his first step of the Cursus Honorum.

This seemed to soften his mood momentarily but he still scowled. "So what is really happening?" he asked. "What's all this bollocks about a dream and a goddess. I don't get it" he said, sitting again and crossing his arms.

I explained again, cutting out the glibness of my father's long discourse to the family and explaining that I still thought the priestess was making up the story to get someone important to investigate the murder. He sat silently as I spoke.

"So it could be true" he stated as I finished my tale, a sudden dawning appearing like a glint of sunlight in his eyes. He clasped his hands together and leant forward to rest his elbows on his knees, brows wrinkled. "Father seems set on this plan, and it's important Secundus. If he's got wheels in motion then you can bet the carts will be loaded and rolling before dawn. You better sit still and enjoy the ride little brother as this surely has profit in it as Father says. He's rarely wrong." He grinned now, his own words starting to make his mind up about the future as he continued to stare at me with a begrudging frown on his face.

"You better not cock this up" he said sharply. "And remember" he jabbed a finger in my direction. "I'm still the eldest and I won't be dragged down with you when it all turns to shit." At that he stood and was gone before I could reply.

It took me a long moment to turn my head away from the closed door. I couldn't believe what he'd said, the anger he'd shown and the lack of trust in me. I stood, water dripping from my body and then sat again, shaking my head. My father had been happier than I had ever remembered him. My mother had started on the best wine in the house and Scavolo was almost being friendly as he'd placed a hand on my shoulder at my father's words to the assembled household, basking in my glory. And now to complete the picture my brother felt as if I'd usurped his place as heir to the family seat and had told me I'd better not cock it up as he clearly felt I would do so as I am incapable of anything worthy of praise. I sighed, thinking I needed a drink and then remembering the acid crap I had in the office and cursing that bastard Scavolo as he'd clearly switched my good wine with some rubbish he'd bought for the kitchens. I sank under the water and rubbed at my hair to remove the muck of the ditch and river. As my lungs started to burn for air I considered staying under and just letting one of Fontes' water nymphs carry me away. I spluttered at the thought and rushed up to gasp air before deciding I'd better make a libation to the god just in case he was listening to my thoughts and drowned me in a well the next time I needed a drink. You can never be too careful.

XVII

Dawn rose with a heavy blanket of grey broiling clouds which presaged rain for the day. It wasn't a good start. I remembered I owed a libation to Fontes as I looked up at the sky outside the house, hearing far away rumblings of thunder. My father had been up before me and pressed us into an early start. I followed him and his men to the temple, keeping my head down and hood up. A slave carried my spare clothes and shoes for when we arrived, the poor child shivering in a woollen cloak and bare feet. He reminded me of the boy at the Fullers' although I'd forgotten his name already. I didn't recall seeing this slave boy before as he trudged along with his heavy bundle and didn't know his name either. Brocchus was on my mind as we gained sight of the temple ahead of us, the sheets of rain now starting to fall horizontally and bouncing off the smoother flagstones once we met the better quality road. Small rivers of water ran along the gutters that sloped down the hill towards the forum and the marvel that was the Cloaca Maximus. The building of the Cloaca had started under the kings and had received public funds for several years to improve the flow of detritus out of the streets.

Houses to my left were shuttered tight to the rain and those to the right, which were sheltered from the wind were starting to open for the day's trade. I spotted Milo berating one of his slaves as the fire in his oven looked like it had gone out, a disaster for him as the morning rush to the temple would pass by without his hot bread being available for the early starters. My father had several clients who would make their journey to pay tribute, some bringing daily gifts of olives, grains, milk and so on as was their duty to him as patron. I wondered if Graccus' father would have to come along every day and pay homage to me. It brought a smile to my face but then I saw my brother in my mind's eye sharpening his blade as he glared at me and jabbed his finger at my face to tell me I was a useless turd just like the one I saw floating past on its journey downhill to the Cloaca.

And then something hit my thoughts.

I hadn't dreamt about the girl.

It was such a shock that I stopped for a second, the slave boy walking behind me tripping on my heel as he had his head down against the rain. I'd thought about her every night, seeing her beseeching eyes admonishing me, but last night I had slept like a babe. The boy cried as one of the older slaves smacked him across the head, apologising to me loudly as he went to strike him again. I cut him off with a scowl and a wave of my hand, turning to the boy and seeing the fear in his eyes along with his shaking, freezing, limbs. "No" I said. "It was my fault for stopping so abruptly." I started walking again, waving to the child to follow me and resolving to behave better towards the slaves when I had time.

Had Somnus finally released me from my nightly terrors? Did it mean that we had actually solved the case and Brocchus was the killer? My mind swam with thoughts as water dripped from my hood onto my nose and ran small rivers ran down my cloak and onto my legs. I splashed through puddles without thinking, men to my left and right glancing angrily at me for my mindless actions in soaking them but unable to rebuke me as I was the master's son. Within a few strides I found I was walking alone, men having stepped backwards or forwards to avoid me. I was so wrapped up in my own thoughts that I didn't realise we'd entered the temple until Philus called me back to the door and I saw I'd walked several dripping steps into the temple leaving a trail of water in my wake. I relieved the boy of my spare clothes and changed quickly, giving him my soaking attire to carry back down the hill and home. It reminded me of the wet clothes at the festival. The slave boy kept his head low and his arms shook under the weight of the soaked garments. I noticed the other men had similar baggage and all had that look that I'd seen at the fullers. "Bring me a fresh cloak for the return journey home later and some dry shoes as well, I think this rain is here for the day" I said to the slave boy, turning away but then remembering my resolution earlier.

"Philus" I said, suddenly. "Give the slaves some warm milk and a bite to eat, they deserve it. Thank you" I said turning to the young boy and the man who had struck him, who both opened their jaws and stared at me as if I'd been hit by a thunderbolt and lost my mind. I was going to pat the boy on the head, but then saw how thoroughly soaked he was and my soft, dry, hand turned quickly into a gentle wave as I spoke. The slaves all thanked me loudly, their faces eager for hot drinks and food. Philus glared at me as four of the slaves rounded on him expectantly.

"Yes master" he said through clenched teeth.

"Boy, what's your name?" I asked before they could move off.

"Micus, master."

"Get some sandals on the way home Micus" I said. You can't go walking about in bare feet in this weather, you'll catch something nasty. Are you his parent?" The man who'd struck him shook his head quickly and mumbled that the boy was a recent acquisition and had no parents. I stared at them both for a moment. "Tell the vendor that I'll settle with him later, get a token." He understood my words and grinned broadly.

I left them to it and headed to my room searching for the amphora and seeing that it was marked with something akin to a number from one of the cheaper houses. As I had expected it had been switched. I cursed Scavolo again under my breath.

"Drinking that shit early aren't you?"

I jumped at the voice from behind me. The bastard had a habit of turning up just at the wrong time. I was going to ask him about the wine but his sneer caught me off guard. "What can I do for you Scavolo?" I asked.

"Spending your fathers money on sandals for the slaves and feeding them at his expense won't get you far in his eyes" he said sharply. That bastard Philus must have run straight to his boss with the news.

"I'll settle the bill, as I said I would" I responded, putting down the wine and narrowing my eyes as I turned back to the ex-centurion. "And looking after your property is a good thing. Can't have the boy crippled by slipping in the mud and breaking a leg."

His lip curled at my response. "We've got Brocchus."

He'd turned and left before I gathered my wits and raced after him, my head spinning again as if I'd downed the whole amphora of cheap vinegar. I followed him like a fawn following its mother as he strode into the back of the building and down a set of dark stairs with the only light available to us coming through a series of high window-like slits above us on my right which led to the open square outside and through which spots of rain splashed. It was barely enough to see the steps and I clung to the wall like a limpet as I followed Scavolo's steps into the darkness. The corridor at the bottom of the steep steps was lit by a series of these narrow slits high to our right, and we slapped along a stone floor wet from the rain outside which came through the openings. The cold of this dark cavern-like passage bit at my arms and cheeks as we reached the end of the passageway. A door stood open and three men turned to us as we entered, Novius one of them. He greeted me with a nod, which I returned. The room was ten or twelve strides across and square, darkness permeated every corner but a number of oil lamps and candles gave enough light in the central space to see the captive.

Brocchus was chained to a wooden post in the centre of the

room, manacles at his feet and hands. He looked worse than Graccus, his face bruised to a dark shade of purple and clothes torn to shreds. His blackened and half-closed swollen eyes caught mine and he licked at his thick lips, hatred written across his face in every shade of bruising imaginable.

"He put up a fight" said Novius at my expression.

"Has he confessed?" I asked to the room at large.

"No, he's stubborn" came the reply. "But he will." Scavolo grinned as he spoke. "Won't you lad" he leant forward as the boy scurried as far away as he could from the looming assailant.

"Why did you run?" I'd asked the question before Scavolo or his men could take the questioning away from me. I crouched to be level with his head height. "Tell me."

His eyes flicked to mine and then to the men in the room but he didn't answer.

"Answer your betters" snapped Scavolo with a kick from the sole of his boot landing squarely on Brocchus' shoulder. A moment later another kick from one of the men on his other side brought a cry of pain.

I swallowed, knowing that I had to endure this treatment as much as he did, although I didn't feel the pain it was alien to me, having lived through a few beatings of slaves but having never seen anyone chained or beaten like this or to this extent, especially a citizen, in my presence before. Why didn't he answer, what did he have to hide? "Marcius" I was using his given name to get him to look at me. "Tell me why you ran? It makes you look guilty, do you understand that?" His eyes caught mine for a fleeting second before he flinched at another blow. "Give me a reason to stop them and I will." It was the only thing I could think of saying and still he ignored me. I could feel the frustration of the whole room and stepped back, shaking my head at his inability to respond.

"Brand him. That'll make the bastard speak." It was Scavolo who broke the silence with the statement of intent.

"No" shouted the captive, his chains screeching as he tried to move. I noticed that he was chained so tightly that he couldn't straighten his arms or legs, the iron manacles holding him in a type of perpetual crouch.

"Then tell us" snarled Novius, taking over and putting his face up to that of Brocchus.

The boy wept and moaned, rocking on his heels in wracking sobs which sent globs of snot from his nose down onto his lips.

"Guilty as fuck. Just won't admit it, not even to himself" said Scavolo. All the men mumbled agreement. "Branding?"

I realised after a few seconds that every eye was now turned to me. He was actually asking me to sanction that the boy was branded with hot irons. The fear in my face must have shown as Scavolo tightened his lips and shook his head slowly at my indecision.

"This is your last chance Marcius" I said sharply. "I have no other choice if you don't tell us what happened and why you ran."

He continued to sob and screech like an animal caught in a trap, which he was. I shook my head at his silence and then nodded grimly to Scavolo, whose teeth showed through his grinning mouth at my acceptance of the interrogation by hot iron.

****

"Well done." It was my father's voice that shook me from my cold thoughts. "I knew it was him, little bastard." Scavolo appeared with my amphora and filled three cups. I took one with a grimace which he ignored, bastard. "And the girl's parents will be here soon so you can tell them the good news." It was another order.

I remembered the boy screaming in pain and eventually

succumbing to the torturous methods, shrieking that he had killed the girl after the heated iron had been pressed to his chest for the third time. Bubbles of spit had come from his lips, his eyes had closed and body twisted in agony. He continued to cry and scream as Scavolo waved the hot iron in front of his face and shouted that he had wasted our time for so long and deserved more. It was a dreadful scene. I'd shouted at him, asking why he had murdered Lucilla but he had simply curled into a ball and cried, shaking with pain and mumbling as more bubbles of spit burst at his nose and mouth. I shook my head as Scavolo asked if he wanted me to press the iron again to get an answer but I said we had a confession, it was enough. He seemed disappointed, as did Novius, who had stayed with us in the cold room to heat the irons and had warmed to the task as quickly as the heat had grown in the grate.

"His case will be called just after Meridiem, but I doubt we'll have many come today" my father waved towards the sound of lashing rain outside to suggest that the downpour would keep many away from the open forum court proceedings which were due later. The sound of dripping water reminded me that I'd not yet made my libation to the god of wells, springs and running water and feared that this lack of submission was leading to the deluge outside. I shook away the notion as my father continued, standing to give emphasis to the words. "Secundus." His use of my name turned my head from my thoughts as much as a shock of lightning would have done. "Tonight we have a visitor to the house." At this he started to walk slowly around the room. Looking into his wine cup as he did so. He then turned toward the wall as he circled before nodding to Scavolo and his alter-ego stepped forwards to continue to explain to me whatever it was that they had agreed would happen next. I sighed slowly as I realised instantly something was coming and that I probably wouldn't like it so I sat straighter and sipped my wine, bitterness coming to my throat despite the excellence of the taste of the grape.

Scavolo took up the discussion, the former centurion standing straight-backed as if he was giving a military report at a war council. My belly started to churn, what had they plotted now? Who was coming to the house?

"Now that you have reached the status of Asidui" by which he meant a landowner "and are at the age for service you will be called for military duties at the next meeting of the Senate, as you are aware." I was aware of this but had tried to avoid thinking about it as my time was filled with finding the girl's killer. I nodded as I sipped my wine. "Your father has considered the matter and believes that your brother and yourself require a mentor, someone with the status that your new god-given support requires and someone with the right level of position in Rome that will guide you through the Cursus Honorum."

I glanced to my father, seeing that he was back to the fixed-faced stoic he was. I was about to shake my head but refrained quickly as he turned his face to mine.

"Your father has invited Lucius Quinctus Cincinnatus and his sons to a gathering this evening which you will attend." My jaw fell, I snapped it shut quickly at Scavolo's change of expression. "You will be given mentoring by Cincinnatus and you will train with his sons, though they are older and they may give the duty to their sons or freedmen" which was common practice. "You will honour your father and family by attending and you will remain sober and judicious in your behaviour." I glanced up at that, clearly they still thought me a drunken wastrel. "It will be your role to explain this prophecy and your part in it for all attendees at the gathering tonight, although your father has prepared a statement that you will learn and recite this evening when asked." He handed me a scroll, duly written with the words I was to learn. I took it slowly, not quite getting past the fact that one of Rome's greatest living heroes was coming to my home and would be mentoring me in the ways of war. My father must be paying for this service in some way, it would cost a fortune to be aligned to such a great man, a former dictator.

This must have something to do with the man they named Callus earlier. It was an enormous social step forward for all of our clan that the man had actually accepted this invitation and the enormity of it was not lost on me. I gaped, before seeing Scavolo's scowl at my expression. Cincinnatus was already close to seventy summers if not more and very rarely stepped from his famous farm. Scavolo stared at me, I shut my mouth and he narrowed his eyes with an almost imperceptible shake of his head at my uselessness.

There was more.

"Your brother Lucius Sulpicius Merenda will act as your guardian in all matters of military training as he has three successful campaigns under his belt. He will guide you so that you learn quickly and you will do his bidding. Do you understand?" I did, it meant that he could kick my arse as hard as he liked and I had to accept it, just like I had to accept being told what to do by Scavolo and every other member of my household despite my newfound status. With his behaviour toward me yesterday I wasn't looking forward to this in the least. It also made it clear that Sul was still the first born and had superiority over me. My father had stopped pacing and turned to me with a frown at this question.

"I do" I responded with more strength in my voice than I felt. "I will be happy to follow his instruction."

Scavolo smiled at that before continuing with a sneer. "Your brother has appointed Gaius Scavolo as your trainer in all these matters and has honoured me with your daily tutelage."

Scavolo grinned, I winced, my father coughed at my lack of decorum and I snapped my expression back to that which I could manage without the anger at how I'd been played evident in my body language. I nodded stiffly, to which Scavolo nodded in reply, bastard.

"Excellent, well done everyone" said my father as if the contract was signed and sealed, lifting his cup and drinking a toast to whatever future these last few moments had created for us all.

****

Milo belly-laughed as he pointed at Graccus. "Heard you'd been kicked in the face trying to sneak up behind a donkey for a shag and now I see it's true" he laughed deeply again. Even the slave at his fire turned a grin towards us.

"Piss off" snapped Graccus, touching his closed eye tenderly.

The rain had slowed and the arrival of my friend had allowed me to slip out of my lesson with Scavolo in reading and re-reading the words I would relay to the evening guests. Graccus had been sent to work by his father despite the fact that he could hardly walk without issuing some sort of pained sigh at every step. I'd quickly brought him up to speed with the situation and Brocchus' confession as we arrived at Milo's, which not surprisingly was completely empty, as were the surrounding streets which ran with rainwater and the sound of the pattering rain landing on the flagstones.

"Anyway lads, it's good to see you, it's been busy today as you can see" he swept a hand across the scene and pointed us towards an indoor seat which was out of the cold and wet. "What do you want? I have beef stew today, good stuff" he claimed.

"Why not" I answered.

Graccus continued our conversation as Milo went off to fetch our meal. "So, the case is solved?"

"I guess so" I replied. "But something doesn't seem right. I can't get it out of my mind that there is something we haven't considered or that we've missed a vital clue" I shrugged at my own words.

"Well, we *are* new to this. Scavolo has solved a hundred cases if not more, so I guess we should just accept it and move on."

We sat quietly at this, neither of us acknowledging that we had quite enjoyed the past two or three days of fact-finding and mystery.

Then Graccus rubbed at his eye slowly before saying philosophically "If the gods haven't done with us yet I am sure they will remind us soon."

At that I jumped up. "Shit."

"What?" came his startled response.

"I need to make a libation down at the well. Shit, I'll be back in a moment." As I jumped up the heavens clashed theatrically and the rain started to pour like a lake had been tipped upside down on our heads to remind me of my failings. I raced past Milo, who was waving two bowls at me with a frown as I disappeared down the road, hands over my head and feet slipping and sliding recklessly as I shouted I would be back as quick as I could manage.

XVIII

I returned soaked to the skin but happier to see Milo and Graccus deep in conversation, three empty bowls on the table. I gave the evidence of my money being badly spent in my absence a stern glare and Milo chuckled as he stood and placed a hand on Graccus' shoulder. "I'll get you another one. You?" he was asking his new best friend, who had the good grace to decline a fourth helping with a sheepish look at the empty vessels that had sailed off with my money as Milo took them away.

"I won't ask" Graccus said as he looked me up and down. I sat dripping with water and breathing hoarsely after my run down and back up the Capitol Hill. I was tight-mouthed as I started to shiver, it wasn't particularly cold but my soaking clothes made the light wind prickle my skin. Graccus placed a hand over his mouth as he burped a beefy smell. "Milo thinks that the weather will change this afternoon" he said trying to change the conversation away from my glowering at the empty table in front of me. He looked up at the sky. "An old woman up the street has a bad toe, she said it'd stop later" he answered to my questioning frown. I nodded my understanding of the mysteries of how old folk often understood the weather through various aching limbs and how invariably they were correct; the gods really did work in strange and unknown ways. At least it brought a half smile to my miserable face.

"I've been thinking. I don't think Brocchus did it." The startled face of my friend greeted my words. "He just doesn't seem the type" I said slowly.

"Do you *know the type*" expressed my beef-stew guzzling friend.

I bit my lip. "No. But I can't see him doing it. He's a born coward. He didn't fight back against Arnth or Aspius and he ran because he was scared. He's just a stupid…" I couldn't finish my words. "It's just a feeling I have. That he's not the killer. Why did Aspius pay those girls for their silence? Where was Arnth when everyone was searching for Lucilla? There are so many parts of this mystery that still don't add up. Is there something simple we just haven't considered?" My lack of certainty and further questions was greeted by a slight head nod.

"Well we have about three hours to prove anything if it isn't Brocchus. And.." he was looking at me through slits as he half closed his eyes "the boy has confessed. It's all the proof Scavolo needs."

We sat in silence as Milo appeared with a bowl of stew. "What were you doing?" he asked with a glance at me, still dripping wet.

"I had to make a libation. I forgot until just then" I shrugged at the inevitability that if I forgot, the god was sure not to have and would remind me of this through some consequence later in the day.

His lip protruded as he grunted his understanding of my sudden disappearance. "Good, it pays to keep the gods on your side. Hey" he had half-turned before coming back to face us. "If you're seeing the Fuller's family today you better get changed quickly, look" he was pointing towards the slope of the hill where a procession of the girls family members could be seen turning through the forum down below.

"Shit" I replied, digging my spoon out of a pocket and starting on the food as quickly as I could.

Milo laughed, turning to Graccus. "You two look like a couple of slave boys beaten and drowned for stealing the family silver. I have to say, your lives have changed a lot recently." Rubbing his chin and giving us an appraising glance he turned at his jest, laughing all the way back to his oven.

His words flashed through my mind and I turned to Graccus, a seed of an idea blossoming in my mind. "I need you to do something. I have an idea that could save Brocchus."

****

Scavolo wasn't impressed at the state of my clothing upon my return to the temple. He'd said he would give up one of his own tunics and grumbled about how the delay and feeding of the group of slaves had been an error of judgement on my part as he fumbled about looking for the clothing before settling on one that was at least two sizes too big for me, providing me with an old worn leather belt to strap across my waist to hold it all together. I guessed it was his idea of a joke, to make me look ridiculous, but I was above his pettiness and would bear it and make the best of it as a good Roman patrician should. As he set to leave I mentioned I had no undergarments and he almost stopped dead as he turned to me and placed his hands on his hips with the thought that I might wear some of his own. Eventually, after I expressed that it might be bad manners to wave my genitals at the guests he rummaged about in a bag and found something that approximately fitted and we were on our way to greet the waiting Arturii. I felt as if I had gotten my own back as I scratched my crotch at his glaring scowl.

Fucilla and Lucius greeted our arrival by standing as they were the only seated couple in the room, the formal chairs for my father and I remaining empty as I had kept them waiting. I noted Larce, his wife and son and four tall men had come with them. I had passed the other members of their group standing in the temple as the room was for honoured family guests only. Presumably the new baby girl was with someone outside as it was not attached to Fucilla as it had been for most of the time I had seen her.

"I am sorry I am late" I said as I arrived. "I had an errand to run and was late back." It was a kind of truth so I said it genuinely.

"We are at your service master" said Lucius formally as we were in the temple and he knew his place, in fact he seemed quite nervous.

"The Quaestores will be here soon. Can I get you all a drink, food" asked Scavolo with a gracious smile and a bow to the assembled company. He waved to a slave in the corner without waiting for an answer, and the man inclined his head before he set off quickly to arrange the delivery. My belly felt warm and full after Milo's stew so I was in no rush.

"Do we have news?" asked Fucilla, clearly unable to hold her tongue.

I was about to reply, but Scavolo stepped in quickly. "In time, priestess" he bowed again. "Please sit. My master will be here in moments and will confirm what we have found. I will hurry him along" he added, bowing to myself with a look that suggested I say nothing of what we had found before he left the room. Clearly my father had to be present to impart the news that they had beaten a confession from the hopeless Brocchus.

Fucilla looked to me with an expression mixed with fear and hope. Her cheeks looked sunken and shadows lay on her face where previously there had been a healthy sheen. I noticed that she wore several silver and gold rings and a heavy gold necklace adorned with pinecones and heavy green gems. They must have cost a fortune. Lucius wore a thick gold band on his middle finger and two thin bands on each thumb, very Etruscan in their make with a horse and a swan etched as a designs. I wondered what they signified. These last few days had taken a heavy price, I thought. I smiled slowly and warmly at her gaze, looking to her husband once more as I did so. I saw bags under his eyes too, as if he hadn't slept for days either. His brother looked worse, his hair unruly and his face tired. Arnth, who I still wished to question, couldn't look me in the face and his dark eyes brooded as he looked around the room at the walls to avoid my own. The only other woman in the room, Larce's wife, glared at me with what I caught in her glance was hostility before she turned her eyes away quickly. Her stance was tense and her mouth taught. I wondered if she had spent every night awake with the baby in support of the mistress of the house, although none of those who faced me looked like they had had any decent amounts of sleep for days. She was a tall woman with large hands and thick forearms, certainly not someone to cross, I thought. Her dark eyes scoured the room as if she expected someone to jump out at them at any moment and I caught her glance to Larce several times but he was doing his best to avoid her eyes as much as he was avoiding mine.

An uncomfortable silence stretched until several slaves bustled in with make-shift tables and trays of food and drink. The small group slowly took morsels of food and relaxed a little, a slight hum of hushed conversation permeating the previous silence.

"How is trade?" I asked of Lucius as I looked at a small bowl of toasted nuts covered in a sweet sauce and then to him and his wife as she also turned to her husband to await his reply.

He looked at me as if I had asked him to bare his backside before understanding dawned on his face and he understood that small talk was needed until my father arrived. My father was the true ruler in this small kingdom inside the temple and we had to await his appearance before we could start any of the important discussions. I waited with a false smile and a tilted head, imitating one of Scavolo's statuesque stances; I am starting to learn some tricks I thought to myself.

"Ah, yes business is good" he shrugged. "Though this weather doesn't help as some of the pots fill with water and are no use for the cleaning process. You need good strong fluid" he said of the terracotta piss pots that dotted the streets and were collected as part of the fulling process. I lifted my chin in understanding, though I knew nothing of the processes of which he talked. "But it is generally good. My brother is looking for new premises on the southern slopes of the Caelian" he said more enthusiastically as Larce nodded solemnly, his mouth working on a braised chicken leg and fingers dripping with grease. I noted he had already wiped his hands on his hips as the glistening fat shone back at me. I was about to shake my head at his lack of manners but held firm as it was not my place to judge him.

My nods and fake smile were followed by a short silence as I struggled to get them to continue to talk. "Expanding the business?" I ventured, trying to get them to say more.

"A new business for the boy when he marries" said Larce inclining towards Arnth.

I raised my eyebrows at this and thought of Scavolo's words. "Congratulations" I said warmly. "And who is the lucky girl?" I asked the question quietly as I looked to Larce, my heart starting to beat faster as I anticipated the answer, recollecting Scavolo's suggestion that the boy would try to keep the business in the family after this tragedy.

Larce looked to his brother with a confused frown, as if the information was a secret that should not be shared but he had been asked by a patrician in the temple of Jupiter and to lie could be an offence against the gods. "It is" he stumbled the words slightly before he continued. "It is Fucilla" he said with a glance to the woman across from me. I gaped at this, questions written across my face as I clearly misunderstood what he had said and all my best patrician training went out of the window as usual.

"The baby" replied Fucilla with a knowing smile at my incredulous look. "We have decided to make a pairing early" at which she touched Boronia's hand "to avoid the sort of unpleasantness that we have been through recently." She cast her eyes down to her feet and was about to say something else when my father arrived, preceded by Scavolo and a priest. I stared at the taller woman, who glanced to me momentarily with a look of anger and hatred before she quickly turned her head to the new arrivals. My mind was whirling. Was this another option I'd overlooked or were the family just being pragmatic. Scavolo had said that the boy could have been the killer so that he gained the future of the business. But Brocchus had confessed. I bit my lip in thought as I turned to the room and thoughts ran through my head like a herd of cattle scattering from a wolf. Aspius and Arnth ranged into my mind as I tried to get some semblance of order into what I knew and what I didn't. Everything was second guesses and half-truths. I didn't really know anything. How could I convict Brocchus when I truly didn't think he was the killer. To be honest I didn't know who it was and the gods were playing with me once again.

The priest intoned a series of old Latin phrases as he paraded around the room in his blue and gold robes, followed by my father who drifted like a ghost in his brilliant white toga and ceremonial white shawl which was aged grey as it was an historic garment from the times of the Kings. He waved some strong smelling incense smoke around to cleanse our minds for a new beginning, intoning Janus and Jupiter to support our discussions and to be our guides through difficult times. It was well played and I watched in awe at the effect the priest had on the assembled group.

My father sat. We all followed his lead, Scavolo standing at his left shoulder. "The Quaestores has good news" started the head man after a moment. Lucius, Fucilla and the family members all seemed to lean forwards expectantly. I watched them intently, staring hard at Larce, then Arnth as I still had reason to watch them. "Secundus Sulpicius Merenda has apprehended a man, who has confessed to the murder of your daughter."

A wail of shocked emotion greeted the words as faces turned to me momentarily. Lucius and Fucilla stared at one another. Larce growled, his lip curling as he stared at me. Arnth dared to look at me, shock in his wide eyes and jaw and shoulders slack. His mother gripped Fucilla's shoulders until she turned and they rose to hug tightly. She glanced to her husband with some sort of relief in her expression as she did so. He avoided her look. Lucius was asking questions as I watched the group with such intensity that I didn't realise he was speaking directly to me for a few seconds.

I bowed, unsure if he had thanked me or asked who the killer was. I looked to Scavolo, who was frowning. Thinking I had given him permission to speak for me, as my father would probably have done, he spoke with such strength that I was, once again, reminded of his role as leader of men in the army and his command of them and situations such as this. "We searched several leads, but by the grace and support of Minerva and Jupiter, Secundus Sulpicius arrested and gained a confession from the boy Marcius Brocchus this very morning."

The announcement brought a gasp from the assembled group. "What?" blurted Lucius. "Brocchus?" He was looking to his wife, whose face showed the astonishment of the revelation. Voices started to rise as others began to ask questions.

Fucilla had her head in her hands as she sat and Lucius, on bended knee, was beside her. Scavolo, his voice growing louder called for calm. "The announcement will be made at the Comitium this afternoon. Details will be read out at the time and questions can be asked there, they are not allowed here as you know from the laws of the twelve tables" he said, informing the group that no further details could be shared lest they were given by mistake to those who wished to defend the boy. That was the way it had to be, those were the rules.

Lucius and Fucilla stood and turned to me. Fucilla bobbed her head and spoke through tear-filled lashes. "Thank you." She said the words quietly, yet with a force that could knock a man from his feet. "The goddess was right to choose you." I saw my father smile, Scavolo glancing to him with a grin.

Lucius stepped forward to grip my hand, his tears streaming down his face. "Justice will be done. Thank you."

"The Quaestores has confirmed that you can remain here in this room until the time of the hearing" called Scavolo. "More food and wine will be provided" he added as my father rose and received a rousing thank-you from the group, others now being ushered into the room from outside where they had waited. I had my hand shaken several times by people I didn't know, and I received a kiss from Fucilla, who gave me a strange look as I thanked her and I thought for a moment that she could sense that I was not sure of this conviction and had set matters in hand to test my theory. I turned to Larce, who gave me the limpest handshake he could muster and stepped out of my way quickly, his son nowhere to be seen.

"Well done." My father was on his way across the temple before I could get a moment to speak of my concerns as the door closed behind us, as much to keep them in the temple before the hearing at the Comitium as to get ourselves out.

Scavolo appeared at my shoulder. "Have you practised for tonight?" My tight-faced reply caused him to furrow his brows. "You better not cock it up" he said as he stomped away towards Philus, who was waving from a doorway.

****

I still had questions and so I hung around by the doorway for a moment before entering again, faces turning to me as I did so. I smiled benevolently and moved across to pick up a small piece of toasted corn.

"Lucius, Fucilla, I have a few questions to ask in private if I may" I said quietly as I approached the small family group. Arnth and his father exchanged a glance and Boronia narrowed her eyes. Despite the evident questions they had the Fuller and his wife followed my steps towards the edge of the room. I allowed a moment to pass as I turned to those closest and they moved away slightly at my silent glare.

"I'm sorry to have to ask these questions" I said quietly. "But they are necessary so that I can close off some gaps in the events of the night and ensure that the conviction is made legally, you understand?" I raised my brows to them both and they nodded expectantly. "I have information that Lucilla was seen by the butchers shop later in the evening" this brought a questioning look to Lucius' face. "She wore a brown and blue shawl" I said, watching them both closely. "Do you know where she got this from or do you remember her wearing it?"

Lucius spoke first. "We have several shawls of various colours" he was looking to his wife.

"Yes, we have a few garments like that. I think I had a brown and blue shawl that night, as did Boronia and Hurnita" she was nodding towards a group of women, one of whom must be the person she'd mentioned that I hadn't heard named before.

"Did you return with yours or did you or anyone else give their shawl to your daughter?" It was a straight question which brought a frown. I expanded. "I have found that the children splashed water and had to change their clothes. Lucilla was seen later wearing a shawl and the last person to see her states that she ran into the streets wearing it. That shawl is a vital clue. It was not on her when I found her and it has not been recovered or seen since" I explained as the significance was clearly lost on both of them if their expressions were to be believed.

Lucius understood and replied. "When we searched we didn't find any clothing, I would know. Are you sure it was not in the ditch?"

I shook my head. "I think I would have felt it or found it, they are quite large items" I added. "Did anyone else appear wearing a shawl like it on that night, do you remember seeing anyone with such an item?"

"I cannot remember who wore what." Fucilla's words were heavy with sadness. "I wish I could" she added slowly. "Shall we ask the others?" she said this to her husband. "They may have seen something." I was nodding at this and so was Lucius.

"Will you find me and send me word if anyone knows anything? Send a message with one of the temple boys" I said. "I'm not supposed to be here, so please, see if you can find anything that helps to close that last gap in information."

They agreed and I left, to disquieted looks from the family members.

XIX

I paced my room for what seemed like an age, waiting for Graccus to return. In that time the slave boy Micus had re-appeared with a fresh set of clothes and shoes. As I dressed in my own clothes I considered something that I might have forgotten. Where had she gotten that shawl, was it truly as important as I suddenly thought or was it another trick from the goddess to muddle and confuse me? Where had it gone? I considered every scrap of information we'd gathered and couldn't remember anyone saying she was wearing it. I certainly hadn't seen it when I had found her. Was it important? I wasn't sure. Micus took Scavolo's garments from me and I asked him to wash the clothes at home so they could be returned to their owner, noting that I still had another garment to add to the pile when I returned home and scratching my crotch once more as Micus hadn't brought me any new underwear. This got me working through other thoughts and I cursed as I'd not questioned Arnth properly yet. I then noted Micus' new sandals, which he wore with pride and he told me that he had never owned a pair before in his life. His happy face cheered me up as I awaited Graccus, but I sent the boy away with another request to return before dark with my cloak in case I needed it for the wet walk home as I didn't trust the old woman's toe as much as Graccus and Milo did.

Graccus came skidding into the room, breathless, about fifteen minutes after Micus' departure. His eyes were almost popping from his head. "It worked. It fucking worked" he said so loudly that a passing temple slave stopped to peer into the room. I waved him away and closed the door.

"Well?" My pained question was asked as soon as I turned, seeing my friend upending the vinegary wine that sat on the table. He winced at the taste and gave me a displeased expression, tongue out as if it had been sullied by the acidic liquid. "Scavolo took the good stuff and replaced it with that piss-water" I explained. "Come on, what did he say?"

Graccus sat heavily, pain in his face at each movement. "I did exactly as you suggested. I changed into a slave's tunic and then went to the kitchen's to get a tray of food. I took it and explained to Novius that you wanted more information from the lad and what the plan was. Novius let me in after a few questions. Brocchus was asleep so I nudged him with my foot and then offered him the food; said I'd heard him being beaten and thought he might need it. He took me for a slave immediately just as you said he would." He slurped more wine, winced again and continued. "He looked me up and down and seeing my face asked what I had done to get such a beating. I gave him the story we suggested and he accepted it without question and I soon had him eating the food and opening up. I asked what he'd done and he said he'd just admitted to a murder he didn't commit." My thoughts started to run, but I reined myself in and listened. "He said that he is in love with a girl called Lucilla and would never hurt her, but he couldn't withstand the pain so had to confess to make it stop. I agreed with him, told him I'd been beaten lots of times and confessed to what I hadn't done just to stop the pain." It was a good ruse as Graccus looked the part of the beaten slave for certain and in my mind I thanked Milo for the comment, thinking once again that I owed a devotion to Minerva. Graccus continued to speak. "I asked what you said I should, getting him to tell me why they thought it was him and what had actually happened." My guts started to tighten with anticipation at this and I found myself biting the nail on the thumb of my left hand.

"He told me how you thought it was him because he was betrayed in love by Lucilla, but that wasn't true. She'd followed him after Arnth had hit him. He saw her in the street of the butchers and went across to her but she said that even if she loved him they could never marry but they could stay friends. He was heartbroken and had run away from her, leaving her in the streets as she called after him. He saw Arnth a short while later and dodged him, staying hidden under a stairway in a dark corner at the end of the street which borders the ditch where the girl was found. He says he saw other figures going past the end of the alleyway but it was foggy and dark so he couldn't make out who they were but stayed hidden in case it was Arnth or others who wanted to beat him again. He then says he heard voices shouting at each other, two women, but he wasn't sure who it was because the shouting was some distance away and stopped suddenly, replaced by a man shouting. Soon after that he saw someone stumbling along and he thought he'd been stabbed in a fight by the way he was clutching his belly, possibly from the shouting he'd heard but then he realised he was swaying so much because he was so drunk. He watched him pissing in the alleyway just ahead of where he was hiding. After that he crept home, keeping to the darkness to avoid Arnth or anyone else and only the next day did he learn that Lucilla was dead. He curled up in a ball after that and I couldn't get him to say any more."

I thanked Graccus as I let it all sink in. "That must have been me" I exclaimed after a moment "in the alley." I let my mind run back to the night. I'd thrown up three or four times, but only once had I turned into an alley to piss. That alleyway was five or six minutes to when I met Ducus and probably ten or fifteen until I'd found the girl. That small window of time held all the clues. If Lucilla was in the butchers street, which was at the western end of the forum, fifteen minutes at the most to when I found her, how did she get to the ditch. I explained these thoughts to Graccus who accepted them with wide eyes.

"You saw no-one else?" asked Graccus.

I shook my head. "I wobbled on my feet in the fog and not long after that alleyway I stopped a few times to retch up bile." I remembered the acid taste in my mouth. "I stopped by the stone of Janus as I said before, holding it and standing there in the silence for a while. I felt as if I was being watched and someone must have pissed on the stone as it was wet, I remember that now" I was shaking my head. "But I saw nobody, not until I came across Ducus and scared the shit out of him with my appearance." We shared a look and then my mouth gaped.

"Bastard" I said loudly.

"Shit" said Graccus, my shocked expletive causing him to see where my mind had run. "It can't be him can it?"

I stared at him. Was this everything that I thought we'd missed? Had Ducus been the killer? Many murders were opportunistic, my father and Scavolo had said as much several times when they had given me the benefit of their wisdom and experience. Pieces started to click. He was alone in the fog, a pretty young girl had stumbled into him, he'd leered over her, tried to press himself on her. I swallowed as my thoughts ran on. Had I come across him just as he'd been attempting to rape her and made up the story of the goats, which I suddenly realised we'd never found? He must have clubbed her with that staff he was walking with, ripped her undergarments from her. And then I stumbled into him and he pushed her into the ditch. It seemed to make sense.

"Get his statement" I said quickly. Graccus ran around looking for it and pulled out a short note made by one of Scavolo's men. I read it aloud. "My goats had disappeared and I searched for them along the road to the Halitorium and then back towards the Boarium but it was so foggy I couldn't see anything. After a while that man who went into the ditch found the dead girl."

"Is that it?"

I nodded. It was poor at best. "Where does he live?"

"From memory his farm is across on the Janiculum. It'll be ten or fifteen minutes there by horseback at least."

"Shit" I replied, using the word that seemed to suddenly be my favourite expletive but accurately described our situation. "Get a

sturdy horse we need to go now, tell Scavolo what we're doing"
I shouted as I ran to find a pair of thick woollen cloaks and
something for my feet which I could wear to ride in as I guessed
we would be soaked by the rain and wet and muddy roads.

Minutes later, Scavolo had met us at the stable and tried to stop
us, saying that the court case would start within the hour and I
needed to be there.

"This is another wild goose chase. You have no proof and Ducus
is a well-respected farmer in the community. You're wasting
your time" he growled.

"Is he married?" I asked.

Scavolo frowned. "Wife died a year ago, plague."

"There you go then. He's sad and lonely and took the chance
when it came to him." It was a weak answer but he understood
my line of reasoning and what I meant and shook his head in
response.

"You're wrong lad, not every man who loses a wife becomes a
rapist. It was Brocchus that killed her. He's confessed, why are
you wasting your time?"

"I can't see him doing it. His confession was due to the branding,
nothing else" I said as I cocked a leg over the horse from the
mounting block.

"It's standard procedure and allowed under the law. He
confessed, he did it" came the cold response.

I explained about my fears, of the lack of certainty I felt that it
was the captive we'd forced a confession from and of Ducus and
what we now knew from Brocchus' story to Graccus.

His eyes narrowed at my telling of the story but I could see
understanding behind the furrowed brows. He continued to
shake his head, saying that the boy could not be trusted. "That
fucker changes his story whoever he speaks to. He's got you
hooked like a fish and he's trying to find a way out of his

situation. He sees you as his only way out of this and he's playing you."

"He didn't know Graccus was a slave" I exclaimed as if I knew everything.

His arms flapped in exasperation. "He saw him at the farm, he's seen him here" he was waving an arm at Graccus. "Well, I see what you mean" he added as Graccus' beaten face turned to him. "But you are wrong, Ducus is too well known to be the murderer and he's no rapist" he added with certainty.

I was shaking my head. "Just because he's well known doesn't mean he's innocent" I answered, as much to reply to his own comment a moment earlier as to make the point. "Minerva gave me this task Scavolo. I need to check this out as I cannot see Brocchus as the killer."

He sighed heavily and boosted a struggling Graccus behind me with an easy lift of his muscular arms. Begrudgingly Scavolo gave us an appraising glance which suggested agreement.

"I'll send Novius along behind you in case you need any extra support. I hope you've thought through what you'll do if he's there?" he said as he started to walk away. "If you confront him and you're right, he's likely to strike out. I've seen it happen many times and you'll need help." He stopped and then turned back to us. "I'll let your father know that you've gone. And" he was fumbling at his belt. "Here" he handed me a dagger, its handle of well used white bone. "This has saved my life many times, you never know if you'll need it. Don't lose it or I'll kick your arses to the Janiculum and back myself, even if you're dead." I appraised him, his eyes softening for a moment as they caught mine. "You better be back in time for the trial" he added before slapping the horses flank.

We jerked and galloped off hanging on for dear life, completely out of control with Graccus bouncing behind me clutching my waist like a beggar clutching a gold coin.

****

At least the rain meant clear streets, but they were slippery and wet and we almost fell three or four times before we hit the dirt tracks which led across the Tiber and to the Janiculum and on which we had better purchase and therefore speed.

Graccus was clutching me so tightly I could hardly breathe and I told him to relax or he'd have us both dead in the ditch before we solved the crime.

"I can't" he screeched. "Every one of my bones and muscles hurts with each stride"

I laughed as I understood. "The gods are punishing you for being an arsehole and eating three bowls of stew" I laughed. He pinched my waist as he gripped more tightly and I squealed, half turning and causing the horse to swerve and almost unseat us both.

"Stop pissing about" he shouted, fear in his voice.

Several people dived out of our path as we galloped past shouting at them to move as I was unable to stop the horse quickly enough if they didn't. There were countless lawsuits against people who had damaged a horse by allowing a slave or a child to step out in front of it and damaging the expensive creature. I didn't want the bother of this so just screamed at people to move. It worked. Graccus, his knowledge of the farms and streets out here far better than mine as he had often visited the farms with his father, pointed me left and right until we came to the lower slopes of the Janiculum hill and the horse had to slow to a fast walk, it's breath loud as it snorted at the effort. The rain continued to drizzle steadily and I was thankful for the riding cloaks that Scavolo had given to Graccus. We eventually came to a well-tended fence which was shoulder height and stretched around a large farm, visible in the distance some way beyond and through a line of olive and apple trees. We rang the bell, a tinny sound ringing out into the quiet of the road. A slave popped his head up from working in the fields to our left and approached as we called out, pushing back his hood and instantly soaking his hair as rainwater dripped into his eyes, legs covered in mud.

His old face looked at us with a squint. He wore an oiled blanket-like covering which appeared to be a home-made cloak. This was draped over his shoulders with the hood now bunched at his neck but still with oil which kept out the rain. The cloak sank to his knees and had two cuts from which his arms protruded, clearly designed to continue to work the land in the worst of the weather. I was unsure if he was half-blind, half-deaf or both as he called out from twenty yards away asking what we wanted.

"To see Ducus the goat-herd" I called back. "Urgently."

"Why?"

"Official business" I shouted and waved the tablet with the temple seal that we'd brought with us in the hope that the man understood its import and therefore ours. "Open the gate or I'll break it down" I said sharply. This frightened him and he started to step backwards. "Come here and open this gate" I called once more, lifting the dagger Scavolo had given me as the old slave seemed to have frozen in indecision. "Is your master at home?" I called through the drizzling rain which was falling steadily.

"He is sir." He replied, now coming froward to the gate with a look of fear. "He won't be happy that he's being disturbed."

No sooner was the gate opened than I barged through, kicking the horse into life and heading straight to the farmhouse as the old man clanged the gate bell in alarm at our rear to alert those in the house. Graccus nearly lost his grip at the surge in speed and I felt his fingers seeking further purchase as he pulled himself back up behind me. "Hang-on" I shouted to his grunting efforts. At the house a woman stood at the door and raised a shout for help as she saw the horse galloping along the track and saw why the man at the gate had raised the alert. "Well, he'll know we're here for sure now" I called over my shoulder. As we came to the dirt yard by the door, where several puddles awaited us, we were greeted by a line of men, all of them armed and all of them tensed and ready for action. I had made the decision to call for Ducus and accuse him of murder when we'd set off, certain that we had our man but now that a small army faced us I wasn't so cocky. I made a quick decision to approach this differently. The appearance of the armed gang made me realise that, just as Scavolo had suggested, we might not have thought this through well enough. I hadn't considered that the goat-farmer might not only have several burly sons but also a full complement of labouring slaves who would be loyal to their master and not take kindly to two boys turning up to lay claims at his feet that he would no doubt deny.

"Shit!" I exclaimed. "We'd better be more tactful. Follow my lead, we can't just accuse him or we'll never get out alive." Graccus squeaked his agreement.

I reined in the horse and descended slowly and purposefully, landing in a deep puddle up to my ankle and cursing under my breath. Ducus was clearly visible behind the front row of slaves, a spear in hand and an Etruscan helmet which looked older than himself on his head.

"Well" I said loudly, holding out the reins. "Is this how you greet guests?"

****

Ducus frowned at us as he led us into a private room at the back of the house after the tense stand-off at the door had been diffused. The room had a clear view of large fields and a herd of goats who were currently sat either under or in low-branched trees to shelter from the rain. A slave had taken our cloaks to brush with the promise that they would add some fat to the wool to seal it from the rain for our return journey. "Of course I remember you" he answered to my introductory question as he walked ahead of us. "How could I forget, you found that girl in the ditch. Terrible it was. I've hardly slept since."

I glanced to Graccus. This wasn't the behaviour of a man we had, in our haste, assumed was the murderer. We shared a worried frown. Had Minerva tricked us again? Was Janus playing us for fools once more? "That is why I'm here, Ducus, as I said" I explained again, his oldest son behind to ensure that his father didn't say the wrong things or just as a guard us as we entered the room and were pointed to seats. The son offered a red grape wine from a clay jug, a picture of Bacchus adorning its side. I nodded acceptance and the son, who was close to my age poured a small measure, stingy bastard, into a dark clay cup adorned with a goat. Very fitting. I ignored the wine, which I placed on the floor at my feet and started with my questions, concerned about small talk, and the passing time, as I now had a feeling in the pit of my stomach that our journey had been wasted and my father would be sat tapping his feet and awaiting my return. I could see Scavolo in my mind's eye and heard him telling my father I'd cocked it up. In my head I'd seen Ducus as a lonely old man, falling on the girl who had come out of the fog in the wrong place at the wrong time like the monster Cacus in the old tales, the goatherd taking her life as he tried to rape her until he was surprised by my appearance from out of the fog at which point I had an image of him throwing her body into the ditch. It had seemed clear to me and I'd said as much to Graccus as we'd ridden to the farm. He'd agreed with every word, proving that he is as stupid as I am. Now I felt like a fool and I still owed Minerva a coin; was this her way of telling me I was late with my prayers and devotions?

I took a slow breath as Graccus sipped the wine and then looked into the cup and raised his brows, evidently his portion was as small as the one I had been given. "Thank you for allowing us to enter your humble dwelling" I started with platitudes. "As you know, I have been tasked to find the girl's killer. A very sad tale and a difficult nut to crack" I was nodding slowly as I spoke.

His eyes were narrowed and his head leant forward as if he was struggling to hear. Maybe at his age that was a concern so I spoke a little louder. "Please, Ducus, I would like you to think back to that morning before I met you. Your report didn't give much detail and I wondered if you could expand on anything else you saw so that I can piece together this puzzle." He was looking at me suspiciously, as if he might be incriminating himself by speaking. "Tell me what you saw before you met me on the road and I went into that ditch to find that girl. Did you see anyone else?"

"Of course I did" he said as if I was an idiot.

My mouth dropped and my eyes widened. "Who? There was nothing in your report."

"I didn't see any report? I was asked by that idiot what I saw and I told him." He was looking to his son, who frowned. He shook his head several times before he started to speak again. "I saw a man and his son, they were heading for the river to fish, they asked directions from the opposite side of the road as the herd had spread out by then and took up most of the track. That was quite a bit before I saw you though, further along the track to the bridge." He rubbed his chin and looked to his son.

"Could you describe them?"

"Not really. It was pretty thick fog as you know." He took a second before adding. "Medium height, medium build. Had a fishing pole and some nets, or rope at least. Looked like rope now I think of it" he shrugged. "The older one spoke in a heavy Latin accent as if he was a foreigner" he said. "Then there was a couple further along the ditch, a woman with a younger man. They hid their faces, probably a married woman with her young lover and moved along quickly towards the city when they saw me coming. Didn't see them again." He scratched his chin and smiled at the thought but then continued. "And then just before you a pair of men came out of an alleyway, rushing down the road they were, one of them wasn't even dressed properly." I knew who they were, cloak and no-cloak.

"Anyone else? Anything else at all which could help us?"

"Not until you appeared. It was damned foggy and cold. The sound didn't travel much in the fog so I couldn't hear anyone walking" he was shaking his head and I considered that if he was as deaf as I suddenly thought he was then it was unlikely he'd have heard anything much on that morning or any other. "And by then I'd lost my bloody goats."

I took a slow breath as I considered what he'd said. "What can you tell me about the woman and her lover? Where did you see them?"

He took a moment to think about this. "Near the old wall but along the track to the Tiber on the path. They were there before me, they stepped back as I approached. I was wary, but they didn't seem harmful and kept to themselves, crossed the road in fact as they were just off the road when I arrived with the herd, the dog saw them first and barked. I had my spear though so I was safe enough. They moved off quickly when they heard the dog." I remembered now that the goatherd had a spear, not a staff, I hadn't recalled it until he said it. I nodded at this as it made sense and I realised that my vision of him as the club wielding murderer was completely wrong, Scavolo had been right again.

"Can you describe them in any way? Was there anything about then or their behaviour which I might use to find them?"

"Describe them" he said this to himself, his eyes drifted towards the ceiling as he considered my question. "She was well built, a tall lady. Had a thick shawl over her shoulders and head and turned away as I approached, she was afraid of the dog so moved across the road quickly, dragging the lad with her. The man had his hair tied up on his head like my son" he nodded to his boy who had an Etruscan knot on top of his head. I suddenly gasped at a memory, and everyone stared at me for a moment until I waved away the thought and asked him to continue. "But

I couldn't say any more about them as I had to keep an eye on the dog, she was barking at them until she stood on something and hurt her foot so was whimpering. When I looked up they'd gone." The dog looked at us from its place at his feet, grey eyes showing that it had lost most of its sight due to age just like the old goat herd had lost his hearing.

"How tall was she?"

He shrugged at my question but stood and placed a hand at about his eye level. I stood and judged the height, nodding my thanks. "Was the lad tall as well?" he nodded. "Any jewellery or other clothing that stood out on any of them?"

"No. As I say they moved away from the edge of the road quickly as I approached. They seemed to be looking for something."

"Looking for something?"

"Yes, they were staring across towards the old walls from the old Boundary stone, you know, Janus' head." He meant the old walls of Romulus which were the old boundary to the city and almost non-existent now and I nodded that I knew the stone as I had leant against it shortly before I stumbled into Ducus.

I let my thoughts run over the scene and I asked, "so they were facing the ditch."

"I guess there were" he added, eyebrows raised at his own words.

"And the fishermen, can you describe them?"

He scratched his head slowly. "The younger lad was skinny and had a long nose. Looked like he'd sucked on a lemon" he shrugged but I had an inkling that I knew who he was. "My eyes aren't as good as they used to be" he said slowly.

"And the older man?"

"I couldn't tell you in truth. The dog was barking and they edged away after that. They looked dodgy though, I can tell you that for sure. I kept looking back over my shoulder after that to check they weren't following. You know what I mean?"

I nodded my understanding.

"You have been most helpful Ducus, thank you. We need to return to the temple" I said as I turned to Graccus, standing and half-knocking the wine over before I apologised and drank the liquid quickly as my throat was suddenly very dry. The wine slipped down my throat like nectar. It tasted heavenly and I stood and looked at the cup for a second, mimicking the action I'd seen from Graccus moments earlier. I couldn't remember tasting such good grape, ever. "This is very good, is it your own?"

"It's Lathius' here" he said with a jutting thumb to his son. "He has the fields above for grapes, only just started making it two years ago, we use the goat dung for the vines, seems to make them grow well."

"Could I purchase some?" I asked quickly to the son, smiling broadly at the question for a second before his face turned to a business-like scowl.

Ducus answered for him. "It's not cheap" he gave me that glance that suggested he was about to attempt to barter with us over the cost. I took a second to think. We had to return quickly as I now thought I had found another option for the killer and bartering for wine might take more time than I had to spend. The son smiled as I turned back to him.

"I'll pay a pound of bronze for twenty amphora" I said, Ducus stopping in his tracks as he stared at his son, who had clearly never been to my tutor as his mouth was slack and his eyes wide in shock. It was a very good price, but I knew the wine was far better than the amphora that Scavolo had stolen from me which was two pounds of bronze for ten amphora and I knew a good grape when I tasted it.

"A pound of bronze for fifteen and you have a deal" shouted the old man, cutting across his son.

"Agreed. I'll send a boy called Micus to sort the transport" I said as he shook hands and sealed the deal. He seemed upset that I'd not bartered harder and I guessed he wondered if he could have asked for more.

At the door I saw several of his beasts, their coats glistening in the rain as their beady eyes turned to the movement at the doorway. "They're healthy looking animals" I said with a nod to the goats as another thought struck me.

"Etruscan stock from my grandfather's time and we have herded them here on this land since the time of Ancus Marcius. We are the only farmers in the whole of the Roman territory to breed this stock and we produce the best meat and milk this side of Veii" he said proudly. "We don't sell them except for meat and we butcher our own when the deal is done." It was common practice for the animals to be shown live and then for the butchery to happen closer to the delivery, otherwise the meat might spoil despite the salt barrels which often contained it. "If you want a deal on meat we could talk more" his raised eyebrows suggested a further lengthy debate and I apologised, stating that we really needed to get back to the temple as there was to be a hearing within the hour.

Back at the doorway we'd regained our brushed and freshly oiled cloaks and I nodded my thanks and climbed aboard the horse, Graccus being pushed up behind by one of the slaves and placing his arms around my waist. A memory floated into my mind as I spoke. "I'm sorry to have troubled you Ducus, but very glad that I did. Thank you" I said. The old man waved as I turned the horse. "Oh" I spoke over my shoulder as the horse was getting edgy at the rain which had started to fall in heavy droplets again. "Did you ever find your goats?"

"No" he said sadly.

"Follow us to the Comitium with some of your men" I called. "I might have something for you. But be quick, the case starts in less than an hour." His puzzled expression followed us as we span in a circle as I tried to manoeuvre the horse out of the yard where it had been groomed and fed and suddenly felt at home and didn't fancy a rain-soaked journey. I didn't hear anything else as the horse spooked at a door that slammed shut at a sudden gust of wind and we shot off like an arrow from a bow.

XX

The return trip was worse than the trip out. The roads were busier as people had ventured out in the rain to get their daily food shopping or collect food from their lands in covered carts which ran with water and were stuck in the mud in several locations. We then met Novius as we crossed the Tiber, his horse having slipped in the mud and dumped him on the ground. He was soaked and the horse was limping as a small crowd had gathered at the scene, but neither man nor horse seemed particularly hurt by their fall. Novius was apologetic as soon as he saw us, his face angry at letting us down and then relieved as we explained that we had been wrong in our theory about the goat farmer. He told us that Scavolo had said we'd be wrong and suggested that it would be a waste of time. It was good to know that the head-man had shared his views of our poor judgement with Novius. He waved us on after we told him what we'd learned and what it meant for the investigation. We left him to the long walk back with the horse, or to await it feeling better so he could ride it as he couldn't risk riding the beast immediately to make sure it wasn't hurt beyond what seemed likely from the slip; horses are expensive creatures.

I ran through my thoughts with Graccus, telling him what I needed him to do, who I needed him to bring to the Comitium and how I intended to play out this mystery as I was now sure we had our killers but were still unsure of motive. He asked several deep questions, checking what he needed to do, and as we approached the forum we agreed that we had our plan. He sniffed loudly and I felt him lean against my back and wipe his nose along my cloak. I wasn't impressed.

The roads to the forum were now busy as people had ventured out and some of the smaller stalls were opened for business. As we caught sight of the temple of the Vestal Virgins, raised on it's plinth as it was, the rain ceased and a ray of sunshine seemed to light our way. Graccus grinned at the warming sun and made a comment about the gods shining on us. I agreed, reminding myself that I owed Minerva a libation as well as another to Bacchus for finding such excellent wine. Fewer stalls were open the further we traversed along the road so those that were, were crowded. We pushed through, knowing that we were late and hoping that Brocchus hadn't been condemned already. People grumbled at our riding through the walking spaces, but we pushed on, shouting that we had official business, with Graccus waving the tablet with the seal of Jupiter, which people ignored and called us pricks or even worse.

At the spring of Juturna Graccus slid from the beast and raced off to do the errands I'd set for him. I hoped he would be able to complete them all in the time we had as I kicked onwards. Eventually I arrived at my destination, the trial had started without us, but only just. Scavolo stood, with his robe of office adorned across his shoulders, a dark blue cloth with a hood which draped down his back. The head man pointed at Brocchus calling out the crime and that he had confessed as the trumpet was played to signal that he had been accused. People hissed at this and I saw that Hastius and his son were in the crowd as well as the Arturii clan, plus several other local families. It was a good crowd for judgement considering the weather. My father sat to the left of the staged area on a heavy wooden seat with his fellow Quaestores who had to be present at all official events even though his main duty was financial. He looked bored, his fat cheeks working on some form of meat that lay on a covered tray at his side along with a cup of wine. I'd forgotten his name but it was Marcus something or other. He'd visited the house often, but I'd always kept out of the way or been ushered out of the way by my father, embarrassed at my presence.

"And as he has confessed" said Scavolo. "I ask if any man here has any words to say in defence of this murderer." It seemed a pointless act for anyone to raise such a claim as the bruised and battered figure on the stage lay in a heap, still sobbing, and had confessed to the crime already, as Scavolo had just alluded to.

"Wait" I called as I approached, my voice still distant but causing several heads to turn in shock.

"Ah. A voice in defence" said Scavolo as he nodded towards my father. For his part my parent simply remained facing the crowd and looked interestedly at the faces of the people. Fucilla stood and turned to me as I came to the stage and threw my soaking cloak to a slave. I nodded to her as I passed and made a motion towards the boy at Scavolo's feet.

"That boy is innocent" I called, receiving a gasp from the crowd and a cheer from a small group of horse-faced individuals at the far end. I ignored the desire to stare at them and turned instead to Scavolo.

"This is irregular Secundus Sulpicius Merenda" he said loudly, his ability to switch to his official voice and play the part of protector of the rules intact. I nodded at his solemn words. "For you are both the prosecutor who found the boy and gained the confession and now you are proclaiming his innocence and suggesting you will be his defender who says that he is innocent." He turned to the crowd theatrically. "Explain yourself." His words were spoken loudly, stepping back with a frown towards my father who creased his mouth into a thin line at this strange turn of affairs.

I looked at him and flicked my head towards the crowd slightly with a worried glance, his keen eyes catching the movement and giving me an imperceptible nod. "I was never sure that this boy was the murderer, but he confessed under hot irons." It was a recognised process and people were nodding at the words as they understood that such treatment might get the result that was wanted but that it was not always the correct one. "I have ascertained that on the night of Lucilla Arturii's murder several things happened. First" I held up a finger. "Spurius Hastius argued with the Arturii family about a recent break in a marriage contract. It is well documented" I said to Hastius, who had stood and was about to claim that he had nothing to do with the murder. His son sat beside him, his head drooped. "Second." Another finger. "That argument led to this boy" and I pointed to Brocchus "chancing his love for Lucilla Arturii at the festival of Minerva. He had loved her for a long time and when he saw a chance to offer his hand to the girl he pestered her, begging for love and her hand. Many of those here today have told me this, so it cannot be disputed. She said no. She told him it could not be and that they were friends but not lovers" People mumbled as I spoke and I saw heads turning to speak to each other, nodding agreement. "We have testimony from many who saw it happen" I replied to several questioning looks from faces in the crowd who had come along despite the poor weather. I noted old faces, wrinkled and weather worn as well as young. The people of Rome felt it was their right as citizens to judge the actions of others, and our laws allowed any member of the citizenship to vote on the outcomes, which the Quaestores would sanction and judge.

I circled slowly, looking into their faces before I held up a third finger. "People saw Lucilla at the wrestling and then afterwards playing with her friends, splashing in water in a horse trough and getting soaked. Then she sang and danced around a fire at the olive grove to dry off and warm her cold bones. All of this is common knowledge." I turned back to the prone body of Brocchus and held my gaze on his pathetic figure. "All of these are facts. We know where she was up to that point. And then she seems to have disappeared from everyone's view." I circled slowly, keeping my eyes on Brocchus, who had looked up at me slowly. "The next aspect of this case that we know" and I turned back to the crowd at this point. "Was that Spurius Hastius told us that he had seen Brocchus with Lucilla by the cloth shops just after this time." I turned to look at the Hastii clan, sat stiffly in the front row to my left. "But we have evidence that this is untrue."

Hastius was on his feet again. "That is a lie, prove it" he called out, waving his arm and shaking his head.

I moved closer to them and looked down at them from my elevated position. "Aspius Hastius, did you or did you not talk to Lucilla and try to change her mind with regard to your marriage contract on that evening at the cloth shop. Tell us here, now in front of the gods." He looked up, fear in his eyes, his father looming over him. "I can provide the statements of two women who saw you there if needed Aspius" I said to his wide eyes which were suddenly filled with dread as he realised that I knew about his contract with the two women.

"Lies" shouted his father. "He cannot claim it was my son, there is no proof" he continued to shout, turning to his clansmen before he placed indignant hands on his hips and glared around him at the crowd. Others in his close circle stood and berated my *lies*, calling out that the boy was innocent. Others in the crowd were nodding their heads, fury burning in their eyes at my comments as others whispered and hissed at the accusation as they shared dark looks towards the Hastii. I remained calm as I stood, waiting for Aspius to reply. He didn't. His features darkened as he looked to his father, shame and fear etched into his visage.

A noise to my right caught my attention as Larce stood and waved a fist, shouting "let the boy speak Hastius. If he has nothing to hide this is the place to let it out. Sit down and let him speak."

I turned a frown to him and noted from the corner of my vision that Scavolo had understood my furtive glance and nod of the head as several of his ex-soldiers and temple slaves stepped into the gaps between the different clans, clubs half hidden under long cloaks but clearly visible to deter any frustration turning to violence. This quietened the proceedings as I called for silence and Scavolo appeared next to me on the Comitium. I was glancing around, where was Graccus? I needed to know he was here before I continued.

Scavolo prowled across the Comitium with his fists on his hips like a schoolteacher giving his class a bollocking. "Remember we are civilised men under the gaze of the gods" he called out to the assembled crowd. His anger held in check but evident. "Keep it civilised" he jabbed a finger at Hastius and then turned towards the Arturii with a grimace. "You too" he added. "Let Secundus Sulpicius speak. I'm sure we will all benefit from following this tale in the proper order" he nodded sharply to me as the crowd voiced agreement.

I turned back to the Hastius clan, the father red-faced as he glared at Scavolo and then to me. "We seek the truth Hastius, nothing more and nothing less. Let the boy speak. Aspius, did you or did you not speak to Lucilla at the cloth shop on that night?"

"Yes" he mumbled quietly, head down.

"What?" the scream was from his father.

People muttered now, the noise level rising. I saw Larce and his wife talking hurriedly and then Larce spoke to Lucius, who stared back at the Hastius clan and balled his fists. I could see it getting very ugly at any moment and so I called out to Aspius. "Stand Aspius Hastius." He looked at me aghast, as if I was about to accuse him of her murder. "Stand and tell us what was said."

"I didn't do it" he yelled. "I couldn't kill her" he said again, staring at his father now as well as the crowd of faces that had turned toward him, the mumbled words suggesting that people were now working their own judgement on the boy from the fact that he had obviously lied. Larce shouted an expletive and several of the Arturii rose from their seats and turned towards the speaker, hands raised in anger. Aspius half turned to the group that were now facing him, starting to shout loudly and wave angry fists at the Hastius contingent. Scavolo moved quickly and was calling the crowd to order and telling them to calm down. I glanced to my father, whose head was bent with his fellow Quaestores, their mouths working as they discussed some element of the proceedings that I couldn't hear.

I stepped forwards, moving closer to the edge of the Comitia and turned to the Arturii as I spoke slowly and sternly. "No action can be taken here until the case is decided. We have a long way to go until we identify the killer. Sit and await the trial conclusion, there are things we have yet to learn in this case so don't be so quick to judge others whilst we have not concluded all of the evidence I have gained." I spoke with such ferocity that Fucilla put her hand over her mouth and whispered loudly enough for all those near her to hear her words clearly.

"Minerva speaks through him."

It caused a gasp, one which actually brought a smile to my father's face and broke his stoic training for a moment. If I hadn't turned to him just as the priestess spoke I would never have seen it. He was almost human after all. His fellow Quaestores looked at me with an appraising glance but nodded for me to carry on before he turned back to my father and their heads closed once more to continue their conversation. The crowd turned their faces to me, some raising eyebrows at the words of the priestess, others talking in hushed tones.

"Aspius, repeat your answer" I ordered loudly to break the spell that Fucilla had caused. I was getting desperate as I searched the back of the crowds for the faces I needed to be present if my planned arguments needed support, but could see none of them, Graccus' dribbling nose nowhere in sight.

The duck farmers son was standing as I faced him, his father tugging at his arm and vociferously telling him that he had nothing to answer to. The boy shrugged him off, finally having the guts to speak against his father's wishes. "I tried to bargain with her. To get her to agree to the marriage contract. I said I would give her time to consider options, and that she could stay at her home for a month each a year. We had been together for so long. I loved her. We were a good match" he said these words with passion, and every face was silent as he spoke. "I didn't kill her. I couldn't harm her." His head dropped, his hands limp at his sides. Spurius Hastius glowered, his face red with anger at this admission which he believed made him look like a fool as everyone knew he had publicly argued with the Arturii and then severed links between them.

"I didn't have a child with another woman either. That was a lie spread by someone to split us up, to stop me marrying her." He'd shouted this last few words with a glare at Lucius. The noise of the crowd grew at this as he fixed his jaw and stared hard at me momentarily before turning back to the Arturii clan. "You spread that lie to stop us marrying. You knew that our flocks had suffered and you wanted a way out of the contract." His words were greeted with jeering from the small crowd of Etruscans, Larce laughing loudly and making obscene gestures.

"I didn't kill her" he shouted again in their direction. "I couldn't hurt her."

"I know that you didn't kill her" I said slowly bringing a moment of silence to the proceedings. Spurius Hastius' face turned sharply to me, eyes narrowed, as his son's jaw dropped at my words. "But what you did to lay the blame elsewhere was wrong." He bit his lip at this and said nothing. "Why did you blame this man?" I was pointing to the prone figure behind me.

His anger flared now. "He must have done it. That idiot did nothing but follow her around all night, begging her, pulling at her arm, pissing her off with his constant whining. Who else could it be but that prick" he stated angrily.

Brocchus' family stood and called out that the boy was innocent and that the gods would find the real killer. The crowd grew restless again, the noise level rising as I saw more and more people joining the back of the crowd and asking what was happening. Faces turned back to Brocchus, who peered at them through a half-closed eye and then curled up into a ball once again as if the fact that he could not see them meant that they could not see him.

"I do not believe you are right Aspius Hastius. I do not believe that Brocchus is the murderer. Please sit Aspius, though I may come to you again." I was about to face the crowd but added "and learn a lesson from this. Money will not buy you freedom if you err again. And yet more might come of your actions on the night of the festival." At this Spurius Hastius' head jerked and he looked at me and then at Scavolo, who was too busy facing the Arturii clan and forcing them to sit to see the glance in his direction.

I turned back to the crowd, who looked confused by my words, Spurius now whispering furiously with his son, who was shrugging away his hurried questions. I continued with my story. "We were told by Brocchus that he and Lucilla were in love." This raised several comments from the crowd, including Lucius who shook his head. "However, this was all in Brocchus' head. Many have told us that Lucilla did not have any feelings for the boy and treated him like a puppy, someone to keep on a leash. Maybe she did love him in a way. Maybe she felt pity for him, but certainly there was no love between them, certainly not as Brocchus saw it. And yet, with Aspius Hastius' accusation that Brocchus had argued with Lucilla we followed the natural trail to a conclusion. A conclusion that Marcius Brocchus killed Lucilla Arturii because she spurned his love. One that was wrong because others led us to believe that he was the killer and led us down blind alleys with their lies or half-truths. And one that was wrong because Marcius Brocchus didn't tell the truth himself." At this I looked to Aspius, the crowd hissing their displeasure at what they saw were his lies.

After a moment I faced the crowd again and spoke. "Arnth Arturii" I said, looking for the boy, who flinched at my naming him. "Why did *you* also tell us that you saw Marcius Brocchus with Lucilla at the cloth shop on the night of the festival?"

Lucius span around and faced his brother's son with a scowl. The boy looked like a ghost, paling as he was faced by many of those around him. I noticed Larce stiffen.

"I thought it was him, that's all" he called back.

I nodded slowly. "And yet you were very clear in your statement that it *was* Brocchus. And later you found Brocchus with Lucilla near the olive grove and you chased him away, striking him. Is that right?"

"I did. He was being a prick" he replied loudly, clearly happy to answer my questions confidently when it showed his ability to punch someone smaller than himself. "He was always hanging around her, acting like an idiot, pretending she was interested in him. I told you that, you have said so yourself." He was crossing his arms over his chest, facing me squarely. It was the first time he had properly looked at me, his usual lowered gaze now able to face me with confidence. I saw a fixed jaw, tense shoulders and fear. His eyes danced despite the strong body language. He couldn't look me directly in the eye after a few seconds and I picked up on this.

To everyone's surprise Brocchus shouted out "You're the prick, not me. You. She loved me." at which Arnth was about to run forward but a guard stopped him, gripping his arm and holding him back.

I held up my hands and turned to Brocchus. "Tell us what you saw and heard Marcius. Tell the people so that they can judge your innocence" I said aloud.

He gaped at me, aghast, his face so badly swollen that it was painful just to look at him. The crowd looked at him with some pity, except for those who still considered him guilty. I waited to see if he would take up the challenge and break the chains of cowardice that had dogged his life. His prone body moved slowly to face the judgement of the people but his will collapsed and he knelt, eyes looking to the skies before his head drooped. One of his clan called out to him to tell them what he knew, to save himself. But the boy was mute and incapable. Pity clawed at me, his beaten form painful to watch as the people of Rome muttered at his inability to speak.

I raised my arms for silence. "We must explore what happened next so that we can understand and judge this case." Arnth had sat, but I stepped across slowly, rubbing at my chin. "Arnth, you attacked Brocchus and he ran away" he was staring at me angrily. "Did you follow him?"

He glanced to his mother then back to his father. "No" he said.

I nodded slowly. "So it was not you that chased him through the streets?"

"No."

I circled slowly, the crowd watching my steps in rapt silence. I continued to rub my chin as I watched the people, still searching for Graccus. "And you were not in the streets late into the night and till dawn?"

He answered even more angrily. "No."

"Lucius Arturii" I spoke to the Fuller, who raised his chin. "Did you see your nephew after your daughter disappeared and before you learned of her body being found?" It was a gamble, I hadn't asked him this question before.

His brows creased and he looked to his wife before he replied. "No, I don't remember seeing him." His face turned to his brother who looked to his wife, who looked to Arnth. "Boronia said he was with her searching the Field of Mars" he added as the woman paled at his words and stared hard at me with that anger I'd seen behind her eyes every time I'd spoken to her.

"I searched for her" said the boy, standing with a look of indignation on his face and twisting from his mother to the head of the family, "as did everyone else."

I had to chance my arm, to push my spear forward to defend Brocchus but without the support I'd sent Graccus to gain my spear was blunt. I was about to the change the subject and try to waste more time when Graccus waved at me from the rear. I beamed, which caught all of those close to me off-guard and they frowned in question at my sudden change of facial expression. It brought a look of fear to Arnth.

"Then why were you seen lurking in the shadows close to the place where Lucilla was found?" It was a harsh accusation and I'd rushed it in my determination to call him out.

Larce stood and shouted. "Rubbish! That is a lie. What proof is there of this?"

Arnth was at his side. "I searched for her, that is all" he said loudly, though his eyes darted around the crowd.

"You said you were nowhere near where she was found" I said slowly as I crossed my arms over my chest and looked down at him from my raised position on the stage.

Lucius turned a look to Arnth and then to Larce. "Where did you search?" he asked. "I didn't see you with the others." I let that sink in as Arnth turned to his father and tightened his jaw.

"I, I went around the roads for a while" he blurted. "Trying to help. I forget where I looked. I was panicked that she had disappeared. I might have been in several places."

Lucius had stood and was about to ask further questions when I called above their voices, trying to get things back on my own track. "Gentlemen" I was calling loudly now to get their attention. I noted Fucilla place her hand over her mouth and glance to her husband with a worried look. "Please, sit. Let me continue, there is more we need to know." They did so, but not without a few choice words to each other in their mother tongue.

"So, Arnth" I placed my hands behind my back and glanced to my father. His eyes narrowed as they caught mine and he nodded slowly with a half-smile to suggest that I should carry on. His fellow Quaestores was eating again, his jaw chewing quickly as his eyes scanned the crowd, he was enjoying the show. "You told us just a moment ago that you were not in the streets on that night, and that you were not seen near the place that Lucilla was found close to dawn. But now you say you might have been and you cannot remember. Is that correct?"

He floundered now like a landed fish. "I said I wasn't there all night. I went looking for a short while" he said sharply, his head turning left and right.

I stopped my circling and turned slowly to him, with a single finger over my lips as if I was thinking deeply and then said, "I've heard a series of confusing answers and I'm not sure where you were and what you were doing on that night."

I let the silence stretch. People craned to see him as he wriggled in his seat. He was about to speak but I lifted my hand to stop him. "Lucius" I turned to the head of the family. "You said that you didn't see Arnth. Tell us more about this. Did you see him before Lucilla disappeared or after?"

His teeth clenched as he took a deep breath and rounded on his brother. "I did not see him after the wrestling match and until he came to say that Lucilla had been found. Did you see him brother?"

Larce bristled, his face tight. He looked to his wife, who had paled and was glancing around quickly. I felt something change in the atmosphere and I took a quick gamble to drag this back to myself before the Arturii started to settle questions and answers with fists.

"Then Arnth" I was calling out loudly now and I lifted my chin to Graccus and flicked it for him to bring forward one of the people he had searched out. "It seems that your story does not add up. Where were you after you hit Brocchus and were seen chasing him into the streets?"

He clammed up. No words came from his mouth as he stared at me with hatred.

"What you saw could be crucial to this case" I added, trying to get him to speak. "No answer?" I shook my head. "The goat herd Ducus saw a bot, with an Etruscan knot in his hair with a tall woman standing by the ditch just before I found the body. Was that you?"

"No" he shouted, head twisting from side to side.

I stood and looked down at him, waiting for the crowd to calm as I saw Fucilla and Boronia share a glance, one which I thought was bringing a realisation to the mother of the dead girl, and one which I had also now confirmed in my mind. I waited a few heartbeats as Graccus came forward with a fair-haired man and an ex-soldier who beamed at Scavolo as he appeared at the edge of the Comitium but his glower at me at having duped him when I'd given him Graccus' name evident on his face as he looked toward me. "Then you should know that this man, a citizen, took a horse-trader from his inn to the stables on the morning of the murder. I saw him myself, and he recognised me the moment I entered his father's inn."

Arnth and his father shared a glance, Fucilla looked over her shoulder and said something curt which seemed to shock Arnth and he looked to his mother quickly. Things were changing rapidly and I needed to get this back on track quickly or it may be lost to flight or fight.

"He saw Brocchus as well as an Etruscan boy running in the shadows on the morning Lucilla died. The horse-trader can be summoned to agree to this story if we need to do so. Gallus" I turned to the boy. "You are a citizen and have the right to speak?"

"I do" he said proudly with a glance to his father. It was important to get that statement out of the way early so that no counter claim could be lodged which would slow the case further as only citizens could make statements at the Comitia.

"You told me that you saw a boy in the shadows on that morning just before you saw me. Can you tell me if you can see that boy here in the crowd?"

He turned and raised a finger. "It was him" he said loudly to gasps from the assembled crowd. And then to my surprise he also added "and wait, I saw that woman too, she was wearing a blue and brown shawl over her head and standing by a house as if she was about to go inside, but it was definitely her I'd recognise her anywhere."

Everyone looked to where he was pointing. I had my murderers, but I now had to confirm it.

XXI

Uproar ensued.

Boronia and Larce were up and shouting, pointing at Gallus and screaming defiance in Etruscan. Graccus was somehow in the fray and I saw his head bob up and down as much larger men pushed him backwards, fists flew as Larce tried to grapple his way out of the melee and Arnth was wrestled to the ground. Fucilla screeched like a bat, her fury and anger beyond anything I had seen from a woman before as she launched at Boronia, catching her hair and pulling at it as the taller woman smashed her fists into her attackers arms. Lucius was throwing his weight into what had quickly become a complete street brawl. I gulped, not knowing what to do. Then three things happened very quickly.

Firstly a whistling sound resounded across the Comitium.

Secondly Scavolo appeared with five men and they marched into the Arturii family group, people parting or being trampled if they were too slow to move. I noted the crowd swell backwards at the start of the fight and then move steadily back into the fight as Scavolo came barging into the frenzied scene.

And finally Scavolo, Novius and one other man came striding from the melee with Arnth, blood dripping from a wound to his eye, Larce, arms tied behind his back and legs kicking out but constrained and Boronia, dress torn and one shoulder bared, dragged forward as she screeched in pain as her arm was shoved up her back by her captor. They deposited the three of them on the floor at my feet as if I were a conquering king. My father caught my glance and after a moment, in which he actually nodded his head with an appraising smile to me, waved for me to continue, the man at his side talking animatedly but with a broad, toothy, grin at what had become a great show and one that they would be talking about for some time to come.

I tried to get a grip of myself as my heart was hammering at the sudden change in mood and the subsequent violence. Scavolo appeared at my shoulder and whispered in my ear, "get on with it lad, and don't cock it up."

Chastened, I turned back to the crowd and raised my arms for silence. Almost everyone was on their feet and several people were still pushing and shoving each other in the crowd. I could see Lucius and Fucilla angrily talking with several others, hands being thrown in the direction of the people on the stage as they conversed in Etruscan. "Silence" I called. "Please. Silence." It took a short moment until people returned their glances to me and things began to calm. I saw Hastius and his son looking more relaxed than I had seen them for days, Brocchus' clan were on their feet shouting to Marcius to stand and claim his freedom as they had all clearly decided that the people at my feet were guilty and their boy was not.

"Silence." I shouted once more and then started to talk, believing that the need of the crowd to hear what I was saying would outweigh the discussions that people had started. "Gallus" I called as the boy stepped forwards once more. "Tell us what you saw on the morning after the festival and then I will call the goat-herder Ducus to add to your story." People looked around as Graccus pushed Ducus forwards, his movement sheepish and slow.

"We left the inn in the early hours to reach the stables as one of the guests had a long journey. As we left I saw this boy" at which he pointed to Arnth, who had the sense to keep his face to the floor. "He was lurking in the shadows and I assumed he was up to no good. And then just behind him I saw this woman standing in a doorway as if she had just come out of the house. She turned away as soon as we approached, but" he lifted his shoulders "she is easily recognisable" his words suggesting that she was very tall and therefore easy to identify. "She was dressed too smartly for someone who had just risen from their bed" he added.

I nodded.

"Boronia Arturii, where were you on the night of the murder of your niece?"

It was a question that got a spiteful mouth full of swearing thrown in my direction, all of it a denial. She finished with a plea to Fucilla. "I did not kill your daughter" she screeched, sobs and then tears coming such that she reminded me of Brocchus. I noted the horse-faced lad was on his knees staring at the scene around him with renewed interest.

Fucilla turned her head away and buried it in her husband's shoulder.

"Thank you" I looked at the man who stood at my shoulder. "I will now call forward the goat farmer and ask Ducus to tell us what he saw." The goat farmer stood still for a moment, fright obviously taking over his senses. "Ducus" I said in a harsh tone to wake him up from his daydream.

"I" he stammered. "I brought the goats over the river and was heading to the Forum. I saw a man and his boy going fishing and then I saw a tall woman and an Etruscan boy standing by the stone of Janus at the old walls next to the ditch." He looked up at me. "The ditch where you found the girl" he added. The crowd broke into a whispering frenzy and Lucius was on his feet shouting at Larce, asking him what had happened. His brother buried his face in his hands and bent his head in sorrow. I noted that the crowd had swollen to hundreds now, the rear-most people pushing to get closer to the front to see and hear what was happening. I called out over the noise as Scavolo started to parade up and down the Comitium to silence people.

"Can you see that woman and boy here today?" I asked loudly over the growing noise from the crowd.

He looked at the three on the floor and pointed. "I would say that it is very likely that woman. The boy I am not sure, but it could be him. It was foggy" he added in his defence. People hissed with gossip as Larce tried to stand and was immediately pushed to the floor.

"It was her idea" the brother shouted, his face to Lucius. "She wanted to keep the business in the family. I didn't know about it, not until today" he claimed, his eyes full of tears. "Brother..." he was pleading, his face filled with the tears that ran down his face. "I didn't know" he yelled.

His wife screeched again like a demon and jumped at him flaying his face with her nails and trying to kick at him before she was pushed back by Novius' man. One of Scavolo's men struggled to get her hands tied and it took two of them to hold her as Larce cried out that he knew nothing and Boronia screamed at the top of her lungs at his cowardice. She then turned on him and started to accuse him, shouting that he had put the seed into her mind, bewitched her.

As they accused each other Arnth sobbed and hid his face, imitating the curled up creature that Brocchus had been on my arrival. The noise level grew once more, people standing and shouting at the stage, telling those accused of murder what they thought of them.

I turned to my father and saw his face was stern. I didn't know at what point to end the trial, and he nodded towards Scavolo and I picked up on his suggestion. "Scavolo" I called aloud. "I accuse these people, Larce Arturii, Boronia Arturii and their son Arnth of the murder of Lucilla Arturii." The Arturii clan all stood and shouted at once, Scavolo pushing them back as they rose like a wave of heavy muscle. A sudden thought struck me and I knew it must be true. I turned to Larce and spoke strongly. I waved my arms and called for silence as something was biting at me, forcing me to do the right thing; was it Minerva guiding me again?

"Larce Arturii, I believe that you did not know about this death until after it had happened. None of my investigations placed you anywhere near this murder. Tell us what you know. Tell us why this happened." His face turned to me, eyes wide with shock at my words as he was struck dumb, so I continued. "For the sake of your brother, for your family. Tell us. I believe that your wife and son caught up with Lucilla near the stone of Janus. They argued with her. Brocchus heard it, he told me that he heard two women shouting at each other as he hid in the alleyway. They were shouting angrily and arguing. And then something happened and a man was shouting. I believe" and at this I turned to Arnth "that you tried to talk her into joining you in marriage to keep your family business intact and give your side of the family a future stake in the fulling business. And then" my mind was racing as I clutched at thoughts which fell into place as if the goddess herself was truly guiding me, "you, Boronia, pushed her and started to fight. That is what Brocchus heard. She argued with you, telling you she wouldn't marry Arnth and Arnth stepped in and pushed her backwards to stop the fighting. She fell and hit her head on the Janus stone and fell into the grassy bank, which is why she had no bruises on her body, the grass was soft and the marble is smooth from years of wear. She must have been killed instantly, her senses knocked from her head. You tried to save her didn't you Arnth? But then Ducus came along and his dog barked at you. You panicked. You picked her up and threw her across the ditch, out of sight in the fog so that nobody could see her. It was natural reaction as you were in shock. You never meant to kill her did you?"

All three of them looked at me as if I were a soothsayer telling their tale as if I knew every detail when in fact I was making up each word based on what I had now guessed had happened. "You moved across the road and Ducus saw you wearing the brown and blue shawl that you'd picked up from the floor as Lucilla fell.

You took it as it would point to her body in the ditch where you left her to die. Is that what happened?"

Silence descended on the Comitia as the enormity of what I was saying became clear.

Larce spoke first, his body turning to his brother. "I didn't know Lucius, I swear. It was only today that I pieced it together. I am sorry, brother. I ..." he fell to his knees as the crowd hissed at his pathetic apology as his words were drowned by a cacophony of shouting.

"I didn't mean to kill her" shouted Arnth, now realising that he was about to be accused of murder. "I didn't" he shouted again. "It was an accident. They were fighting. It was you, you bitch" he snarled at his mother. "Always pushing me to ask her to marry me. She didn't like me but you wouldn't listen. Then you attacked her. Struck her and I stepped in to stop it" he put his hands to his face. "And she fell. Hit her head" he was looking to me now, eyes wet with tears, snot dribbling from his nose. "She fell. Hit her head. I didn't kill her" he was shouting now, his anger turned toward his mother.

"Shut up you little bastard" called Boronia, kicking at him but missing. Novius knocked her over with a slow push of his foot and got an angry glare from Larce which was met with a snarl. The crowd were in uproar still, Lucius and Fucilla the only people who were motionless.

I turned to my father with a pleading look as I did not know the correct process to accuse them and my arms lifted slowly in question. Understanding what I was trying to say he turned to his fellow Quaestores and spoke in a whisper before both men nodded.

He stood. "Scavolo, in the name of the Senate arrest these people on a charge of murder and being an accomplice to murder" at which the head man stepped forwards and started to grapple with the larger Etruscan and his wife, Arnth simply accepting the man-handling and having his hands manacled whilst he whimpered about not meaning to kill the girl. Lucius and Fucilla were on their feet, standing in silence as they clasped hands and stared at the scene in front of them with shock written across their faces. I stepped back and away from the crowd who were on the Comitium, moving Ducus and Gallus away and thanking them for the part they had played in solving this case.

Graccus appeared at my shoulder and slapped me on the back. "Bloody brilliant" he said quietly. "When did you work it all out?" he asked.

"About ten seconds ago" I replied.

****

The scene began to quieten as the three accused were being removed, but I wasn't finished yet. "Ducus" I called to the old man, his half-deaf head looking around for who had called his name. His son was with him. "Here" I called to them and then whispered into their ears, the son giving me a hard stare, followed by a stern-faced grimace. I noticed the crowd turn their faces towards us, some nodding to the friends and pointing back at us.

"Are you sure?" asked the old man, his keen eyes starting to show his anger.

"Absolutely, and Graccus here saw it too." My friend nodded agreement. "Get Fastus, quickly before everyone leaves" I said sharply knowing that the trick was to do it in public. Graccus ran over towards the end of the Comitium where the trumpeter was just about to leave, both men looking back towards us as I instructed Lathius in what he had to say.

My father was just standing to dismiss the crowd when Fastus blew his trumpet, the tone immediately recognisable as a summons. Every pair of eyes in the vicinity turned towards the trumpet player as he strode forwards, Lathius at his side, Ducus behind him and Graccus and I behind them. Scavolo scowled, my father looked back over his shoulder and narrowed his eyes and Hastius, seeing the trumpeter moving towards him opened his mouth in fear. I waved to my father to come across, I knew he would appreciate this.

"Spurius Hastius" shouted Lathius as the trumpet finished its call. "I accuse you of stealing my father's goats. On the morning after the festival of Minerva you were seen with your son Aspius near the river Tiber. You stopped and asked my father if there was a good fishing spot, when in fact you were there with theft in your minds and to steal our goats. I declare that I believe you are trying to build a herd of goats as your duck farming business has hit hard times. You believed that you could steal from my family to profit from our livestock." It was good enough as a summons and I nodded.

Hastius shouted back "You have no proof, piss off."

Ducus grinned at this and Fastus blew the trumpet one more time, Scavolo coming across to listen as the crowd moved closer too. "This citizen" at which Lathius pointed to Graccus. "Saw your son Aspius Hastius with two of our goats when they visited your farm not more than two days ago. Only my family farm that breed, there are no others in Rome so you must have stolen them from us or received them as stolen goods, in either case you are liable under the twelve tables. And also" he was enjoying this "this citizen, Secundus Sulpicius Merenda saw the goats at the same time."

Fastus blew the trumpet.

Scavolo laughed aloud.

My father clapped loudly.

Hastius turned to his son and slapped him across the face.

XXII

Cincinnatus was god-like.

He had the face of man thirty years younger, but his arms and legs were of a man much older. Stiff joints and aches from old age dogged him as he moved, but his stories, his charm and his eloquence made up for it. He held centre stage for over an hour and was clearly enjoying being amongst our family and friends if the humour and loud laughter were anything to go by. I sat enthralled at his military tales, the story of returning the dictatorship as he went back to his farm and jibes at the modern men who profited from their term of office all endeared him to everyone in the room. My father looked like a pig in muck and Scavolo, always at his side beamed.

The Fuller and his wife, who had been invited to our close gathering, were in awe of him, as was I. As I recited the lines my father had written, and Fucilla backed it up with a long recitation of the dream she had, one that I was sure my father had also written, the room had burst into lengthy discussions on the role of the gods. Cincinnatus and one of his sons were well versed in history and added line after line of knowledge to the debate, ranging from Castor and Pollux to Hercules himself. By the time the moon had crossed the sky people had only just stopped talking about the case I had solved, the dream and what it portended for the future and the state of modern day Rome when people murdered family members for greed. Cincinnatus had laughed that Romulus had begun the city with murders so it was no surprise to him that it continued. Time had gone so quickly and not one guest had made an excuse to leave early. My father offered people beds for the night or spots by the fire. It was a triumph akin to that which Cincinnatus had held.

I was as exhausted as the old man himself looked, although he seemed to have an energy beyond his years. His retinue donned their cloaks as they prepared to leave and my parents attended him like slaves, checking his every step, offering to send their own staff as additional security for his trip home and also offering him an amphora of the excellent wine I'd procured from Lathius, which he had enjoyed so much he'd almost supped a whole jar on his own. Even Scavolo had commented on how good it was and scowled at me as the stuff he'd bought was seen as inferior. The former dictator left in a decorated Benna, a light people carrying cart with one horse. He could be heard singing along to a ditty as he traversed the slope and set off for his farm.

I returned to the house to find Lucius and Fucilla in conversation with Scavolo, their cloaks wrapped around them and their retinue standing waiting for their departure.

"Thank you Secundus" said the priestess as she took my hand and then reached up to kiss my cheek. I blushed. Lucius shook my hand warmly and I apologised to them both.

"For what?" said the Fuller.

"For finding that it was your own nephew and sister in law that had caused the death of your daughter" I said slowly, the wine pulling at my senses. "I do not think your brother was involved and I hope that this is clear when judgement is made" I added.

"The will of the gods is never clear" said Fucilla. "I wish it was not so, but I cannot change it. I pray that my new child has a better life and lives to old age, like Cincinnatus" she smiled at this and I agreed with her. "One thing" she asked, catching me off my guard.

"Yes."

"Scavolo says you broke into my house and replaced the scroll."

I looked to the former centurion and cursed him under my breath. I was about to blame Graccus, who was standing over her shoulder and suddenly stepping backwards sheepishly before I nodded and sighed, letting my head drop. I was about to explain the reasons but she looked at me with humour in her eyes. She let the edges of her mouth lift slightly. "Well, you didn't break anything of value, just an old jar of olives in oil that my mother had left me. I'd stored it with her Lare as it was the only thing that she left me when she died." I wondered where this was going and tightened my jaw in anticipation. "When we awoke the next day one of the slaves brought me several of the olives in a cup." I was screwing up my eyes at the story, concerned as to where it was going and what these olives had to do with anything. My mother was standing at my shoulder and, in her cups, she looked as confused as I was. "Well" she took a small cloth bag which had been suspended on her thin green leather belt and opened it slowly. In her hand was a small golden ring, adorned with a bird, a green gemstone which was big enough, if it was an emerald, to buy a small townhouse and a ruby, as bright as blood and likely worth more than the emerald ring. Two further gems shone back in the light of the oil lamps and I gaped at the treasures held on her palm. My mouth opened as she continued with her story. "These were pressed into the olives, hidden where the pips had been. I never knew, and my mother had passed her inheritance to me without being able to explain it to anyone as she died very suddenly. We never knew where her treasures were and had assumed they had been stolen when she died." She looked at me and her eyes flashed, reminding me of her daughter and filling me with sadness. "If you had not come to the house, if you had not tried to pass the dream to your man Graccus, then we would never had known" she said, a brief glance to her husband. "Minerva has given me this gift in our time of sorrow." Her large eyes were filled with awe as she turned her face to face once more.

"We owe you so much" said Lucius, his deep voice filled with emotion.

Fucilla took my hand and pressed something into my palm as she bent to kiss me. "Take this" she whispered as her mouth came close to my ear. "It is the will of Minerva."

I felt the cold stone of one of the gems in my palm and was shaking my head. She held my hand closed, Lucius nodded and placed his hand over hers. "You have brought us closure for the spirit of our daughter, Secundus. We cannot thank you enough. These gifts were not ours until you found them. It is the will of the goddess that this is yours" she whispered again so that no-one could hear.

I was waving it away as my mother spoke over my inebriated noises. "Minerva has placed us together my dear" she put a hand over Fucilla's shoulder. "It is clearly written in the stars. When do you next meet, how can I join your group?"

I left them to it, escaping to the back of the room and an empty chair. I clutched at whatever she had placed in my hand, not daring to open my fingers. It could be way out of this house. A new beginning away from all of this. I closed my eyes. Was it truly what I wanted? I opened my fingers. It was the red ruby, as large as the end of my thumb and worth a small fortune. I could get my own house with this. I felt elation and joy, and then sadness as I remembered the dead girl, but this time my memories were filled with visions of her happily splashing water at the festival and dancing and singing as the slave boy Rupio had told me.

Graccus fell in beside me, sitting on the floor and wiping his nose on his sleeve. I sighed at him. "What an adventure, Secundus. What's that?" he asked with a glance to my closing hand. I waved away his question, his bruised face turning to look up at me. "But all things come to an end. What will you do tomorrow?"

I hadn't considered it and I smiled at him. "Stay in bed and nurse a hangover." We laughed. "I really don't know" I said. "I have lands to go and visit as I understand one of my clients has found a new home for some pigs that I might be given." He laughed at his and looked to his father, who was chatting to an olive seller that my father knew. I shrugged. "You should come along, you know more about that sort of thing than I do" I said to his blackened, half-closed, eye. He nodded slowly.

"My father says I need to go back to work at the temple" he answered slowly and quietly as he watched people donning cloaks and starting to leave, dawn not far away. I stared into the room, seeing nothing and contemplating his words.

"I guess that I will return to the temple too, though I'm not sure what I'll do now that this case has been resolved. My father will no doubt have a plan for me."

"Mine too" said Graccus, sniffing again and raising an arm to his nose. I grinned at him, his pathetic face looking up at me confused. I started to laugh, water soon streaming from my eyes as I got a fit of giggles.

"What?" he asked, sitting up and starting to laugh as I creased up with the pain of the continued laughter. He started to laugh too. "What's so funny?" he was belly laughing now, gaping at me in-between streams of water dripping from his eyes and nose. People stared at us from across the room. I laughed louder, slipping half-off my chair. Graccus let out another guffaw and he honked, his nose dripping with snot. I almost choked. He stretched out on the floor and rolled over giggling. I fell off the chair beside him and rolled over, my sides hurting as I sucked in breath but could not stop the fit of laughter that had taken over my body.

After a moment I felt a kick. It was Scavolo, sober and upright whilst I was rolling on the floor with Graccus, both making honking noises and struggling to breathe as we continued to giggle like children.

"You better get up, your father wants you."

I wiped my face, trying to stifle the laughter as Graccus, his nose as wet as his eyelashes tried to stand-up by placing a hand on the chair where I had sat. It slipped backwards and he fell on his face, which set me off again. Scavolo grabbed my toga and pulled me across the room, growling in my ear about sobering up or getting my arse kicked. By the time we reached my father's private room I realised that I'd not seen him since Cincinnatus had left. "What does he want?" I asked as we reached the door.

Scavolo just grinned and replied, "You'll see." He slapped me around the face to wake me up and pulled at my toga to straighten it. I was shocked, but too surprised to react. He knocked on the door and a voice called us in.

We entered to find a small group of people sat around my father's desk, his fellow Quaestores and four others. One of them I knew, it was my father's patron, a great man who had been Consul some years before, Agrippa Furius Fusus. He was on my left and looked at me with his cold brown eyes. He'd never liked me, or so I thought. Another man I didn't recognise sat at the end of the table and turned an interested face to me. He had a broad forehead, soft eyes with an intelligent gleam and a well-trimmed short beard. I guessed he was in his early forties, and his lean stomach suggested he remained fit despite his years. I noticed heavy gold rings of senatorial style on his fingers and I was immediately impressed. He watched me as I looked him up and down. Another man sat to his left, a short man with fat hands and a sweaty brow. Despite his lack of height he reeked of power and after a short moment I realised that it was the Pontifex Maximus, Marcus Papirius. I bowed deeply, his narrowing eyes acknowledging that I had recognised him. There was one other person in the room, someone I did not know, a woman of about my age. She kept her face forward but didn't look at me directly. Her hair was dark, braided under a thin hood which narrowed her features. Her eyes were light brown, framed in dark lashes which made them shine. Her lips were full and told of happy years but right now they were fixed in that Roman stoic state. She wore an extensive dress of soft blue with green edging, a thin gold band at her neck and I saw a glimpse of a heavy gold ear-ring with a blue stone. She was likely a few years younger than me but sat proudly, almost haughty despite being in the presence of these great men. My eyes must have widened as my father coughed lightly to remind me that he'd paid a ridiculous amount of money for a tutor to help me to fix my face into the bored expression of a Roman patrician in these social situations but I was still failing.

I nodded to the room. "Father" I said slowly. "Gentlemen, may I apologise for my appearance. I am afraid I have had little to eat and one too many cups of wine. It has been a long day." I bowed again, hoping that my pathetic attempt to explain why I was as pissed as the local drunkard at the feast of Bacchus was a good enough reason for my staring at them all with an open mouth, but guessing it was not. I gained a glower, a shake of the head and a tiny smile from three men and a bored expression from the Pontifex and the beauty that I was attempting not to stare at on my right. I bent to one knee to Fusus, saying how pleased I was to see him again and kissed his hand as he held it out; it was the proper thing to do. "Sir, madam" I said in turn to the other guests as I stood back and nodded to them one at a time.

"Secundus" my father waved for Scavolo to bring a chair closer, probably in case I fell over. "Sit, we have some things to discuss." I was suddenly on my guard and I noticed that Scavolo wasn't the only *significant other* in the room. Behind the door were three further men, hardened old soldiers like Scavolo who bore the marks of many victories in campaigns as well as faces that looked like they'd sucked on several bitter tasting lemons and their features had since been permanently fixed. I ignored them, they were below me in status.

"You know the Pontifex and Marcus Valerius" started my parent, inclining to the two men I knew as well as Fusus. "And may I introduce Marcus Fabius Vibulanus and his daughter Fabia."

I knew instantly that he was of the gens Fabii, a leading family in the Republic and the son of a three times Consul. I realised that these men had been in the room as Cincinnatus and I had told our tales, their faces flashing in my memory, but I could not place the girl. I stood and bowed more deeply than I should, my head spinning slightly as I quickly returned to my seat. I saw the girls lips curl in distaste but I tried not to stare at her. Either the drink was turning my mind or she was one of the most beautiful creatures I'd ever seen. She stared coldly at the wall and looked totally pissed-off at being in the room with a drunken lout like myself. Her knuckles were white as she gripped her hands on her lap and her bottom lip quivered in either fear or anger, I could not tell which. At that exact moment I sobered, the dawning causing my father to make a small cough as my face betrayed my thoughts and I stiffened. They were going to announce to me that this girl was my new bride. What had happened to the snotty faced kid? I faced my father with renewed attention and breathed slowly through my nose to keep my focus.

"Marcus Fabius Vibulanus has interests in horses and is keen to support a new venture" said my father. It made sense after the conversation of a day earlier regarding the horse trader. I nodded to the powerful man, a good ally to have. "His daughter rides" he said, with some difficulty as I knew he thought it a frivolous hobby for a woman, "and she also manages the stables for the family, so has some skill in this area." I was immediately impressed. A woman from a wealthy family managing the estate, not unheard of but rare. I inclined my head to her and she deigned to glance at me before her mouth turned down and she looked out of sorts, I wondered why. "We have discussed an arrangement" he said. Here it was, the arrangement was clearly the hard-faced girl being aligned to me, a convenient marriage of the two houses. Thoughts about Aspius and Lucilla flooded my mind but I held them back as I attempted to keep up with the conversation. My mouth was suddenly dry and I tried to swallow but was thwarted and stifled a cough. "Fabia Vibulanus will manage your new estate in our agreement. Scavolo will support if needed but Fabia will have the final word" my jaw crept open and I closed it quickly as my father's face dropped. Not marriage then, of course not, she was too high status for me. I was disappointed and then angry for no reason at all. I saw the girl curl her lip once more at my pathetic attempt to keep a straight face. "She will have the final say in all matters of horse and management and the Fabii will gain four stallions per year from the estate in payment once the estate is up and running." It was a hefty sum for a piece of land that we didn't yet own, added to which my entry into the world of horse flesh management contained no stock. I was confused. I wasn't keeping up. Bacchus had done it to me again. Given me a night of feasting and drinking in which I'd dropped my guard and then slapped me with a complex problem involving total concentration which I had absolutely no hope of attaining.

I looked to her, she allowed her gaze to flick to mine but then turned away just as quickly with tightening lips which suggested distaste at my drunken appearance; she wasn't as good at this as she thought. I didn't know what to think but nodded sharply as my befuddled brain tried to keep up with the conversation. So, the girl was going to manage a new horse business for which I'd be in debt to these men. It wasn't making sense? I shut my eyes and opened them again to see all of the men in the room glowering at me.

My father was continuing, as usual he had it all planned out. "Marcus Fabius has a piece of land in mind for your new estate" here it was, the cost to me would be enormous, I'd be in debt to one of these three men for the rest of my life, turning up a like a pauper at their door as a client until the day I died. I felt my shoulders start to sag, but I lifted them and straightened my back to accept whatever my father had agreed. It was the Roman way and I had no escape route that my stupid brain could see. I was cursing Janus for his duplicity as I listened.

Marcus Fabius smiled. He had a warm face, one which I suddenly thought would drag you in with false platitudes before he clubbed you around the head and took everything you owned. "The land is five Jugera of grazing just outside Laurentina." I knew it, a place north of Lake Albinus and about four miles along the Via Laurentina. I nodded although I was still trying to keep up with the conversation. "We have been offered the site with a small farm building and six stables. It is adequate for a start-up business" at which his daughter inclined her head. "I have several horse which I could use to populate the business as a starter."

He was rambling on as I stared at my father, his eyes not moving from the wall behind me, expression fixed. I narrowed my eyes as I tried to contemplate how he was going to pay for this and I had a sinking feeling in my stomach. I turned slightly to look at Scavolo. As usual he was statue-like, the bastard. I knew what was coming, a life of servitude to these men. Anger bit at me and I saw the girl glance to me with a momentary worried expression. My face had clearly betrayed my thoughts.

"Is there a problem Secundus?" It was Marcus Fabius, his voice calm but he, too, had seen the change in me. Fabia turned her face to me with a look of curiosity. She really was very pretty. She then turned to her father and they exchanged a strange look. My father's eyes narrowed and Scavolo shifted on his feet. I could hear him saying *you cocked it up you prick*. The Pontifex allowed a small gleam to cross his face as he inclined his head with interest.

I shifted nervously in my seat, suddenly feeling very self-conscious and biting back the anger that was rising inside my head. Would I ever get away from the power of my father. Should I have taken the gold and run as Scavolo had said right at the start of this adventure. I bit down my anger, there was nothing for it. I couldn't get out of this plan, with the Pontifex, Fusus, my father's fellow Quaestores and Vibulanus all in some sort of pact I was out-manoeuvred. Not only would it be suicidal for my family and clan for me to decline this offer, but it would be foolhardy for me personally if I were to have this glittering career that my father and his patrons were creating for my future. Despite the hardship of having this snooty woman telling me how to run my business I'd have to beg and scrape to these bastards for years as the cost of starting up a business was high and we didn't have the political clout that they had to get the best deals on grain, transport, wood and so on. I wanted to tell them to shove their plans up their arses and to stride from the room a free man, but I couldn't. Scavolo had been right all along, I was a coward just as much as Brocchus had been. I could see nothing for it, and so I put my hand into my pocket.

"This should cover the costs of the estate and what is needed" I said as I placed the large ruby on the table in front of them all and stared hard at my father with anger burning in my mind at his suggestion that I tie myself to these idiots. I didn't need anyone telling me what to do. His face turned to a picture of confusion. I was going to show him that I was above his planning and would prefer to pay for the estate up front and hold no clientship however important the man in front of me was. I'd endure the girl managing everything if that was what it took, but I'd stay away from the business, leave them to it and just take the profit. I'd had enough of being under someone's thumb all the time. That ruby must be worth at least twenty Jugera of land my stupid brain was telling me.

Vibulanus and his daughter looked to each other with expressions of shock.

The Pontifex smiled and couldn't take his eyes off the ruby.

Fusus turned to my father with raised eyebrows as did his fellow judge.

I heard Scavolo sigh.

The Pontifex Maximus lifted the ruby and inspected it. "Well this is a turn-up in your plans" he said as he nodded his head to the large gem. "Ancient, very, very good quality. I'd say this is worth fifty or more" by which I believed he was talking Jugera but he could be talking ingots of silver or bronze.

Fusus took the gem and lifted it to the light. "I'll give you fifty" he said suddenly, a glint in his eye.

My father's face grew cold although I could sense the anger burning inside him. He turned to Scavolo and they shared a moment in which I could see them both tying the knot at the top of the sack and personally kicking me to death before they discarded my useless body in the Tiber.

Vibulanus held out his hand and Fusus passed the gem across. He was inspecting it closely. "I am confused Marcus Sulpicius" said the statesman. "I believed we had an agreement, and now this?" There was anger in his voice. The daughter seemed disappointed, her face now turning to me as her lips tightened into a straight line. Her eyes caught mine and I saw disappointment and pity flaring behind the gaze that enveloped me. What had I done to upset her? She looked genuinely saddened at something.

Scavolo stepped in and gave me a look of frustration. Had I cocked it up? What was going on?

"Gentlemen there has been some confusion." He gave me that hard look, the one which suggested if I wasn't the bosses son he'd happily kick my head from one side of the forum to the other and back again. "If I may" he was asking permission from my father who nodded with a glare in my direction. He asked for the gem, which he placed on the table before me. "Secundus Sulpicius" he was addressing me, taking control, but looking at me as if I were a student who didn't know how to add two and two together. "Marcus Fabius Vibulanus is offering the hand of his daughter Fabia in marriage. *The dowry* will be an estate which she will manage and build for you both as she has some skill in this area...."

He was continuing to talk but my face fell. I was starting to swallow hard. Not only had I cocked it up, but I'd insulted the Fabii clan by offering to pay for the land instead of marrying the girl. That was why they seemed so shocked. Fucking Janus had tricked me again. The others were here to seal what was quite an important contract and to confirm the details which no doubt Scavolo would write up after the meeting. Scavolo was continuing to talk to me as if I were a dimwit; which I was. The girl turned her face away from me, clearly slighted at my offer to pay for the land and not, in her eyes use her dowry. What an idiot I'd been, Scavolo was right, I'd cocked it up. Vibulanus placed a hand over his daughters as she seemed about to run from the room to escape the insult to her person. Fusus grinned at the awkward situation and kept his eye on the gem. I needed to rescue the situation and stop Scavolo treating me like an idiot. Both would be hard to do in my drink-enthused state.

I looked to the girl, who turned her head slightly further away as I did so. From the side she had a perfect profile, olive skin and soft eyes like her father. "I'm sorry" I said to her directly. She half turned but then looked down at her hands. I picked up the gem, Scavolo tensing as I felt he was about to smack me over the head if I dared to speak again. "Bacchus has twisted my words and turned them into confusion. It is the way of the gods" I glanced to the Pontifex who was watching me closely now but smiled at my statement. "This will help to build a better stable yard, better fences, buy more slaves and workers, more breeding mares. That is what I meant when I said it would cover the costs. A new venture, as Janus will tell us, needs capital, and I offer this to you Fabia to do just that." I slid the gem across the table to sit in front of where she sat. "To let your imagination run free, to buy what you need without having to ask for permission." I inclined my head to her father, he glanced to me and his warm eyes narrowed slightly as his lips curled to acknowledge my comment. My father glanced to Scavolo, who was pursing his lips and then tightened his jaw. "To build the best stock and the greatest horses that Rome has seen." She'd turned to me now, interest lighting up her pretty face. Her father was watching her, she was clearly his favourite. Had I gambled too much? My father narrowed his eyes once more and steepled his fingers as Fusus sat back and with an uncommon gesture placed a hand on my knee and grinned.

"I can replace the farm buildings" she was smiling, her father starting to smile too. "Put in the olive grove and pear trees I had designed." Her enthusiasm was infectious as people began to relax.

"Buy some horses" I said with a grin.

"Buy some horses" she said, looking at me and radiating goddess-like brilliance. She picked up the gem and turned to her father, kissing him on the cheek.

It was obviously some sort of sign as Vibulanus stood, held out a hand to my father and they clasped to seal the deal. My father was beaming as hands were shaken around the room. I couldn't take my eyes off Fabia as she looked back at me.

And then Scavolo edged into my sight and whispered in my ear, "you nearly cocked that up, prick."

THE END

Thank you for reading this book, I hope you enjoyed it. If you did, please add a review on Amazon to support my work.

Below is a short extract from Book 2 – The Case of Vulcan

****

It was big news so I wasn't surprised that Milo was in my face fishing for gossip from the moment I arrived at his roadside eatery.

I'd tried to ignore him, slurping my soup noisily and giving him my sternest frown as Graccus sat back and rubbed vigorously at a red lump on his arm. I looked at it with disgust as my friend licked his finger and wet the sore-looking area, rubbing his finger up and down to leave a trail of saliva over the bite. He proceeded to pick up a lump of bread and tear off a chunk which he then offered to me. I shook my head slowly with a glance to the wet patch on his arm, the bread and the soaking finger. At that moment I lost my appetite.

"Come on lads you know more than you're letting on" stated the food-seller irritated at our silence and with his thick eyebrows dancing in disbelief.

"We don't know anything Milo, honestly" I replied to his intense stare. "I've just come back from Laurentina so I missed the fire." I was waving my arms and shrugging my shoulders as I continued. "I haven't spoken to my father yet as he's been in meetings with the Senate all night and he didn't come home. I hear all the officials are chasing about like flies around shit. It's a big problem but it's not *my problem* and I don't have any news for you" I added with a further glance at his disbelieving face and dancing eyebrows. "And it's not a problem that I particularly care about either. You probably know more about it than me."

Graccus upended his bowl and licked at it for a moment as Milo sighed heavily and rolled his eyes. We were obviously not the purveyors of red-hot gossip that he'd expected when he greeted us with open arms and ushered us to the best table in his street-front food shop. To be fair the best table was the one out of the late morning sun under a rickety roof and containing less of a swarm of flies than all the others. It was becoming our usual table and we were probably his most regular customers.

"Well I can't believe they got away with all that treasure." Milo was shaking his head but watching us with the intensity of a hawk in case we gave any indication that we knew more than we were giving away. "I heard that there were five ingots of silver and thirty of iron and bronze at least, but they left some of the iron. Too much to carry I guess?" His knowledge of official records seemed accurate from what I'd heard from Graccus just moments earlier. My friend looked at me sheepishly above the lip of his bowl and I held back from a sigh lest I turned into my mother and started to wag a finger at him. "How can they have made off with that much without anyone seeing them? And why burn the place down? And that poor priest, he died a hero's death trying to save the Temple. Poor bastard." He was walking away as he spoke, a customer approaching. I continued eating, wondering if he would come back before I had a chance to speak to Graccus.

I'd sent Micus ahead to get Graccus to meet me here as I was only just out of my bed after a long journey overnight and a lie-in till almost Meridiem. In honesty I didn't know much more than Graccus had already said to me before Milo arrived with his questions, which from the sound of it was the topic of gossip across the city. I yawned deeply. It was strange that I'd slept so well but still felt as if I needed to go back to bed for a few more hours. I'd heard the news of the fire from my mother shortly after my arrival at home, she was up late drinking with a new friend from the Temple of Minerva, a lady who lived on the Vaticano whose family grew olives and also seemed to have a passion for Bacchus' water. Through mouthfuls of the green berries my mother and her friend had explained that the Temple of Vulcan at the foot of the Capitol Hill had been raided the night before and a priest who was guarding the site was killed before the Temple was set ablaze. My father had set his team, Scavolo as their leader, onto the case immediately and had hardly returned home since that moment. This was a *big* problem, a religious institution attacked, robbed and a priest killed. It was state funds that had been taken, so it was everyone's problem to some degree, however small. So far, according to Graccus, they had found no clues to why the temple had been burned to the ground and what treasures had been taken. I assumed Milo knew that too as I looked to my friend, soup on his nose and chin as he placed the bowl on the table.

"Tell me again Graccus" I asked, stifling another yawn, "what do they know so far?"

To his credit he looked over his shoulder to see if Milo was listening, which he wasn't. "Novius said this morning that

Scavolo has been bashing heads to get information but the priests of Vulcan are like mutes, they have nothing to say." I knew what he meant, they were a strange order, one of Rome's oldest and said to have started their cult at the time of Romulus but also notoriously close knit and difficult to work with. To join the order you had to give up all formal rights beyond that of citizen and live a basic life, despite the fact that they usually held vast sums in their vaults. They wore dark blue tunics with gold thread at their necks and they maintained a very simple life, devoting their days to praying to their god, helping with local disputes and completing devotions and sacrifices brought by locals. It was the sort of thing I'd dreaded when the priestess of Minerva, Fucilla, had suggested that I had been granted a goddess-given power to find the killer of her daughter. My fear that I might end up being forced into some kind of priesthood had kept me awake for nights, with the face of her daughter, and my own dead wife, staring back at me each night as I slept. It was what people did to their unlucky second sons, stick them in a Temple and leave them to rot.

The priests of Vulcan followed the old ways, shunning modern ceremonies and sticking to the humble rites which focused on the aversion of harmful fires. I smiled, that one didn't seem to have helped them in this case as the place had been gutted from what I understood. Apart from that, the main duty they'd held since the time of Romulus, and the one for which they were most renowned, was to receive all the metal spoils of war which they melted down into ingots and handed back to the State and citizens as and when there was demand. To this end they had contracts across the city to smelt their goods and stored all of the ingots in their own vaults until they were collected. That was simplifying what was an institution in Rome but in essence the Temple kept a small fortune in a sunken strongroom, with iron bound doors and a guard or two. This break-in and the theft of the treasure had caused a major uproar as much for the robbery as the burning of the site. The fact that one of their priests had been killed in the robbery had caused as much of a stir as the theft of the silver and bronze.

"The priest who was on guard that night was killed and they took all of the precious metals and about half of the iron" finished my friend as I looked to him and held back another yawn.

"How? What did they do to get all that metal out of the temple?" I asked.

"That's the problem, nobody can tell."

I let out a huff. "What do you mean nobody can tell? There must have been a fair few of them, carts and horses to move that much metal?" Graccus was lifting his shoulders and moving his head from side to side to suggest that nobody seemed to have an answer, particularly him. "Someone must have seen or heard something at least, you can't move that much stuff in silence?"

"Ghosts in the night. That's what Scavolo said."

"And the priests? I thought they slept in the Temple?"

Graccus inclined his head, "yes, the priest who died was left as a guard. The others had been on a vigil at the Temple near Ostia and came back to find the place ablaze."

That seemed like a convenient occurrence and I huffed at his words and rolled my eyes. "Well, I don't give a shit. Who cares if a few bars of bronze and silver have been taken" I said promptly. "I have better things to do now" I said to his sad eyes. "What?"

"So it's true." His voice was downcast. "You're not coming back?"

The tone of his voice made me realise that he was still my client and that he'd been offered a job at the Temple on the basis that he was supporting me in whatever I did for my father. Since I'd suddenly gained a wedding proposal from a socially superior family and a new farm a few miles out of the city I hadn't given this any thought. "Anyway, who says I'm not coming back?" I'd spoken more cheerily than I felt as the last thing I wanted to do now was slog my guts out with that bastard Scavolo looking over my shoulder and telling me I was a prick every few minutes. My future was set and I was looking forward to greeting it with open arms, basking in the gaze of Minerva and Janus as my new patrons.

"Philus."

"*Philus?* What does that prick know" I slapped my friend on the shoulder and gave him my broadest smile. His glum countenance suggested that he didn't believe a word I was saying, which was probably true. I really did need to engage a new tutor to improve my ability to take the patrician stance of holding little or no emotion in my face or bodily expressions. "More?" I was pointing to the bowl of soup to distract him.

With an expression of utter despair my friend shook his head and started to stand. "No, I have work to do. Scavolo has me scribing some of the reports from the fire, with Novius and Pemptor." Graccus turning down another bowl of soup indicated the depth of his despair. My jaw fell slack as he said goodbye to Milo and then slumped off up the hill, shoulders sagging and head down. I was watching him shuffle along the steepest section of the Clivus Capitolinus in silence, not quite sure what to make of it when Milo came up and sat next to me, elbows on the table and head down. I edged away at his familiarity and gave him a look of distrust.

His head turned towards the hill and he watched my friend for a few seconds before speaking. "Graccus has been talking about you coming back and solving this case all morning" he was shaking his head as he looked at the forlorn figure that was now turning the corner towards the Temple of Jupiter Optimus Maximus. "He's been really excited that you could solve it." His shaking head continued to admonish me without saying it directly as I bit my lip. He gave me his broadest grin. "Anyway, prick can't do anything on his own can he? Heard he ballsed-up your last investigation" his eyes were conspiratorial now as his eager face stared at me and his teeth showed though his grinning lips. "Probably lose this job too if you're not around. You going to get on this case? More soup?" He'd assassinated my friend, tried to get some gossip about my actions and moved to selling more of his food faster than my mind could keep up with his furtive eyebrows.

"I have no interest in the problems at the Vulcanal" I said angrily, giving the Temple its local name. "Why do I care if it's burned to the ground and everything taken? I couldn't give a fig for those priests, they probably stole it all themselves to go whoring."

Milo stood urgently and looked down at me for a moment with concern written across his face. "You want to watch it cursing the priests and the temple out loud" his beetle like eyebrows danced again as he spoke and his hand rose to his chin. I glanced to him, a modicum of fear shooting through me at my mistake and I turned to see Graccus' heel disappear around the corner. Had I said a curse out loud which would come back to haunt me? I decided I better make a devotion to the gods quickly.

I watched Milo return to his urns and shook my head at my own insecurity. I really couldn't give a shit about the temple of Vulcan and its priests. Things were on the up for me and I was looking forward to a bright future. Let that prick Scavolo solve this case, I had absolutely no interest in it whatsoever. I'd make a small devotion, but with Minerva, Janus and Jupiter all looking after me, I was sure it was all fine. It really didn't interest me at all. I sat back and closed my eyes, smiling at my luck in finding the dead girl, Lucilla, and the positive change it had made to my life.

(please note that by time of publication I may have edited some of the above)

Go to the Amazon store now to continue reading .....

Also by Francis M. Mulhern
The Dictator Of Rome series

Dawn of the Eagle (Book 1)

The Fall of Veii; part one (Book 2)

The Fall of Veii; part two (Book 3)

Vae Victis (Book 4)

The King of Rome (Book 5)

The Last Battle (Book 6)

Also in this series

The Ancilia Shield (prequel to Book 1)

The Thracian; a short story

In Fantasy Adventure Fiction (as Fran Mulhern)

Witch Hunt

In Murder and Mystery

Secundus Sulpicius Series

The case of Minerva (Book 1)

The Case of Vulcan (Book 2)

Printed in Great Britain
by Amazon